Classroom Interactions
as Cross-Cultural Encounters

Native Speakers in EFL Lessons

ESL & Applied Linguistics Professional Series
Eli Hinkel, Series Editor

Youmans • *Chicago-Anglo Conversations: Truth, Honesty, and Politeness*

Birch • *English L2 Reading: Getting to the Bottom, Second Edition*

Luk/Lin • *Classroom Interactions as Cross-Cultural Encounters: Native Speakers in EFL Lessons*

Levy/Stockwell • *CALL Dimensions: Issues and Options in Computer-Assisted Language Learning*

Nero, Ed. • *Dialects, Englishes, Creoles, and Education*

Basturkmen • *Ideas and Options in English for Specific Purposes*

Kumaravadivelu • *Understanding Language Teaching From Method to Postmethod*

McKay • *Researching Second-Language Classrooms*

Egbert/Petrie, Eds. • *CALL Research Perspectives*

Canagarajah, Ed. • *Reclaiming the Local in Language Policy and Practice*

Adamson • *Language Minority Students in American Schools: An Education in English*

Fotos/Browne, Eds. • *New Perspectives on CALL for Second-Language Classrooms*

Hinkel • *Teaching Academic ESL Writing: Practical Techniques in Vocabulary and Grammar*

Hinkel/Fotos, Eds. • *New Perspectives on Grammar Teaching in Second-Language Classrooms*

Hinkel • *Second-Language Writers' Text Linguistic and Rhetorical Features*

For a complete list of titles in LEA's Communication Series, please contact Lawrence Erlbaum Associates, Publishers at www.erlbaum.com

Classroom Interactions
as Cross-Cultural Encounters
Native Speakers in EFL Lessons

Jasmine C. M. Luk
The University of Hong Kong
Angel M. Y. Lin
The Chinese University of Hong Kong

IEA
2007

LAWRENCE ERLBAUM ASSOCIATES, PUBLISHERS
Mahwah, New Jersey   London

Lawrence Erlbaum Associates, Inc., Publishers
10 Industrial Avenue
Mahwah, New Jersey 07430
www.erlbaum.com

Cover design by Tomai Maridou

Library of Congress Cataloging-in-Publication Data

Luk, Jasmine C. M.
Classroom interactions as cross-cultural encounters : native speakers in
    ESL lessons/Jasmine C.M. Luk & Angel M.Y. Lin.
            p. cm.—(ESL and applied linguistics professional series)

    Includes bibliographical references and index.
ISBN 0-8058-5083-X (cloth : alk. paper)
ISBN 0-8058-5084-8 (pbk. : alk. paper)
1. English language—Study and teaching—Chinese speakers—Social
    aspects. 2. English language—Study and teaching—Chinese
    speakers—Research—Methodology. 3. English language—Study
    and teaching—Chinese speakers—Psychological aspects. 4. Hong
    Kong (China)—Social life and customs. I. Lin, Angel, 1962- II. Title.
    III. Series

PE1130.C4L852006
428.007105125—dc22   2006011750
                                                          CIP

Books published by Lawrence Erlbaum Associates are printed on acid-free paper, and their bindings are chosen for strength and durability.
Printed in the United States of America
10 9 8 7 6 5 4 3 2 1

Contents in Brief

Preface   xv

1   Introduction   1

2   The Native-Speaking English Teachers (NETs)   11
    in Postcolonial Hong Kong

3   The Native-Speaking English Teachers in the Global   21
    ELT Industry

4   Culture and Studies of Interaction   33

5   Understanding Cross-Cultural Classroom   45
    Interaction—An Ideological Framework

6   The Participants in Context   57

7   Making Sense in the Lessons   83

8   Having Fun in the Lessons   113

9   Performing "Teachers" and "Students"   139

10 Implications—Toward a Pedagogy of Connecting   185
    for the Development of Intercultural
    Communicative Resources

Notes 207

Appendix: Conventions of Transcription 219

References 221

Author Index 233

Subject Index 237

Contents

Preface   XV

1   Introduction   1

The Authors' Experiences of Learning English   2
   (written from the first-person perspective)

    Jasmine Luk   2

    Close "Encounter" of a Cross-Cultural Kind   3

    Angel Lin   3

    Constructing Alternative and Expanded Selves   4
      in English

The Cultural-Chemical Reaction Through   5
   Cross-Cultural Contacts

How Were the Data Collected?   5

    Ethnographic Observations and Recordings of   7
      Interactions

    Recordings of In-Depth Interviews and Reflections   7

      Preclassroom Observation Interviews   8

      During Classroom Observation Interviews   8

      Interviews With Students   9

      Postclassroom Observation Interviews   9

Questions for Reflection and Discussion   10

2   The Native-Speaking English Teachers (NETs)   11
   in Postcolonial Hong Kong

The NET Scheme and Its Precedents   12

The Roles and Functions of the NETs in Hong Kong   14
    Views of the Policymakers   14
    Views of NETs and LETs   16
    Views of the Students   17
The NET Scheme—An Act of Linguistic Imperialism,   18
    Strategic Pragmatism, or a Postcolonial Re-membering
    of the Past?
Questions for Reflection and Discussion   20

3   **The Native-Speaking English Teachers in the Global**   21
    ELT Industry
On Defining Native Speakers   21
On the Pedagogical Effectiveness of NETs   24
    The Positive Arguments   24
        Native Speakers for Cultural and Linguistic   24
            Exemplification
        Native Speakers as Facilitators of L2 Learners' 24
            Use of the Target Language
    The Negative Arguments   26
        Native Speaker Models Create Unrealistic and   26
            Unattainable Goals for L2 Learners
        NS Teachers Often Lack Knowledge of Local   26
            Students' Cultural and Language Backgrounds
    On the Sociopolitical Privileges of NETs   27
    The Synergy View   29
The Stance of This Book—Problematizing "Nativeness"   30
    as a Pregiven Entity
Questions for Reflection and Discussion   32

4   **Culture and Studies of Interaction**   33
Understanding Culture   33
Understanding Cross-Cultural or Intercultural Interaction 35
A Discourse Approach to Cross-Cultural Interaction Studies 36

Investigating Classroom Interaction   38
    The Discourse Analysis Approach   38
    The Sociocultural Contextual Analysis Approach   41
    The Critical Approach   43
Questions for Reflection and Discussion   44

5   **Understanding Cross-Cultural Classroom**   45
      Interaction—An Ideological Framework

Settings—Sociohistorical Context and School Context   46

Activities   47

The Participants, Their Identities, and Interactive Resources   48
    Identities and Positionings   48
    Interactive Resources   50

Asymmetrical Power Relations   53

Mediated Dialogic Interactions   54

Questions for Reflection and Discussion   56

6   **The Participants in Context**   57

The Education Context in Hong Kong   57
    The Banding, Streaming, and Evaluation Systems   58
    The Medium of Instruction (MOI) Policy   59
    The Education Logistics, Curriculum Culture, and   60
        English Language Teaching (ELT) Methodology

Ms. Berner   63
    Academic and Professional History   63
    The School Context   64
    Professional Beliefs   65

Mr. Williams   66
    Academic and Professional History   66
    The School Context   66
    Professional Beliefs   67

Mr. Nelson   68

  Academic and Professional History   68

  The School Context   68

  Professional Beliefs   70

Ms. Hung   71

  Academic and Professional History   71

  Professional Beliefs   71

Miss Logan   73

  Academic and Professional History   73

  The School Context   73

  Professional Beliefs   74

Mr. Sze   75

  Academic and Professional History   75

  Professional Beliefs   75

The Students   76

  Views about Learning English   77

    Attitudes Toward Learning and Using English   77

    English Learning Experience   77

    English Learning Strategies   79

  Views about their English Teachers   80

Summary   81

Questions for Reflection and Discussion   82

7 **Making Sense in the Lessons**   83

Tuning-In Discussion   83

Sense-Making Resources   84

Exploring Successful Sense-Making Practices   86

  An Ability to Travel Between L1 & L2 Linguistic   86
    and Cultural Borders

  An Ability to Capitalize on Students as Linguistic   91
    "Brokers"

An Ability to Repair in the Face of Communication   95
    Breakdown

Exploring Unsuccessful Sense-Making Practices   97

    Linguistic-Based Interaction Breakdown   97

    Culture-Based Interaction Breakdown   104

    Institution-Based Interaction Breakdown   108

Summary   110

Questions for Reflection and Discussion   111

8   Having Fun in the Lessons   113

Tuning-In Discussion   113

Phonological Play   114

Social Talk   119

Verbal Challenges and Friendly Teases   123

Taboo   133

Summary   136

Questions for Reflection and Discussion   138

9   Performing "Teachers" and "Students"   139

Tuning-In Discussion   139

Performing "Teachers"—Getting Students on Tasks   141

    Directives for Procedural Control   142

        Illustrating the Least Authoritative Directive   143
            Discourse

        Illustrating the Most Authoritative Directive   145
            Discourse

    Directives for Advisory Purposes   146

    Engaging Reticent or Nonconforming Students   148

        Exercising Authority   148

        Making Concessions   153

        Appealing to Students' Sense of Face   161

Performing "Students"—Participating in Tasks   168

    Enacting a Teacher-Designed Agency Role   168

    Transforming a Teacher-Designed Identity   173

    From Resisting to Participating: Shifting   177
       Positionings

Summary   182

Questions for Reflection and Discussion   184

**10 Implications—Toward a Pedagogy of Connecting   185
    for the Development of Intercultural
    Communicative Resources**

Revisiting the "Native"Speaker Communicative Resources   185
    in Cross-Cultural Settings

    Native Speakerism—A Myth or a Reality?   186

    Privileging Situated Communicative Resources in   187
       Intercultural Communication

    The Plurality and Multiplicity of Students' Linguistic 188
       and Cultural Experiences

    Multiple Identities of Students   190

       ID1. Learners of a Socially Important Language   191

       ID2. "Native" Speakers of a Language Closely   191
         Related to Their Everyday Sociocultural
         World

       ID3. Adolescents Closely Attached to Everyday   192
         Cantonese-Based Popular Youth Culture

       ID4. Interlocutors in a Conversation That   192
         Involves Cross-Cultural and Interethnic
         Elements

       ID5. Adolescents Developing Into Adults Who   193
         Are Capable of Independent Thinking

    Capitalizing on the Multiple Identities of Students 194

Toward a Pedagogy of Connecting   196

Conclusion   204

Questions for Reflection and Discussion   205

Notes   207

Appendix: Conventions of Transcription   219

References   221

Author Index   233

Subject Index   237

Preface

This book is written for English language teachers working in contexts that involve intercultural communication. Central to the book are issues concerning teaching English as a global language in non-English speaking countries by "native" English speakers. Although the term "native English speakers" has been found by many sociolinguists and TESOL researchers (Canagarajah, 1999a; Phillipson, 1992; Rampton, 1990) to be problematic in its essentialist overtones by many sociolinguists and TESOL researchers, the term is still used in this book because four of the six teachers reported in this book were recruited under a scheme called the "Native-speaking English Teachers Scheme" (NET Scheme) in Hong Kong. A major official defining characteristic of this group of English teachers when the Scheme was introduced in 1997 was that English should be their "mother tongue"[1] (Education Department, 1997[2]). The notion of "native speakers" defined as such will however be revisited and problematized throughout this book.

Apart from focusing on native English speakers, we shall also focus on native Cantonese-speaking teachers and students. The study involved four native English-speaking teachers (NETs) and two bilingual Cantonese-English speaking teachers engaged in *intercultural classroom dialogues* with their Cantonese Hong Kong students. For convenience, we will call the bilingual teachers LETs (local English teachers) because most of these teachers were born, raised, and received their basic education in Hong Kong.

Through analyzing naturally occurring dialogic encounters under three thematic categories (making sense in the lessons; having fun in the lessons; and performing "teachers" and "students"), we discuss the multifarious ways in which teachers and students utilized diverse communicative resources to construct, display, and negotiate their identities as teachers, learners, and language users, with different pedagogic, institutional, social, and political implications.

This book addresses a variety of issues in applied linguistics, including linguistic imperialism (Pennycook, 1994; Phillipson, 1992), postcolonial theories (e.g., Childs & Williams, 1997; Gandhi, 1998), micropolitics of classroom interaction (e.g., Bloome & Willett, 1991), language and identity (e.g., Miller, 2000; Norton, 2000), and bilingual classroom practices (e.g., Lin, 1990, 1999; Pennington, 1999a, 1999b). The classroom data analyzed in this book have come from the first author's qualitative study of classroom interactions in Hong Kong secondary schools from 1998 to 2000. The data are naturally occurring interactions collected through video and audiotaping with the first author taking the role of a classroom observer.

The context under focus is postcolonial Hong Kong. On July 1, 1997, the sovereignty of Hong Kong was returned to China after being colonized by Britain for more than 150 years. During the late colonial days, English was the official language side by side with Chinese (Chinese became one of the two official languages only in the mid-1970s), and English has been playing a significant role in business, economy, education, and the officialdom. What implications will a territorywide recruitment of native English-speaking teachers in postcolonial Hong Kong have on the status and functions of English in the postcolonial era, and the development of localized varieties of English as in other postcolonial settings are also explored in this book.

Below are some special features of the study reported in this book:

- Different from other ethnographic studies on cross-cultural or intercultural communication (e.g. Alfred, Byram, & Fleming, 2002; Byram & Fleming, 1998; Guilherme, 2002; Scollon & Scollon, 2001), the present study investigates cross-cultural interactions *in ELT* (English Language Teaching) *classroom contexts.* It is also different from classroom interaction studies on NS (native speaker) teachers and NNS (nonnative) students that focus on interactions from an SLA (second language acquisition), psycholinguistic perspective (e.g., Long & Sato, 1983; Pica, 1992). The present study has a key emphasis on the sociocultural meanings and micropolitics of classroom interactions that reveal the complex realities of power and identity negotiations.
- It revisits, deconstructs, and reconstitutes the notion of "native speakerness" and repositions the roles of "native" and "nonnative" English teachers in the TESOL profession in the context of decolonization, globalization, and the need to mobilize intercultural communicative resources for global communication. It will challenge some of the conventional expectations on NS/NNS interactions, which give the NS dominating positions in shaping the content and direction of the dialogues (e.g., Long, 1981). The present study reveals the important role of the NNS students in coconstructing, transforming, and reconstructing the interactions through their creative discourse practices.
- The present study addresses two major concerns of EFL (English as a foreign language) classroom researchers and teachers, namely *student resistance,* and *learning motivation* by providing a thick description and fine-grained, microanalysis of students' interaction practices through which students are constantly negotiating and performing different identities.
- The present study examines and analyzes the changing (both explicit and implicit) ideologies of teachers and students about English learning in the context of a postcolonial society, Hong Kong, and how these ideologies are being enacted, reproduced but also sometimes contested in EFL classroom interactions.

This book provides education researchers and policymakers with rich naturally occurring classroom data and in-depth analyses. We hope that this book would help TESOL professionals of different cultural backgrounds working in different sociocultural contexts to critically understand how nonassimilationist, dialogic intercultural communication with students could be achieved and capitalized on for mutual cultural and linguistic enrichment and empowerment.

AN OVERVIEW OF THE BOOK

In chapter 1, "Introduction," we present the backgrounds and personal English language learning biographies of the authors. Through the anecdotes, we explain how cross-cultural encounters with English users coming from different sociocultural backgrounds may have created far-reaching impacts on our perceptions and attitudes toward the language and the learning of the language. In the second part of chapter 1, we also present the general design and methodology of the study.

In chapter 2, we provide a background of the native English speaker teacher scheme in Hong Kong. A brief history of the Hong Kong government's initiative to recruit NETs to teach in local schools, and its sociocultural and sociopolitical implications are discussed. Chapter 3 extends the issue to a wider perspective to explore how the notion of NETs has been constructed and deconstructed, problematized and rejected in the field of applied linguistics.

In chapter 4, "Culture and Studies of Interaction," we explain the conceptualization of the current study by reviewing the findings of similar studies. Apart from the issue of native speakers, studies of cross-cultural interaction and classroom interaction are the two key theoretical strands of this book. The chapter discusses how some representative studies under these two strands have come to be conceptualized and what they reveal about cross-cultural interactions that are classroom based. With insights from these previous studies discussed in chapter 4, the authors present in chapter 5 the conceptual design of the study through a theoretical framework: "Understanding Cross-Cultural Classroom Interaction—An Ideological Framework." This framework facilitates our investigation of cross-cultural classroom interactions. A cross-cultural classroom interaction model is proposed that encompasses ideologies from sociocultural and critical approaches to classroom discourse analysis.

As its name suggests, in chapter 6, "Participants in Context," the main characters of the book, the teachers and students, are introduced. We begin by highlighting significant features of the education contexts at the time of the study; for instance, the education systems, policies, teaching orientations, and the curriculum culture. We also describe the teachers' professional and academic history, their school contexts, and their professional beliefs about ELT as well as the students' attitudes to learning English, and their views on being taught by NETs and LETs.

Three chapters, chapters 7, 8, and 9, examine what seemed to be happening in the classrooms both between the teacher and the students and among the students.

These three themes were constructed to organize our discussion of the recurrent patterns of all the classroom episodes that are representative and significant in illuminating the features outlined in the cross-cultural model of classroom interaction (chap. 5) such as power relationships, sociocultural and linguistic identities, interactive resources, and mediated dialogic activities. Chapter 7 shows the discourse practices of the teachers and the students in getting meanings across. We analyze both successful and unsuccessful sense-making practices. Chapter 8 shows how students frequently usurped the pedagogic space for fun-making purposes and how they achieved this by taking advantage of the NETs' lack of L1 resources. Chapter 9 shows how the teachers and students performed their institutional roles as "teachers" and "students" through discourse. It shows that both parties did not always conform to the institutional expectations, and deviations from the institutional norms might reflect the wish of the teachers and students to negotiate multiple identities.

All the selected classroom events are presented in transcripts. Readers may refer to the Appendix for the conventions of transcription.

The last chapter, chapter 10, "Implications—Toward a Pedagogy of Connecting for Intercultural Competence," integrates the data analysis and findings in previous chapters and refocuses readers' attention to two key issues; (1) the role of "native" speaker communicative resources in intercultural contexts; and (2) the impact of the plurality and multiplicity of students' linguistic and cultural experiences on their discourse practices. Instead of reinforcing the hegemonic status of native English speaker communicative competence in TESOL settings, we propose "a pedagogy of connecting" to help TESOL practitioners of different ethnicities to see the importance of connecting the local and the global in intercultural communicative encounters (also see Canagarajah, 2005a), and to develop the ability to capitalize on the multiple identities, and linguistic and cultural resources of students in the process of encouraging students to invest their time and energies in the English learning tasks.

QUESTIONS FOR REFLECTION AND DISCUSSION AND TUNING-IN DISCUSSIONS

Each chapter contains Questions for Reflection and Discussion (appearing at the end) to promote critical thinking and understanding of the issues discussed in the chapters. Tuning-in discussion questions are provided in the three chapters on classroom data analysis (chaps. 7, 8, & 9) to activate the interpretive schemas of the readers before they examine the actual classroom episodes. The authors believe that the three chapters on classroom data analysis provide useful pedagogical materials for courses on classroom discourse analysis from sociocultural perspectives in EFL teacher education programs.

ACKNOWLEDGMENTS

The authors want to thank the teacher participants, their students, the school principals, and their colleagues for making this study possible. Without their generous agreement to participate in this study, this book would not have been possible at all. What they have opened to us was not just their schools and their classrooms, but also their hearts. They contributed to this book not just by making available the classroom and interview data, but also by their commitment to teaching and learning and their interesting, insightful, and sometimes critical and original perspectives on some of the classroom issues. In many respects, they were the "authors" of the core parts (the data) of this book, and in this sense, they were not only contributing to this study and this book, but also to the wider research and professional communities in TESOL and applied linguistics.

We also want to thank Greg Myers at the Lancaster University, United Kingdom, for his most enlightening and intellectual comments on this study and earlier versions of the data analysis.

Special thanks go to Naomi Silverman of Lawrence Erlbaum Associates for her interest in and support for this book project, and the three reviewers of the book proposal—Ryuko Kubota, University of North Carolina, Chapel Hill; Brian Morgan, York University; and Timothy Reagan, University of Witwatersrand; for their encouraging and inspiring comments.

Last but not least, we thank the two reviewers of the book manuscript—James W. Tollefson, International Christian University, and Anne W. Roberti—and Eli Hinkel, series editor for the ESL and Applied Linguistics Professional Series, for their comments on the book manuscript. The authors are deeply grateful for their practical, critical, and insightful suggestions that show concrete directions for how the book could be further improved in its theoretical framework and data analysis. We hope that this book will contribute to the teaching and learning of many teachers and students from different cultures and language backgrounds when they coconstruct their understanding of one another in the cross-cultural contact zone of the language classroom.

1

Introduction

T he following incident happened 7 years after Hong Kong ceased to be a British colony in 1997: Due to declining birth rate, dozens of publicly funded primary schools in Hong Kong could not recruit enough Year One (aged 6) students and were closing down. A couple of such schools appealed and obtained special approval from the education authority to run the schools in a self-financed mode. Press releases by these schools highlighted one major measure to prove to the public the schools' determination to provide quality education—the hiring of several more "native-speaking" English teachers (termed *NETs* in Hong Kong) to teach English in the new school term. Media coverage of the new student orientation day of one of the schools highlighted one major event—three to four NETs were playing games with a group of 6-year-old schoolchildren. There were smiles on the students' faces. The television coverage has sent out a strong unspoken message to the public. The parents have made the right choice to send their children to the school because students there would receive the best possible type of English language education (which is the greatest concern of most parents in Hong Kong)—to be taught by NETs who have a reputation for being able to teach the language in authentic, lively, and innovative ways. The availability of NETs is the strongest warranty of quality education that the schools have pledged to provide. The generous recruitment of NETs is believed to be something that would make the schools stand out from the rest, a promising step toward becoming a prestigious school.[3]

The incident previously described reflects the symbolic (or perhaps consensual or hegemonic) status and value of NETs in a post-British colonial, as well as a cosmopolitan city such as Hong Kong. To most schools in Hong Kong striving to survive or maintain the established reputation, NETs seem to have become an essential trademark of quality English language education that is highly priced and valued by the whole society. NETs are also the main characters of this book. However, the term "native speakers" in the book title does not only refer to native "English" speakers but also to "native" speakers of Cantonese[4]—the local students and English teachers with Chinese parentage, born and raised in Hong Kong.

The reader might be interested to know why the authors, two female ethnic-Chinese English language teachers and teacher educators born and raised in Hong Kong, wanted to write this book and what our stance is in the controversial issue of the power and status of NETs in EFL settings. Some readers might suspect that from their local sociopolitical positions, the authors might hold the view that NETs are not better than LETs (local English teachers). In fact, we are going to show that the scenario is much more complex than can be reduced to any simple binary sets of conclusion (e.g., "good" or "bad"). To help readers better understand the background of this book, let us begin with the authors' experiences of learning English.

THE AUTHORS' EXPERIENCES OF LEARNING ENGLISH

Jasmine Luk

My path in learning English was nothing unusual. I was born to a working class family with virtually no English-related linguistic and cultural capital. Like the majority of children born in the 1960s, English entered into my life at the age of 4, when I attended kindergarten. The only person I could turn to for problems about English was my eldest brother who began learning the language 7 years earlier than me. Throughout my primary and secondary schooling, I had not been taught by any native English teachers.

Because my results in English and math in the Secondary School Entrance Examination[5] were not outstanding, I was allocated a school place in an academically average secondary school close to the government-subsidized public housing estate[6] where I lived. The school was run by a Chinese Buddhist Association. Perhaps due to this religious background, the English learning culture was not strong compared with that in Christian and Catholic missionary schools in Hong Kong. There were seldom any activities to promote an English-speaking culture in the school. Even though most of the English teachers were well qualified to teach English and used almost 100% English in the lessons,[7] English remained a language inside the classroom for purely study and examination purposes. In the corridors and on the playground, seldom a word of English was heard among the teachers and students. At the end of my matriculation, I obtained distinctions for all my Chinese language-related subjects in the advanced level examination whereas my use of English was just a good pass. None of my classmates received a distinction or a good credit for their use of English in that examination. To sum up, although I have both intrinsic and extrinsic motivation to learn English, my investment in learning English from primary to secondary schooling was solely driven by a desire to pass examinations, and to climb up the social ladder by entering the English-medium university.

Close "Encounter"[8] of a Cross-Cultural Kind

Despite my average result in English,[9] I was admitted to the University of Hong Kong, the most prestigious English-medium university at that time because of my good results in other subjects. After entering the university, I took English as my major in the university even though I attained excellent grades in the Chinese subjects in the A-Level examination. The sociopolitical situation of Hong Kong in the early 1980s convinced me that obtaining a degree in English would furnish me with, in Bourdieu's (1991) terms, more economic, social, and cultural capital for my future development than majoring in Chinese. Due to the university policy that English should be used as the medium of instruction for all disciplines other than Chinese, I obtained more opportunities to use English to express myself. However, the most remarkable experience for me was a 15-minute casual conversation I had with an expatriate lecturer from Britain. To use English to answer questions and express myself was, of course, not a novel experience. What is most intriguing about the effect the interaction had on my subsequent development as a language learner lies in the fact that the lecturer and I shared information and exchanged views over topics arising from our respective "culture." We talked about differences in forms of address in the kinship systems in British and Chinese cultures, and how addressing someone inappropriately might result in embarrassment. For the first time in my life, I saw the value of knowing a foreign language. If I had not known English, I would not have been able to introduce and explain the intricacies of my own culture to a "foreigner." *I saw how my knowledge in a foreign language has opened up and widened my capacity for social interaction.* The ability to converse successfully over spontaneous issues other than those related to academic studies has also increased my confidence in my English proficiency.

Angel Lin

I do not belong to the small number of people in Hong Kong who have been born into families and communities that provide them with ample English linguistic and cultural capital (Bourdieu, 1991; Delpit, 1988) to succeed in school in a British colony, where English is the key to academic success, overall success, and socioeconomic advancement. My parents do not speak any English. People we know all speak Cantonese, which is our daily language. I grew up in a home and community where few had the linguistic resources to use English at all, and even if anyone had, she or he would find it extremely socially inappropriate (e.g., sounding pompous, putting on airs) to speak English.

My chances for learning and using English hinged entirely on the school. However, I lived in a poor government-subsidized apartment building complex (called "public housing estate") in the rural area (the New Territories) in Hong Kong, where schools were mostly put up in the early 1970s and they neither had adequate English resources (e.g., staff well versed in spoken English) nor a well-established English-speaking and English teaching and learning tradition or school culture.

My parents were poor manual workers. They put all their hopes and expectations in their children: Illiterate in English as they were, they did not fail to be keenly aware of the fact that their children's future depended on doing well in school, and doing well in school depends on mastering the English language in the Hong Kong schooling system. They have passed on the work ethic to their children. We were urged day and night to "study hard" and especially to study English hard.

Upon leaving the primary school, I got good results in the secondary school entrance examination and got admitted to an English-medium secondary school. I would spend hours and hours looking up in the dictionary all the new words of my textbooks and writing down their pronunciations (in phonetic symbols), meanings, and examples in a vocabulary notebook and read them whenever I had time.

Constructing Alternative and Expanded Selves in English

In my circle of girlfriends in my secondary school, having pen pals had become a topic and practice of common interest. Through organizaions such as Big Blue Marble or International Youth Service, I got penfriends from England, Austria, Canada, and the United States and we communicated regularly in English by air mail letters. Sending letters to our overseas penfriends and waiting eagerly for their replies had become our everyday hobbies.

I also started to write my own private diary in English every day about that time. I started this habit when a pen pal sent me a diary book as my birthday present and suggested writing a diary as a worthwhile activity to me. I chose to write my diary in English because someone (a teacher? I don't remember now) had told me that finding a chance to use English daily would improve one's English. I felt that I could write my feelings *more freely* when I wrote in English—less inhibition and reservation—I seemed to have found a tool that gave me more freedom to express my innermost fears, worries, anger, conflicts, or excitement, hopes, expectations, likes and dislikes, or my alternative selves, without constraint or inhibition—as if this foreign language had opened up a new, personal space (a "third space," so to speak, see related discussion in chap. 10), for me to more freely express all those difficult emotions and experiences (typical?) of an adolescent growing up, without feeling the sanctions of the adult world. I guess I was creating an expanded self in English, and English seemed to provide me with the additional resources I needed to explore myself in a somewhat different manner, in a somewhat different value system, one that appeared to be less prohibiting than my native language in some areas, for instance, in the area of explicitly articulating one's emotions like anger.

English, it seems, had opened up a totally new space for me to express and entrust my secrets and innermost feelings—I felt safe to confide in Gretchen, my U.S. pen pal, and to my diary. I also felt that English had provided me with a tool to broaden myself, to reach out to new friends in new lands, to invent and recreate for myself a somewhat different self from the one my parents knew. It gave me excitement when new and lasting friendships across cultural and geographical boundaries were formed, and it gave me satisfying feelings like those that an adventurer would have exploring a new land and new culture.

THE CULTURAL CHEMICAL REACTION THROUGH CROSS-CULTURAL CONTACTS

There are indeed a lot of similarities between the English-learning histories of the two authors. The most significant similarity lies in the opportunities to interact with speakers across cultures in the language that they were learning to acquire. Such experience affords the language personal meanings that were difficult to obtain in linguistically and ethnically homogeneous classroom situations in Hong Kong.

Therefore, even though the authors are fully confident in the valuable contribution that local Chinese-English bilingual teachers could make to English language education, especially in their sensitivity to students' learning difficulties, and their ability to negotiate with students in their shared first language, we are also convinced that the nature of contact with LETs is never quite the same as that with the NETs. We believe that the difference is not entirely due to language proficiency, but more to sociocultural perceptions and identities, which have been historically and institutionally constructed.

Having come from the same sociocultural worlds and backgrounds, LETs and their students probably have more to share in terms of interactive resources, cultural heritage, and practices, mental frameworks and ideologies that might not be shared by NETs. The little crossing over of the sociocultural backgrounds between NETs and local Chinese students, on the other hand, might be a key factor leading to creative dynamics in interactions. This is similar to chemical reactions arising from the blending of two both similar and differing substances, which result in unexpected, sometimes desirable but sometimes undesirable, consequences. How such chemical reactions take place, and to what effects on foreign language learning, constitutes the main thesis of this book.

HOW WERE THE DATA COLLECTED?

The data for this book were collected with ethnographic and case study approaches. With its research tradition rooted in anthropology, an ethnographic approach produces writings about contexts and societies with a focus on the "cultural interpretation of [people's] behaviour in naturally occurring, ongoing settings" (Watson-Gegeo, 1988, p. 576). The ethnographic approach is by far the most appropriate research instrument to discover the implicit sociocultural norms and resources shaping social interaction patterns and interpretive meanings of naturally occurring human actions and interactions.

The sites of research in an ethnographic study, the "ethnos," need not be a nation, or a village, but "any social network forming a corporate entity in which social relations are regulated by custom" (Erickson, 1984, p. 52). The sites of research of the present study are secondary school classrooms situated in the larger sociocultural and sociopolitical contexts. As pointed out by Watson-Gegeo (1997), classroom ethnography emphasizes

> the sociocultural nature of teaching and learning processes, incorporates participants' perspectives on their own behaviour, and offers a holistic analysis sensitive to levels of context in which interactions and classrooms are situated. (p. 135)

Schools are without doubt interesting social and institutional contexts sufficiently similar to other local communities for research to be done ethnographically. The structure of schools is characterized by a network of communication, rights, and obligations between different classes of persons (students, teachers, administrators, paraprofessionals, parents), with specified roles and statuses, and different rates and modes of interaction. Externally the school is also linked to larger social units (the education department, the tertiary institutes, the government, religious organizations, or even some big business enterprises), influencing them as well as being influenced by them. In his paper explicating the significance and relevance of school ethnography, Erickson (1984) concluded by saying that "because of its holism and because of its cross-cultural perspective, [ethnography] provides an inquiry process by which we can ask open-ended questions that will result in *new insights* [italics added] about schooling in American society" (p. 65). The same of course applies to the Hong Kong society. The changing political situations in the postcolonial period leading to changing language policies and societal attitudes toward English create desires, pressures, and conflicts in the language classrooms among teachers and students with different identities or subject positions. The intricacies of the patterns and meanings of interactions can be better captured and interpreted by the researcher being there in the context, continually observing, questioning, examining, and analyzing the interactions transpiring in the classroom.

Multiple methods have been used to collect data to minimize possible weaknesses and deficiencies of any one single method. Basically, ethnographic lesson observations and transcriptions of tape-recorded lessons provide the core body of data, whereas data from interviews and field notes complement and enrich the interpretations of the ethnographic classroom data.

Ethnographic Observations and Recordings of Interactions

Ethnographic observations of classroom interactions of six teachers (four NETs and two LETs; see chap. 6 for details) and their students were conducted by the first author, Jasmine Luk, in the middle stage of the second term of the school year. That time of the year was chosen because the teachers and the students should have already established some kind of rapport, and were not yet under the pressure of the final examination. With every teacher, the first author spent 5 to 6 consecutive days in the school. By observing lessons over a few consecutive days, the first author was able to see interaction patterns in different types of lessons. Any undesirable consequences resulting from the "observer's effect" on the teachers and students can also be reduced to a minimum. According to the teachers, some of the students displayed slightly different behavior on the first 2 days of the visits but returned to their normal selves and behaved naturally from the third day onward.

During the visits, the first author followed the teachers around in the school as far as possible, and video and audiotaped most of the interactions they had with their students, which took place mainly in the classrooms. Inside the classroom, the first author undertook nonparticipant observations. She usually stood at the back of the classroom, with the camera facing the teachers. This arrangement was felt to be the most acceptable by the teachers as some students were quite sensitive to the camera. The audiorecorder was usually placed on the desk of one of the students sitting in the front row. Two male teacher participants agreed to carry the recorder in the pocket of their shirts or jackets. This enabled the first author to record more private interactions between the teacher and the students.

To follow the teachers all the time was usually not possible in most Hong Kong schools as the staff rooms were very crowded. During recess time, many students would come into the staff room to see their teachers and there was little space. Besides, most of the teachers preferred to "take a break" and be "off our hook" during rest time. They told the first author that they felt a bit uneasy being observed all the time. Therefore, interactions outside the classroom were difficult to capture, and when they did occur, they could only be observed but not recorded because they always occurred in fleeting and unpredictable moments. Observations of this type are, therefore, supplemented with field notes often made during breaks or retrospectively at the end of each day's visit to record any points of interest; for instance, efforts made by students to get meanings across or a possible misunderstanding between the NETs and their students.

Recordings of In-Depth Interviews and Reflections

Along with ethnographic observations, three in-depth semistructured interviews were conducted with the teacher participants at three stages; they are the *pre-, during, and postclassroom observations.*

Preclassroom Observation Interviews.   Preclassroom observation interviews were conducted to gain access to the teacher participants' academic and professional history, their perceptions of local students' learning styles and strategies, and their professional beliefs. These interviews were done before or on the first day of the visits with the following focuses:

- their knowledge and perceptions of the sociocultural and educational contexts of Hong Kong;
- their perceptions of the strategies of local students in learning English;
- their perceptions of local students' attitudes toward learning English;
- their perceptions of their roles as an English language teacher in Hong Kong; and
- their perceptions of the major differences between NETs and LETs in teaching English in Hong Kong.

With the NETs, two additional questions were asked:

- the reasons why they decided to teach English in Hong Kong; and
- their prior experience of teaching ESL/EFL students similar to those in Hong Kong.

During Classroom Observation Interviews.   There were two types of during classroom observation interviews. One type included several informal chats that the first author had with the teachers about the lessons just observed to capture their instant feedback and feelings. Due to the tight teaching timetable and heavy workload of teachers in Hong Kong schools, these exchanges were done in an informal way. Usually, they took place during recess, lunchtime, or on the way to the next classroom. In addition to these informal exchanges, a more formal interview was conducted with each teacher toward the end of the visit. Issues for both the informal and formal exchanges centered on the following:

- general evaluations of the teachers' and their students' performance;
- their favorite teaching activities;
- practical constraints, if any, on their teaching; and
- whether any communication problems have arisen, from their point of view, how they occurred, what could be the possible reasons, what strategies were used to redress the problem and whether they were effective

Information obtained from these reflections were used to supplement the data about the interaction patterns and features obtained during the lesson observation.

Interviews With Students.   Semistructured interviews with students were arranged to listen to the other side of the story in these interactional encounters. Each teacher participant was requested to identify a sample of students, balanced in gender and English proficiency level, to do the interviews. The interviews were done in the students' first language and more or less revolved around the following issues:

- their perceptions of the need to learn English;
- how motivated they were in learning English;
- how did they usually approach the task of learning English, for example, their most and least favorite English learning tasks;
- whether they have come across difficulties in lessons with the native or nonnative English teachers;
- whether and how these difficulties were overcome;
- whether they perceived any differences between having English lessons with the native and local English teachers

When time allowed, students were required to comment, explain or discuss why certain phenomena happened during the lessons observed, for example, Did they understand a particular point raised by the NET? Why did they provide an answer like that? Why didn't they respond to a question asked?

Postclassroom Observation Interviews.   Postclassroom observation interviews were conducted with the teacher participants. During these interviews, interesting parts of the lessons in the form of transcriptions were brought back by the first author to understand the teachers' interpretations of possible causes of certain phenomena. The major purpose was to allow an opportunity for the participants to express their views on issues that appeared to be intriguing or puzzling to the researcher. Getting to know the perspectives of the participants may reduce biased interpretations of the data. The most frequently asked questions were:

- Can you think of any possible reasons why the students use (e.g., Cantonese) in this situation?
- Is there any reason why you conducted this exercise in this way?
- How would you interpret your behavior in this incident?
- How would you interpret the students' behavior in this incident?

The data collection process generated two major types of data; (1) the primary data from the video/audiotaped lessons; and (2) the secondary data from the in-depth interviews and reflections. Both types were carefully transcribed for microanalysis. Our framework for analysis is presented in chapter 5.

QUESTIONS FOR REFLECTION AND DISCUSSION

1. Why do people in non-English-speaking countries learn English? Take your country or the place where you teach as an example.

2. What role does English play in your everyday life? How about your students?

3. As a LET, do you have a lot of opportunities to come into contact with native English speakers? If yes, who are they and what do you usually talk about with them?

4. As a NET, how often do you communicate with people in a language other than your own first language? On what occasions? What advantage can the experience of being a bilingual give to an ESL or EFL teacher?

2

The Native-Speaking English Teachers (NETs) in Postcolonial Hong Kong

[When I first learnt that I was going to have a native English teacher], I felt very happy because foreign teachers are more fun; but at the same time, I am worried about communication problems. It could be just like a hen talking to a duck

—secondary year 1 schoolgirl (1998)

I like local teachers more than foreign teachers because when I have problems, I can ask the local teachers in Cantonese. It's very difficult to understand foreign teachers.

—secondary year 2 schoolboy (1998)

I could have more contacts with foreigners and raise my English ability. They [the NETs] could raise our English standard, and we could learn western culture from them.

—secondary year 3 schoolgirl (1998)

These utterances, originally in Cantonese, were made by Hong Kong secondary school students who have been taught by NETs. They reflect different and yet typical perspectives about the *tensions* and *potentials* of the interactions that take place inside the classroom between NETs and some Hong Kong students. "A hen talking to a duck" vividly depicts the predicament in which some local students and probably, the NETs found themselves by being mutually unintelligible. On the other hand, some students found that contacts with the NETs opened up opportunities to explore cultures other than their own, an experience that is generally acknowledged to add value to learning a second/foreign language.

To understand the dialogues between the NETs and the Hong Kong students, readers should first understand the sociohistorical background and sociopolitical connotations of the NET scheme in Hong Kong. The NET scheme provides a context where the cross-cultural dialogues take place. How the scheme was presented by the Government, and how it was received and interpreted by the public have a direct impact on how the NETs, the local English teachers (LETs), and the Hong Kong students (HKSs) perceive their roles and responsibilities, and help shape the sense of identity of all parties involved in the interaction.

In this chapter, we introduce a brief history of the construction and implementation of schemes to recruit NETs in Hong Kong, and discuss how these schemes were received and interpreted by different stakeholders that include the local school personnel, the NETs themselves, and the students.

THE NET SCHEME AND ITS PRECEDENTS

The emergence of schemes to recruit NETs in Hong Kong cannot be viewed in isolation from the status and perceived standards of English in Hong Kong. As the national language of the former colonial government, the high status of English in the government, education, and business sectors has been widely documented (Lin, 19996a; Luke & Richards, 1982). On July 1, 1997, the sovereignty of Hong Kong was formally handed over from Britain to the People's Republic of China after the former had ruled Hong Kong as a colony for 155 years. Whether the change of sovereignty will lead to a corresponding change in the status and functions of English has been keenly discussed by many sociolinguists. Will the majority of the Hong Kong people who had been disadvantaged under the colonial rule due to insufficient mastery of English, display the kind of ultranationalistic ideologies that the Tamil community in Sri Lanka displayed after independence, and adopt a strategy of opposition "to reject English lock-stock-and-barrel" (Canagarajah, 2000, p. 127)?

Views were of course diverse, but one representative view held before 1997 tended to envisage declining importance of English in Hong Kong. For example, in his paper discussing societal accommodation to English and Putonghua[11] in Hong Kong at the 20th century's end, Pierson (1998) quoted several references (e.g., Godfrey, 1992; Harris, 1989; Lau, 1991; Purves, 1989; Surry, 1994) published a few years earlier predicting a decreasing value of English as one of Hong Kong's greatest assets. It was reported that demand for English instruction had already experienced a noticeable slump leading to the closing down of some commercially operated English tuition centres (Godfrey, 1992). It was even suggested by Surry (1994) that the ability to use English well is no longer of much concern to the business community. Lau (1991) speculated that Putonghua would replace English as the "language of success."

After 1997, however, the status and power of English have remained unchanged, or have even become stronger in Hong Kong after the official status of English was stipulated in the Basic Law. The obvious determination of the government of the new Hong Kong Special Administrative Region (HKSAR) to maintain the importance of English in Hong Kong after 1997 as a *global* language was asserted by the first Chief Executive as a measure to increase the competitive edge of

Hong Kong's future generations. Language policies were the major issues in the Chief Executive's maiden policy address in October 1997. A community that is *"biliterate* and *trilingual"* was the overarching goal. It means that the younger generations in Hong Kong are expected to be proficient in two written languages (Standard Chinese and English), and three spoken varieties (spoken English, Cantonese, and Putonghua). To achieve this goal, a series of language policies have been introduced, including education through the mother tongue,[12] compulsory Putonghua education, and a huge investment in improving students' English proficiency in tertiary institutions using mechanisms such as exit language assessment tests plus language enhancement programs. The NET scheme was one such mechanism implemented at the secondary school level.

However, the high status and power of English alone was not the only consideration for policymakers to import NETs to teach in local contexts. The perceived falling standards of English by the businessmen and government officials seems to be the major catalyst. Actually, the initiative to recruit native English speaker teachers from overseas to teach at secondary level (equivalent to Grades 7–13 in the North American system) was not a new issue in Hong Kong, nor were worries about the English standards a new discovery. More than 10 years before the sovereignty transfer, reports and discussions on the falling English standards of the younger generations have prevailed in the mass media (see Evans, 1996, and Bolton, 2002 about the "complaint tradition"). To academics familiar with the situation in Hong Kong (e.g., Bolton, 2002; Joseph, 1996), this may be a natural outcome of compulsory education,[13] which results in a growing population of English literate citizens. However, most local employers (mainly businessmen) of school graduates tend to attribute the perceived falling standards to inappropriate teaching methods and the declining quality of the English teachers, the majority of whom are local teachers sharing the L1 of the students.

To remedy these problems, native English-speaking teachers were recruited under the Expatriate English Teacher scheme (EETS) as early as 1986 on a very small scale[14] in response to a recommendation of the 1984 Education Commission Report[15] (see Boyle, 1997b). However, the EET scheme was not well received by local teachers and school principals in general due to a multitude of administrative, pedagogical, and cultural complications. When it comes to job opportunities, expatriate English teachers became competitors of local teachers. The high hope placed on the scheme by the Hong Kong Government to raise English standards among students and even local teachers has been interpreted by most local teachers as a form of discrimination and an insult to their English-teaching competence.

In an unofficial review of the EET scheme by Johnson and Tang (1993), findings from interviews are reported that reflect a rather skeptical attitude of some local teachers, and some senior form students, concerning the "seriousness" as well as the professional and academic qualities of the EETs. This perception was formed mainly because the EETs emphasized communication games and having fun with language, which ran contrary to most students' major concern with the need to pass examinations. There was only limited evidence showing enhanced language proficiency among the students taught by EETs in specific modalities such as listening and, marginally, in speaking competence (British Council, 1989; Education Department, 1990).

The EET scheme continued to operate on a very small scale until 1995 when a similar scheme was relaunched and renamed as the Native English-speaking Teacher scheme (NET), again, as a recommendation in the Education Commission Report No. 6 (Education Commission, 1995) to raise English standards. Although more schools joined the scheme, the scale remained small[16]. However, the measure was reinstated as an official initiative in the first Chief Executive's first policy address in October 1997 under an Enhanced NET scheme (which is the current scheme). The scheme aimed to recruit up to 700 native English-speaking teachers as an extra workforce[17] to teach in local secondary schools in order to, in the Chief Executive's words, raise the quality of English-language teaching and learning with "immediate effect" (Chief Executive, 1997). Schools that had to adopt Chinese to be the medium of instruction (the so-called CMI schools) under the new Medium of Instruction policy in 1998 (see chap. 6) were entitled to hire two NETs so as to counteract the effects of decreased exposure to English after most of the school subjects were taught in Chinese.

THE ROLES AND FUNCTIONS OF THE NETS IN HONG KONG

Importing NETs from Anglo countries to teach English locally is not a unique phenomenon in Hong Kong. Similar schemes have existed in many Asian-Pacific places including Japan, Brunei, Korea, and some prosperous parts of Mainland China such as Beijing, Guangdong and Shanghai, and NET schemes are becoming increasingly popular. The roles and responsibilities of the NETs vary slightly from place to place. Such variations often reflect the views of the policymakers on how best to use NETs (see Walker, 2001, for more information). In the next few paragraphs, we present views on the roles and functions of NETs from different stakeholders, which include the policymakers, the LETs, the NETs, and the students.

Views of the Policymakers

Lai (1999) reported an interesting comparison of native-speaking English teachers schemes in Japan and Hong Kong. She finds that the JET (Japan Exchange and Teaching) scheme tried to enhance "internationalization" in Japan, fostering ties between Japanese youths and the JET participants from western countries more than actually trying to improve foreign language standards. No teaching experience or professional training is required from the English native-speaker applicants recruited under the ALTs (Assistant Language Teachers), a subprogram with heavy weighting under JET. Instead the ALTs must be young university graduates interested in learning more about Japan. They were expected to be cultural ambassadors more than expert language teachers. The contracts were strictly limited to a maximum period of 3 years, which showed that the Japanese Government did not see the value of accumulated teaching experience. In the classrooms, the ALTs worked as coteachers with the local regular English teachers with all teaching materials prepared by the latter (former ALT to first author, personal communication, March 23, 1999). What is more interesting is that all JET participants were strongly advised to learn the Japanese language before and after arriving in Japan to enhance the mutual cultural exchange.

In many respects, the NET scheme in Hong Kong is very different from the JET program in Japan. From the outset, the policymakers in Hong Kong have presented the NET scheme as a panacea to arrest the perceived falling standard of English. It has always been the government's belief that recruiting native English-speaking teachers from overseas would raise the standard of English among students and teachers in Hong Kong, and a high English standard is of paramount importance to the economic prosperity of Hong Kong. Therefore, not only are NETs required to be well-qualified teachers, they should preferably have experience in teaching English to speakers of other languages. All NETs normally serve on a 2-year contract, but all contracts are renewable subject to satisfactory performance. Unlike the JET participants in Japan, the NETs in Hong Kong were discouraged by the government from learning Cantonese for fear that local students would stop using only English with the NETs (NET informant to first author, personal communication).

Whereas the JET program in Japan aims to enhance internationalization in Japan and young people's cultural exchange with people from English-speaking countries, the NET scheme in Hong Kong has more linguistic and narrowly instrumental purposes in that its introduction has always been presented as a means to raise the standard of English (see Boyle, 1997a). According to Johnson and Tang (1993, pp. 205–206), EETs are expected to achieve three major goals:

1. To change the sociolinguistic climate of the workplace, that is, to change the school from an ethnocentric, monolingual, Hong Kong, Cantonese-speaking environment, to a bilingual, bicultural, internationally oriented workplace:

   (a) by providing a need for Chinese staff to use English for professional, administrative, and social purposes;
   (b) by providing opportunities for students to interact with non-Chinese, non-Cantonese-speaking members of staff outside as well as inside the classroom.

2. To raise the quality of English language teaching in the school.
3. To improve the standard of English of the students taught by the ETS (expatriate teachers).

Although these descriptions do not suggest very concrete duties, a strong implication is for the NETs to be agents of change in schools, and this implication might have been the major reason causing friction between the NETs and the LETs (Tang & Johnson, 1993; see next section). According to a more recent review of the roles and responsibilities of the NETs in Hong Kong by Walker (2001), when the NET scheme was relaunched in the mid-1990s, guidelines issued by the then Education Department[18] show attempts to downplay the change-agent role of the NETs. The guidelines[19] (listed later) are more specific compared to those found in Johnson and Tang (1993) and they seem to suggest roles "that were to be largely similar to locals' but to some extent complementary and supportive" (Walker, 2001, p. 55):

1. To be responsible for classroom teaching and assessment.
2. To provide support to the English panel chairperson, including assisting in the tailoring of the curriculum and the preparation of teaching materials.
3. To assist in conducting extracurricular activities related to the English language, such as speech, drama, debates, choral speaking and extensive reading.
4. To assist in running more oral activities for students after school.
5. To assist in setting up an English corner in the school where students can come together to practice oral English and read English books under their guidance.
6. To act as an English language resource person for other teachers in the school.

This new set of guidelines suggest a more supportive and supplementary role of the NETs (note the use of the verb "assist"). The availability of NETs is to be viewed as extra resources.

Views of NETs and LETs

According to Johnson and Tang (1993), friction occurred between NETs and LETs under the EELT scheme because many NETs "carried with them [the sense] that they had a mission or at least a responsibility to bring about change" (p. 44). However, they were employed at the lowest managerial level, as classroom teachers, whereas "the positions of power within the administrative structure were held by Cantonese/English bilinguals" (p. 207). Tension appeared when the LETs felt that the NETs were too aggressive whereas the NETs felt that they were isolated and marginalized. That may be the reason why the EET scheme was not well received.

The relaunched NET schemes since the mid-1990s with the revised guidelines seem much better received by the principals and LETs, probably due to changing global situations and increasing awareness of the importance of international communication for economic success. However, Walker (2001) identified intriguing discrepancies in the perceptions of role priorities of the NETs between the NETs and the LETs (mainly English panel heads). According to Walker (2001, p. 68), all NETs being surveyed and interviewed "tend to prioritize more highly than locals professional solidarity with local teachers" in terms of "assisting in syllabus development," "fitting in with local practices," and "learning from existing practices in ELT." However, English panel chairpersons (EPCs) and teachers in both Chinese-medium and English-medium schools tended to give significantly higher priority than NETs to the NETs' role as "creator of an English-speaking environment" and "cultural ambassador," *not ELT practitioner*" [italics added]. These LETs in general do not welcome NET assistance with syllabi and do not appear to encourage NETs to "fit in." As implied by Walker (2001), NETs are still not valued for their competence to teach English well, but only for their inherent characteristic as a non-Cantonese speaking native English speaker. Their major roles were perceived by many panel chairpersons surveyed to lie not in the day-to-day teaching of the language, but in their ability to get the HKSs to talk more in English. Such mismatch between the NETs' and LETs' perceptions was considered to be "unfortunate" by Walker. Readers might, however, want to compare findings from Walker's (2001) survey with views expressed by the NET participants in this book in chapter 6.

Views of the Students

> I read with shock the report suggesting that the Native English-speaking Teacher (NET) scheme should be dropped. When we had our English lesson with a NET we often burst into laughter and had so many different topics to discuss. We were encouraged to share our views and learn from each other. That's why we loved our NET and strongly believe the scheme helped us a lot.

> I was a student who was not particularly good at English. However, I was lucky enough to have a NET from Australia for 3 years and he changed me completely. His teaching methods were revolutionary. He taught me that just memorizing facts was a foolish approach to learning and raised our interest in English, which motivated us to learn by ourselves. He was interactive too, and gave us the chance to watch English movies and listen to music. Most importantly, he shared his culture and differences with us and tried hard to create a relaxing atmosphere.

The above piece of writing appeared in a letters column of the *South China Morning Post* (December 20, 2003, entitled "Local teachers can't replace a NET"). The writer is a secondary student in Hong Kong. Although what it says about the merits of the NET and the NET scheme only represents the viewpoints of one student, it seems to provide the "consumers'" perspective on an education "product." In this short piece of writing, the student attributed all the positive impacts on his/her English learning to the work of the NETs. She or he described the teaching methods of the NET to be "revolutionary" and without hesitation labeled "memorization," a stereotypical Chinese learning approach, as "foolish." Like the first author of this book, this student values in particular ("most importantly") the sharing of different cultures with the NET. Whether a local English teacher would have generated the same improvements is beyond verification here, but a strong message being sent by this piece of writing is that the NET has created innovative experiences of learning a foreign language (in terms of cultural knowledge and learning approaches) for the students that local teachers may fail to match. Even though being interactive, and using English movies and songs to teach English should by no means be unique abilities of the NETs, how these are done and who does it seems to matter equally much as what is being done.

The student previously mentioned was of course not alone in harboring this feeling of being taught by the NET. Johnson and Tang (1993), after reporting a multitude of factors affecting the successful implementation of the EET Scheme, conclude with a comment about the impact of the scheme on the students:

> For some students at least, there was a sense almost of a *cultural revolution* [italics added]. It was their first contact with live native speakers and it made a *difference* [italics added] to their attitude to the language and to themselves as users of the language. (p. 213)

The description of the students' experience as a "cultural revolution" no doubt sounds a bit condescending because if this experience did exist, it should be mutual to both the teachers and the students. However, it certainly merits further investigation concerning what exactly is the "difference" in the students' attitude to the language and to themselves. It cannot be denied that Hong Kong students in general are developing a positive ethnolinguistic attitude toward NETs. Findings from a small-scale survey on 212 secondary students (aged 13 to 15) in two middle-banding secondary schools conducted by the first author (Luk, 2001) revealed that the majority of the respondents were in favor of having more NETs in schools because "the presence of the NETs increases the opportunities for them to speak English" (p. 31). Moreover, they mentioned one intriguing point that has not been mentioned by any NETs or LETs: Many students felt that "the NET's English is better or more standard" (p. 31) compared to that of the LETs. However, it must also be mentioned that the majority of student respondents who were against employing more NETs revealed their anxiety over communication difficulties with the NETs because of the latter's lack of knowledge of the students' L1. Even though students' views may have little impact on policymaking, their perceptions of and reactions to the NETs' teaching directly affect the dialogic interaction in the classroom and the institutional functioning of the NETs and the Hong Kong students.

In the last section of this chapter, we attempt to summarize different perspectives of the NET schemes in Hong Kong.

THE NET SCHEME—AN ACT OF LINGUISTIC IMPERIALISM, STRATEGIC PRAGMATISM, OR A POSTCOLONIAL RE-MEMBERING OF THE PAST?

Even though no empirical findings have ever been provided to support the correlation between NET teaching and enhanced proficiency, the scheme was implemented on a territorywide scale and has continued to expand to the primary schools in Hong Kong. A widely held belief among the Hong Kong Education Department officials about the merits of employing native English teachers is that students' exposure to English will be increased (Education Commission Report No. 6, 1995). To many local teachers, however, the repeated introductions of the NET scheme is a clear sign of the government's lack of faith in their ability to achieve what the native teachers are expected to achieve.

When Hong Kong had just entered the postcolonial era, a large-scale expansion of the NET scheme inevitably conjured up intriguing political and ideological connotations in many people's minds. Some local academics, for example, Law (1997) and Lai (1999), view the first SAR government's measures to preserve the status of English and recruit native English speakers from the West as *neocolonizing* measures to extend British interests by offering more job opportunities to the British.[20] The NET scheme in particular was criticized by Boyle (1997a), who is a well-known native English-speaking academic experienced in English language education in Hong Kong, as an example of "linguistic imperialism in the story of English in Hong Kong" (p. 178). Ever since the term "linguistic imperialism" first appeared in Phillipson (1992), subsequent sociolinguists have cautioned against the possible spread of cultural and political dominance by the English-speaking world powers through "linguicism," which refers to the "ideologies, structures, and practices ... used to legitimate, effectuate, and reproduce an unequal division of power and resources (both material and immaterial) between groups" (Phillipson, p. 47). Linguicism is usually perpetuated by manipulating language terminologies such as mother tongue, and speakers of "other" languages to serve political interests. Rampton (1990) holds that "the supremacy of the native speaker keeps the UK and the US at the centre of ELT ... Governments may use the notion of mother tongue to imply that certain languages are of interest only to particular minority groups, thereby denying either a language or its speakers full involvement in mainstream education" (p. 98).

Although the views of Boyle (1997a) and Lai (1999) seem to be alluding to an outside conspiracy or to a secret deal in action, the Hong Kong government's high expectations on the NETs might be conveying a *sociohistorically cultivated mentality* explicable by the postcolonial theories that originate from the works of Gayatri Spivak, Edward Said, and Homi Bhabha (see Gandhi, 1998). In Gandhi's (1998) critical introduction of postcolonial theories, it was said that colonized people in the postcolonial period would experience an ambivalent stage of "postcolonial re-membering." The colonized tend to long for a certain form of continuity with the colonizer who has often portrayed itself as "the disinterested purveyor of cultural enlightenment and reform" (Gandhi, 1998, p. 14). When the colonizers have left, people in the former colony might suffer a "stigma of unauthenticity" because "[t]he Europe they [the colonized] know and value so intimately is always elsewhere. Its reality is infinitely deferred, always withheld from them" (Gandhi, p. 12). The repeated introductions and continued expansion of the NET scheme may be an unconscious instantiation of the mentality of "postcolonial re-membering" (p. 9) of the first Hong Kong Special Administrative Region (HKSAR) Government whose first batch of ruling parties was mainly constituted of the former key civil servants under the former British colonial government.

To many other people, however, postcolonial theories may appear to be too radical or overreacting. Li (2002), for example, after making a comprehensive review of Hong Kong's colonial history and language attitude development, argued that perpetuating the status of and demand for English in the postcolonial period (as evident in the parents' strong preference for English-medium education) revealed a pragmatic self-pursuit of English as a "value-adding commodity" (p. 50) rather than a passive acceptance of social control through linguistic imperialism. In view of the current globalized economy, it seems to be perfectly reasonable to expect Hong Kong young people to be proficient in English to conduct transnational communication in English.

It must be noted that the native English-speaking teacher controversy is not specific to Hong Kong. Elsewhere in the world of applied linguistics and TESOL, heated debates have been going on. There seems also to be an uncontainable force in EFL/EIL places aspiring for more NETs. Is this worldwide trend favoring more NETs in TESOL a confirmation of their unique achievements in enhancing English standards, or is it just some more evidence of "linguistic imperialism" (Phillipson, 1992)? Will this continued demand and supply of native English-speaking teachers in places outside the so-called Centre powers[21] (e.g., United States, Britain) perpetuate the pernicious effects envisaged by academics such as Pennycook (1994, 1998), Phillipson (1992), and Lai (1999)? Or should we view the issue with more openmindedness, acknowledging the potential positive impacts of NETs on the students? In the next chapter, we examine the issue of native speaker teachers from a global perspective. This will form an important background for our interpretation of how native English-speaker teachers function or are expected to function in EFL settings.

QUESTIONS FOR REFLECTION AND DISCUSSION

1. Why and how is English able to maintain its status and functions in postcolonial Hong Kong? Are similar phenomena observed in other former colonies of Britain such as Singapore, Malaysia, or India?

2. What are your views toward the growing quest for native English-speaking teachers to teach English in EFL settings such as Hong Kong?

3. In your opinion, what major role(s) should NETs assume in schools in EFL settings? Should they take a greater leadership role in the English curriculum panel, or take a more auxiliary role mainly as an L2 cultural and linguistic resource person?

3

The Native-Speaking English
Teachers in the Global ELT Industry

I n chapter 2, we briefly presented the history of the NET schemes in Hong
Kong and pointed out the inextricable connection between the emergence of
the NET schemes and the status and perceived falling standards of English in
Hong Kong. We also explored the nature of the NET schemes as compared to
similar schemes in other Southeast Asian countries, and discussed how the
NET schemes were received by different stakeholders such as LETs and HKSs. We
ended chapter 2 by presenting two controversial views of the NET schemes from local academics in Hong Kong. One view tends to see the NET schemes as a kind of
neocolonialism, whereas the other view only reiterates the pragmatic value of learning a language from its native speakers.

What has been presented in chapter 2 is a complex scenario of differing expectations and perceptions of the roles, status, and symbolic meanings of the NETs by
different parties in postcolonial Hong Kong. In this chapter, we temporarily move
away from the specific situation of Hong Kong to look at how the issue of NETs
has been a hot topic for debate in the global arena. We approach the issue by presenting concurrent but contesting views about NETs with three focuses, about defining "native" speakers, about their pedagogical effectiveness, and about their
sociopolitical implications in TESOL.

ON DEFINING NATIVE SPEAKERS

Debates from this perspective tend to focus on the validity of attempts to define "native" speakers of a language. To many people, a native speaker is that idealized per-

son with a complete and possibly innate competence in the language (Pennycook, 1994). They are the models we appeal to for the "truth" about the language; they know what the language is and what the language isn't (Davies, 2003). It seems to be a commonsense view that we are all native speakers of a certain language. In laypeople's terms, it is our mother tongue.

The notions of native speaker and mother tongue have come under severe attacks since the 1980s mainly by sociolinguists. For example, Charles Ferguson (1983, p. vii) concluded that concepts such as native speakers and mother tongues are only items from "the linguist's set of professional myths about language." Rampton (1990, p. 98), summarizing the viewpoints of Ferguson and other sociolinguists such as Braj Kachru, argued that there are two problems with the concepts of mother tongue and the native speaker:

1. They spuriously emphasize the biological at the expense of the social. This is reflected through constant reference to ethnicity and nationality when talking about native speakers and their mother tongues.
2. They mix up language as an instrument of communication with language as a symbol of social identification. In the recruitment of teachers, this has been translated into "who you are" instead of "what you know."

To counteract the unjust effects created by these concepts, Rampton (1990) proposed two parameters to describe the ties between a speaker and the language he or she speaks; language expertise and language loyalty (or language allegiance). With these parameters, biological inheritance would no longer be the sole criterion for a native speaker identity. Since then, it has become generally acknowledged that "nativeness" in a language can be assessed based on expertise, psychological allegiance, social affiliation, and confidence (Boyle 1997b, synthesizing views from Davies, 1991; Rampton, 1990; Tay, 1982). These criteria will enable people whose ethnic origins are not one of those English-speaking countries to claim to be native English speakers if they have met the other four criteria. There were also attempts to displace the debilitating connotation of "nonnative" with other more neutral constructs such as outer/inner circle speakers (Kachru, 1986), speakers of English as a lingua franca (Jenkins, 2000), international English professionals (Brutt-Griffler & Samimy, 1999), or experts/novices of language variants (Canagarajah, 2005a).

Amid a general atmosphere to deconstruct the notion of native speaker and mother tongue, Davies (2003), in the second revised edition of his book exploring how the notion of native speaker should be understood in applied linguistics, boldly claimed that "the concept of the native speaker is not a fiction but has the reality that 'membership,' however informal, always gives ... [The native speaker] carries the tradition, is the repository of 'the language' ... expected to exhibit normal control especially in fluent connected speech ... [possesses] an intuitive feel [about another native speaker based on] an assumption of shared cultural knowledge." (p. 207)

In Davies' (2003, p. 210) configuration, a native speaker can be distinguished from L2 learners of the language along six characteristics including (a) the age of acquisition; (b) intuitions in grammaticality judgment of idiolectal grammar; (c) intuitions in grammaticality judgment of group language grammar; (d) a unique capacity to set clause boundaries by pausing; (e) a unique capacity to write creatively; and (f) to interpret and translate into the L1 of which he or she is a native speaker. However, it does not rule out the possibility of an L2 learner developing into "an L2 native speaker." He proposed understanding the concept of native speakers from two senses, the "flesh and blood type," and the "ideal type." Whereas the ideal type represents the mythical definition of native speakers as products of the homogenized, error-free linguistic Eden, the flesh and blood type of native speakers can be understood along five definitions (Davies, 2003, p. 214):

1. native speaker by birth or by early childhood exposure,
2. native speaker (or native speaker-like) by being an exceptional learner,
3. native speaker through education using the target-language medium (the *lingua franca* case) [italics in original],
4. native speaker by virtue of being a native user (the post-colonial case) and
5. native speaker through long residence in the adopted country.

Davies' (2003) attempt to define native speakers along these lines seems to be one that accounts for the biological, linguistic, and social aspects of the native-speaker construct. Although he does not rule out any possibility of L2 learners becoming "native speakers," he proposes a number of restrictive criteria that suggest the high-level difficulty (mainly in terms of age learning and length of residence) for most L2 learners to attain "native" speaker competence and status. The native speaker identity remains a lofty target for many learners. Very often, it is beyond the L2 learners' autonomy to claim membership of the native speaker community even though they might have fulfilled most of Davies' definitions. Kramsch (1998b, p. 23) asked two thought-provoking questions: "What prevents potentially bilingual outsiders from becoming integrated into a group? What is the authority of the speech community based on?" As suggested by Bruff-Griffler and Samimy (2001, p. 102), "factors determining whether the given international speaker of English is a 'native' or 'nonnative' speaker are not primarily linguistic, but *socially* constructed" (italics in original). The dichotomy between NS–NNS is often drawn according to "a perceived notion of what a 'native speaker' or 'nonnative speaker' should look like and sound like." Amin (1999) illustrated it well with her personal experience. Even though she considers herself a native speaker because English is the language she knows best, she was not positioned as a native speaker by most of her colleagues because she carries a Pakistan accent. We return to the sociopolitical implications of the "native speaker" construct in later sections.

ON THE PEDAGOGICAL EFFECTIVENESS OF NETS

Although NETs have become a much sought-after identity and "product" in ESL/EFL settings, their pedagogical effectiveness has never been conclusive enough to support the quest. In the following paragraphs, we present both positive and negative arguments and evidence regarding NETs' pedagogical effectiveness.

The Positive Arguments

At first sight, learning a language from somebody who is a native speaker of that language seems highly reasonable and natural because there should be no doubt about his or her expertise and experience in that language. Except for a minority of people, the language we acquire as we grow up is usually our strongest language. We may learn a second or third language afterward, but to many of us, the language(s) we learn subsequent to our acquisition of the first is seldom comparable to our first in terms of expertise, and emotional and sociocultural affiliation. It is therefore not difficult to understand the rationale behind most people's quest for native speaker models in language learning if we examine the issue from these two perspectives: (a) Native speakers could provide L2 learners cultural and linguistic exemplification of the target language; and (b) native speakers could facilitate the participation of L2 learners in the negotiation process in communicative activities.

Native Speakers for Cultural and Linguistic Exemplification. The growing awareness of the intertwining relationship between language and culture has laid emphasis on learning a language as learning a set of linguistic symbols with socially situated meanings. Interpreting the meanings of these socially situated linguistic symbols involves knowledge of the "cultural models" (or our mental frameworks; Gee, 1996), which may be developed best through constant engagement in the discourses of the target speech communities (Donato & McCormick, 1994; Hall, 1993). As evident in Barratt and Kontra's (2000) survey, native speaker teachers were viewed by the student respondents as "authentic, walking, breathing resources about other cultures" (p. 20). Native speaker teachers were also felt to be demonstrating the "subtle differences of usage" (p. 20).

On the other hand, difficulties of nonnative English speaker teachers of English to answer spontaneous questions from the learners on the sociolinguistic and cultural aspects of the target language due to insufficient sociocultural and linguistic competence and confidence were reported in the study by Burnaby and Sun (1989) on Chinese teachers' views of western language teaching. Therefore, it seems highly reasonable to argue that given the same academic and professional qualifications, native speakers of a language should naturally be felt to be the ideal teacher of that language.

Native Speakers as Facilitators of L2 Learners' Use of the Target Language. The role of native speakers in L2 acquisition has gained importance with the advent of the communicative language teaching approach and the emergence of interactionist theories of second language learning (Long, as quoted in Savignon, 1991). Interaction strategies such as negotiation (which involves adjustment of one's speech phonologically, lexically, and morphosyntactically to resolve difficulties in mutual understanding) is felt to be conducive to L2 learners' (or NNS[22]) use of the target language and such negotiation seems to be best promoted with one of the interlocutors being a native speaker (NS) of the target language. Through NS–NNS negotiation process, L2 learners will obtain L2 structural and semantic information, feedback on interlanguage production, and opportunities to modify their interlanguage for successful communication (Pica, 1992). Interaction between two NNSs who share the same L1 may not promote the same amount of L2 use among themselves as they are more likely to resort to their L1 for off-record talk, in the absence of the teacher (Hancock, 1997) and when disruptions appear (Platt & Brooks, 1994).

Two studies (Tsang, 1994; Tsui, 1985) conducted in Hong Kong seem to offer positive evidence in support of the facilitative role of native speaker teachers in second language learning. These two studies, conducted almost 10 years apart, compare the input and interaction patterns of two English teachers in Hong Kong, one being a "native English speaker" and one being "nonnative" (terms used in the papers) using a classroom interaction analysis method with a predetermined speech acts coding system. Findings show that teachers' and students' interaction practices in the native speakers' classes were more conducive to second language acquisition. For example, Tsui (1985) found that the native speaker asked more reasoning questions, gave more comments on students' responses, and made more simplifications in input and interaction. In Tsang's (1994) study, the native English teacher was observed to have more bound exchanges[23] with the class, a pattern that helps to maintain a longer interaction. Students in the NET's class also took more responsibility for participating in and initiating during classroom interaction. It seems that both Tsui's and Tsang's studies are implying that NETs are better able to provide a more favorable classroom environment for second language acquisition.

Although neither Tsui (1985) nor Tsang (1994) has explored whether it was the nativeness, or the pedagogical techniques and styles of the teachers that resulted in the differences, the perceived value of the native English-speaking teachers as facilitators of ESL learners' use of the target language has also been confirmed elsewhere. In a survey done by Barratt and Kontra (2000) in Hungary, NNSs showed their preference for NETs "because they do not speak Hungarian, it is in itself a great motivation to think and speak in English," wrote one student (Barratt & Kontra, p. 20). Similar findings have also been reported by Luk (2001) in Hong Kong. Up to 70% of a total of 212 secondary students of different levels stated their desire to have more NETs in school because the availability of the NETs would "force" them to use English more because the NETs do not normally speak and understand their L1. It seems, therefore, that in places where English is not used for intracommunity functions (as in Hong Kong), the presence of native English-speaker teachers can serve as a motivation for students to use the language for communication. This is precisely the main reason put forward by the policymakers in Hong Kong when recruiting NETs.

The Negative Arguments

Despite all those positive findings in support of the native speakers' role in L2 learning mentioned earlier, voices against using native English-speaker teachers have been gaining in volume. There are two major views: (1) Native speaker models create unrealistic and unattainable goals for L2 learners; and (2) native speaker teachers are often deficient in knowledge of local students' cultural and language backgrounds.

Native Speaker Models Create Unrealistic and Unattainable Goals for L2 Learners.   Cook (1999) criticized the favor of native speaker teachers as creating unrealistic expectations on the L2 learners by taking the native speaker models as the goalpost. He claimed that L2 learners are in fact "multicompetent" language users rather than deficient L2 speakers, and that "the prominence of the native speaker in language teaching has obscured the distinctive nature of the successful L2 user and created an unattainable goal for L2 learners" (p. 185). He calls for adopting the language of the skilled L2 users rather than a native speaker variety as the source of information in designing the ELT curriculum. Leung, Harris, and Rampton (1997), in addition to pointing out the redundancy of the "binary native speaker versus other" in multilingual social contexts, called for TESOL pedagogy that is more "pupil sensitive" and that caters to individual needs of ESL students (p. 558).

NS Teachers Often Lack Knowledge of Local Students' Cultural and Language Backgrounds.   One of the representative studies on this issue was done by Guthrie (1984) who compared students' behavior in a bilingual Chinese-English teacher's lessons with that in a monolingual English-speaking teacher's. He found that the monolingual teacher's lesson demonstrated a "certain lack of control" (p. 44) of students' behavior. As for the bilingual teacher, her knowledge of students' L1 enabled her to assess more efficiently how well the students understood the lesson. It seems that knowledge of students' L1 stands as a valuable resource to the bilingual teacher. Even before Guthrie's paper, a study on foreigner talk in classroom settings had shown that the NET's speech when teaching ESL students tended to show ambiguous oversimplification on the one hand, and confusingly redundant overelaboration on the other (Chaudron, 1983). The writer called for "a better understanding of L2 learners' comprehension of the varying structures that teachers employ while attempting to simplify their instruction" (p. 142).

Teaching and learning English in an EFL situation inevitably have to be localized, with participants bearing cultural, ideological, and social norms that may be totally foreign to the "native" speakers of English. Native speaker teachers being imported to teach in such a setting usually lack the "local knowledge" of the students and are in a less favorable position than the local teachers to acknowledge the complexities of the meanings students with limited language skills are trying to produce (Holliday, 1994; Pennycook, 1994). Similar views were shared by Boyle (1997b) and Tang (1997) who claimed that even though the native speakers are at a distinct advantage over the nonnative speakers in terms of language ability, "linguistic and cultural affinity with the students often favour the non-native speaker" (Boyle, 1997b, p. 169).

On the Sociopolitical Privileges of NETs

Although applied linguists such as Davies (2003) would argue that every person is the native speaker of at least one language, any attempt to understand and interpret the "native" speaker as a generic notion across languages may meet with criticism because languages in the world are often socially hierarchized, and being a native speaker of a certain language may not enable the person to enjoy the same amount of privileges and status as the native speakers of some other languages. The situation is particularly acute with English. When people talk about the native speakers of English, they tend to think of Britain and America as the two centers of native speaker origins. The sociopolitical implications of native English speaker teachers were most effectively brought to our attention by Robert Phillipson in his book named "Linguistic Imperialism" published in1992. A working definition of English linguistic imperialism is that "the dominance of English is asserted and maintained by the establishment and continuous reconstitution of structural and cultural inequalities between English and other languages" (Phillipson, 1992, p. 47).

Phillipson (1992) argued that the global ELT business contributes in education systems to the reproduction and distribution of political, economic, and cultural power in non-English dominant, or periphery places. He revealed how this agenda was effectuated by Britain in the Makerere Report published in 1961 arising from a Commonwealth Conference on the Teaching of English as a Second Language, held at Maderere, Uganda in 1961. For the first time, the report establishes the privileged status of expatriate teachers from English-speaking countries:

> Expatriate teachers from the English-speaking countries will be needed for many years to come; they should be employed increasingly as teacher trainers or university lecturers rather than as teachers in schools, since the world demand is so great that the so-called "resource countries" may not be able much longer to provide a substantial supply of school teachers. (Makerere Report, 1961, p. 6, quoted in Phillipson, 1982, p. 184)

As suggested by Phillipson (1992), these statements established the authoritative role of the Centre English powers in supplying resources and expertise for the world's ELT business. Phillipson (1992) criticized this ideology as the "native speaker fallacy" to denote the tenet, which he feels to be false, that the ideal teacher of English is a native speaker simply because of the language model they provide.

Such linguistic credibility of native speakers follows the Chomskyan notion that native speakers are the most ideal language informants because of their greater facility in demonstrating fluent, idiomatically appropriate language, and in appreciating the cultural connotations of the language. Grammarians such as Quirk (1990) also endorsed the value of native speaker teachers in standardizing English because it is feared that periphery variants of English will spoil the purity of English and affect mutual intelligibility among speakers of the language (Canagarajah, 1999a, p. 82).

Since Phillipson, there appeared a deluge of arguments against relying on native speakers as English language teachers, particularly in situations where English is learned as a second (ESL), or foreign/international (EFL/EIL), language (e.g., Holliday, 1994; Pennycook, 1998; Rampton, 1990). Some of these discussions have been mentioned in the earlier sections of this chapter. The general arguments go that because English is considered a global language, it does not belong to any particular country and the concept of native English speakers has become hard to define (see for example, Widdowson, 1993). The increasing number of speakers learning and using English for a variety of social and academic functions in the outer and expanding circles (see Kachru, 1986) of English users has resulted in the phenomenon of world Englishes that denote the phonological and syntactical variants employed by EFL users. Some of these variants have already been institutionalized as indigenous English varieties (such as Singaporean English, Indian English, Philippine English, etc.; see Bolton, 2002 for a discussion of potential Hong Kong varieties of English), which often assert a sense of national identity of the people in these former British and American colonies.

However, despite all these attempts to caution against the native speaker fallacy, native speaker teachers continue to be a privileged commodity in high demand. Advertisements of English tutorial schools in most places still flaunt the use of native speaker English teachers (see Canagarajah, 1999a; Cook, 2000, for evidence). In some instances, the word "Caucasian" is even specified, (A. Pennycook, personal communication, June 2002, during the Knowledge and Discourse 2 Conference). The privileged position of NETs in TESOL settings establishes them as "the custodians and arbiters not only of proper English but of proper pedagogy as well" (Widdowson, 1993, p. 387). It is the public's general belief that because native speakers have acquired the language and culture as an integrated experience and have a feel for the nuances and idiomatic usage of the language that the nonnative speaker cannot claim to possess, native speakers must know more about the knack of teaching and learning the language than do the nonnatives. For example, in Hong Kong, the NETs are always presented as being better able to implement more innovative methods of teaching English such as using task-based and student-centered approaches, in contrast to the more traditional teacher-transmission model believed to be employed by most local teachers (Young & Lee, 1987). It has therefore been suggested by some people that NETs should work as consultants (which implies a higher status than ordinary school teachers) in ELT teacher development programs.

According to Canagarajah (1999a), an "undue emphasis on the linguistic status/proficiency of the teachers excuse them from understanding the local languages, cultures, and social conditions of the communities where they are teaching" (p. 84). It implies that although LETs may be discriminated against in ELT by their non-Centre based accents and nonidiomatic use of grammar, NETs are by no means criticized for their lack of knowledge of the larger social, political, and cultural conditions of the communities from which their students come. Such a phenomenon has also generated undesirable impacts on the TESOL profession and the quality of the pedagogical services associated with the ELT enterprises—such as the production of textbooks and other teaching aids. To satisfy people's desire for native speaker models (which is considered more "authentic"[24]), ELT publishers (which mostly are situated in the Centre) would most conveniently produce textbooks and audiovisual aids based on their own norms and expectations. Thus, most ELT textbooks would contain discourses, situations, and cultural content unfamiliar to the teachers and students in EFL settings.

The Synergy View

Whereas many TESOL scholars are working on deconstructing the notion of native speakers, some researchers such as Canagarajah (1999a) have suggested a reconfiguration of the ELT profession and associate the relationship between "centre" and "periphery" professionals with the English use in a particular situation:

> Distinguishing ESL and EFL situations, we can say that Periphery professionals have an advantage in teaching students in communities where English is learned as a second or widely used language for intracommunity purposes (often with indigenous communicative norms). On the other hand, Centre professionals may make a greater contribution for students learning English as a foreign language for use in Centre communities for institutional/formal purposes or for specialized purposes in restricted contexts of use. (i.e., English for specific purposes; p. 89)

Based on Canagarajah's (1999a) views, the NET scheme in Hong Kong seems well justified as English performs less an *intracommunity* function. However, viewing either centre or periphery professionals as a totalistic unity is itself problematic. The fact that centre or periphery professionals do not come from the same Centre or Periphery renders the talk of a "linguistic norm" futile. The worldwide diasporas and increasingly globalized nature of interactions have also resulted in people from different peripheries coming into contact, making the intra/intercommunity language-use dichotomy difficult to maintain.

However, it cannot be denied that NETs constitute a kind of resource in TESOL, not so much the exemplification of language norms/standards, but the provision of intercultural language experience to the students. Luk (2001) argued that "[t]he availability of English professionals from an international arena would enrich the manpower and resources for learning English for international communication in the local region" (p. 35). The personal history of the two authors in learning English is testimony to the potential positive impacts of opportunities of cross-cultural interactions on their development as English users. The need for local students to have the experience of direct interaction with English users from all over the world has become more acute than ever, particularly under the influence of the advance of information technology and globalized economy (Warschauer, 2000). Increased interaction with NETs might be the beginning of a development of students' intercultural communication resources (see further discussion in chap. 10).

THE STANCE OF THIS BOOK—PROBLEMATIZING "NATIVENESS" AS A PREGIVEN ENTITY

It is beyond the scope of this book to explore whether the huge investment in recruiting native English speaker teachers in non-English dominant places around the world is purely a strategic move to develop citizens' competence in engaging in global communication for economic and political purposes, or an unconscious subscription to linguistic and cultural hegemony[25] of the Centre English powers to perpetuate the latter's economic and political interests. What must be pointed out is that as a reality, native speakerism is a *sociohistorically constructed*, rather than a pregiven, entity. The distinction between native and nonnative traditionally hinges on the degree of mastery of a language code. As a notion advanced by Noam Chomsky, the native speaker is the authority on the language and he or she is the ideal informant providing grammaticality judgments on the language. Over this point, we would like to draw on Pennycook's (2004) concept of "performativity,"[26] which argued against a foundationalist perspective on language and identity. Language, as a system of linguistic signs and meanings, is not a pregiven entity, but a sedimented product of repeated acts of identity through discourse. It goes against many laypeople's thinking that there exists out there a structured system of linguistic signs and meanings on which some people could claim innate ability and authority. Pennycook (2004) enlisted Hopper's (1998, p. 156) idea of an "emergent grammar" that asserts the view that the apparent structure or regularity of grammar is an emergent property that "is shaped by discourse in an ongoing process." Speakers using the grammar of a language and engaging in talk in interaction are at the same time making reference to and being engaged in a dialogic process with former users and uses of the particular language code. "Our speech, that is, all our utterances," is therefore "filled with others' words, varying degrees of awareness and detachment. These words of others carry with them their own expression, their own evaluation tone, which we assimilate, rework and reaccentuate" (Bakhtin, 1986, p.89). Therefore, a language is socioculturally and sociohistorically *coconstructed* by all those who use it repeatedly for actual communications. In the case of English, it should be the contributions of all who use it and every context in which it is used that make it an international language (Chacon, Alvarez, Brutt-Griffler, & Samimy, 2003), but not to be viewed as the exclusive property of the White ethnic British and Americans.

Drawing on Pennycook's (2003, 2004) interpretation of performativity in our current case of the native speaker notion, we argue that "native speakership" of a language should not be seen as a pregiven natural identity and ability, but should be seen as being interpolated through dialogic and repeated acts of discourse in different contexts. No language codes, or systems of grammar, preexist before humankind. We are not born to be native speakers of a particular language. Rather, we develop the ability in a range of language styles and varieties through repeated acts of discourse in interactions, and through these discourses, construct our "identity" as speakers of the particular language. The "native" speakers are generally felt to be different from the "nonnatives" not because of the former's possession of the innate and pregiven linguistic abilities in the language, but because they have been engaged since childhood in different discourses that call for different aspects of manipulation of linguistic uses and meanings, through which linguistic and cultural resources appropriate to changing moments of talk have been acquired.

A native speaker, however, should not be understood as that idealized person who knows all about the language, or has idealized "competence" in the language. As "native" speakers of a certain language ourselves, we all understand that we do not always feel adequate with our currently available linguistic resources in some contexts. For example, although both authors of this paper are native Cantonese speakers, due to social class and age differences, we sometimes experienced difficulties in understanding the slangy expressions used in Cantonese movies that feature the gangster world and youth gangster cultures. To understand what has been said, we often need to refer to the Chinese subtitles, or sometimes, even the English translations. Some years ago, when the first language proficiency test for English teachers[27] was administered in Hong Kong, there were reports in the newspapers (e.g., "Even NETs Fail," 2003) about some NETs having failed the test on grammatical error analysis and explanations. Native speakers may also be weak in some registers such as academic writing even though they may be very fluent in everyday social discourse. Therefore, the depiction that native speakers are fully competent users of a language whereas nonnatives are forever learners could be misleading.

All the previous evidence points to the phenomenon that nativeness is not a stable trait essentially attached to a person, but constantly needs to be (re)constructed, (re)performed, (re)learned, and (re)achieved through repeated discursive acts. Anybody, irrespective of their ethnicities, could perform as a native speaker of a language in a specific context as long as they have demonstrated the skills for communication useful in that particular context. NSs and NNSs of a language should, therefore, not be defined along features such as ethnicities, place of birth, or speech accents,[28] and should not be seen as fixed or immutable categories. A person who in some contexts is recognized as a native speaker of one language could become recognized simultaneously as a native speaker of another language in some other contexts provided that he or she has achieved the relevant communication skills and knowledge pertinent to those contexts through repeated discursive acts.

We believe that in teaching and learning a language in cross-cultural encounters, possessing native speaker proficiency of the target language (or the language being taught) but lacking in knowledge of the native language and culture of the students may not enable the NETs to efficiently and effectively fulfill their communication facilitator role, or to fully maximize their teaching effectiveness. Classrooms with NETs and students with limited English proficiency in an EFL setting constitute interesting and intriguing cross-cultural communication sites imbued with problems of equality and control (van Lier, 2001) in terms of the utilization of linguistic and cultural resources. The asymmetry thus arising may not however slant in favor of the NETs because of their general lack of "native" (or local) knowledge of the linguistic and cultural resources possessed by students in the host country. For successful dialogues to take place in such encounters, both parties need to develop their awareness of both cultural similarities and differences between themselves and how best to negotiate, adjust, transform, and connect (see more discussion in chap. 10).

QUESTIONS FOR REFLECTION AND DISCUSSION

1. Do you have problems claiming yourself to be a native speaker of a certain language? If yes, why? What are the problems? If no, which language, or languages? What are the criteria used?
2. As a TESOL professional, do you agree that your native or nonnative speaker status has, to some extent, advantaged or disadvantaged your career opportunities as TESOL practitioners?

4

Culture and Studies of Interaction

In chapter 3, we discuss concurrent and contesting views about the notion of native speakers and their roles and statuses in the global ELT industry. Although it may be a myth or a fallacy to believe that the best teachers to teach a language are its native speakers, the need to develop intercultural communicative resources in the present-day world due to increased movement and contact between people is no doubt a reality, and the need to cross the communication boundary is the concern of both interacting parties. The growing popularity of the NET schemes in EFL contexts has brought this issue into the classrooms. In this chapter, we discuss the relationship between culture and discourse. We focus on how a situated understanding of cultural practices informs studies of interaction in both classroom and nonclassroom contexts, and how discourse[29] practices revealed in interaction studies inform us of the role of culture as an active process of meaning construction. We begin this chapter by exploring how culture should be understood in light of the present study. We then discuss studies of interaction with a cross-cultural or sociocultural perspective that we believe will help readers to interpret and understand the data presented in chapters 6 through 9.

UNDERSTANDING CULTURE

Traditionally, "culture" as part of school curricula is closely related to *civilization.* Courses on cultural knowledge tend to emphasize what people usually called the "Big C," or "achievement culture" (Tomalin & Stempleski, 1993)—history, geography, artifacts, technology, literature, art, and music, and the way of life. "Little

C," on the other hand, refers to the culturally influenced beliefs and perceptions, especially as expressed through language, but also through cultural behaviors that affect acceptability in the host community, such as customs, habits, dress, foods, leisure, and so forth, and is termed "behaviour culture" by Tomalin and Stempleski (1993, pp. 6–7).

"Big C" and "little C" in these senses represent mainly an iconic or symbolic view of culture, focusing on observable and surface features of culture. However, we should not overlook the more ideological and mental view of culture that refers to how culture can be understood cognitively through investigating people's beliefs, values, and reasoning systems. This view attempts to describe the principles and ideologies that guide and shape people's behavior and manners. For example, whereas the British are usually described as having a preference to begin a conversation by talking about the weather, many Chinese that the authors know, particularly those from the older generations, would greet others by asking if they have eaten yet. These discourse practices reflect what the two peoples believe to be their greatest concerns.[30] This mental view of culture also attempts to capture how people understand and interpret the world or universe around them with a shared but tacit set of assumptions (Garfinkel, 1967). For example, it was mentioned in Scollon and Scollon (2001) that whereas a westerner would consider addressing a Chinese business partner by his Chinese first name as a gesture of "symmetrical solidarity" to show close, friendly, and egalitarian relationships, the Chinese man, on the other hand, prefers "symmetrical deference" and feels embarrassed and uncomfortable with his western partner's insensitivity to cultural differences because only very intimate relatives would call a Chinese person by their Chinese first name (see Li, 2003). Such difference in interpretation of a seemingly universal semiotic system probably reflects different outcomes of different cultural socialization histories of the two people.

Over the last 10 years, a strong message conveyed by academics engaged in cultural studies is the danger of *essentialization* of culture. That means when we attempt to interpret people's practices from a cultural perspective, it is important that we avoid subscribing to unidimensional stereotypical cultural categories. Although it is often useful to talk about people's beliefs and value systems as culturally constructed, they should be viewed as representing tendencies and general patterns as abstracted by the analyst only, and not as cultural fixities. For example, from the authors' experience, beginning a conversation by commenting on the weather seems a common practice across nationalities, particularly when people travel abroad and experience different types of weather. Weather often becomes the most noticeable marker of a change of circumstances. Talking about the weather may, therefore, not be the British's distinct cultural trait, as many people have suggested. In this book, discourse practices are interpreted in the light of cultural tendencies and patterns instead of as cultural stereotypes.

Particularly relevant to the current book is the view of culture as a *verb,* rather than a noun (Street, 1993). Instead of asking what culture is, we should ask "what culture does." As argued by Street (1993), the term "culture" is a signifying process related to the active construction of meaning. Rather than pitching our focus on defining culture, sociocultural researchers should investigate how culture does the work of "defining words, ideas, things and groups ..., under what circumstances and for what reasons" (p. 25). This view of culture as an active process of meaning making is crucial to the data interpretation in this book. As is shown in the subsequent chapters, the joint construction of interaction practices by the teachers and the students, and their mutual interpretation of each other's interaction practices are not static and consistent processes, but are context dependent, and potentially gender and social class specific. For example, even though all students reported in the present book were Chinese by ethnicity, they often displayed rather disparate and unpredictable discourse practices during the interaction. The idea that culture constitutes resources for sense-making and interpretation (Heap, 1976) is further elaborated and exemplified in chapters 5 and 7.

UNDERSTANDING CROSS-CULTURAL OR INTERCULTURAL INTERACTION

As its name suggests, "cross-cultural" involves two cultures. The term is often used to refer to "the meeting of two cultures or two languages across the political boundaries of nation-states" (Kramsch, 1998a, p. 81), and the term often appears in studies involving comparisons across cultures. The terms "cross-cultural" and "intercultural" are sometimes used interchangeably (see Swann, Deumert, Lillis, & Mesthrie, 2004; Kramsch, 1998a). In some cultural studies, researchers found the term "cross-cultural" too restrictive because it implied a comparison between cultures (Samovar & Porter, 1995). Austin (1998) attempted to distinguish the two terms by denoting the successful achievement of understanding with the term "intercultural" while reserving the term "cross-cultural" to only the act of crossing back and forth between two cultures. In this book, the authors will use both "cross-cultural" and "intercultural" to denote contacts of speakers from different cultures, with Austin's (1998) distinction in mind. As is shown in subsequent chapters, some NETs and their Hong Kong students were placed in interaction encounters with or without the successful achievement of understanding. We would like to reserve the term "cross-cultural" particularly for this type of encounter whereas we would employ the term "intercultural" to signify the more desired communicative performance across cultures.

With global increase of diasporic activities, even laypeople are aware that the "one nation–one culture–one language" equation on which the definition of "cross-cultural" predicates, rarely stands. More and more people begin to realize the futility of talking about the "culture" (in its singular form) of a nation. For example, Holliday (1999) employed the term "small cultures" to denote the existence of distinct cultural practices constructed by any cohesive social groups within a large ethnic, national, or international culture. Applied in the educational contexts, if a school generally communicates a unique large culture (e.g., Catholicism or Buddhism), particular classes within the school, or particular groups of students within a class, may constitute small cultures that run counter to the large culture (e.g., speaking vulgar language). Along this vein, the emergence of cross-cultural or intercultural interaction should cover communication between "people from different ethnic, social, gendered cultures within the boundaries of the same national language" (Kramsch, 1998a, p. 81). To this, we would like to add "generation-based" cultural differences. For example, a talk between an English expatriate and a Hong Kong Chinese about the customs and food of Halloween is normally considered to be cross-cultural in nature. A talk between a middle-aged university professor and a teenager about whether and how they would celebrate Halloween could also involve cross-cultural interaction even though both may be considered "local Chinese." The university professor and the teenager may have different cultural interpretations of Halloween, particularly if the former is conservative and the latter is heavily invested in popular local youth culture. In the present book, we focus on cross-cultural contacts that are ethnic based whereas data that are generation, social class and/or gender based would also be drawn on as appropriate.

A DISCOURSE APPROACH TO CROSS-CULTURAL INTERACTION STUDIES

The close connection between *culture* and *systems of discourse* is not a novel issue and has been a major focus of interest in the study of culture (see Kramsch, 1998a). On the one hand, language is itself a cultural creation or artifact in its anthropological sense. On the other hand, language is also considered a major vehicle through which cultural practices are constructed and conveyed, and also through which a person's membership in a sociocultural community is mediated (Kramsch, 1995). Kramsch (1991) proposed an approach to the teaching of language and culture that "takes discourse as the integrating moment where culture is viewed, not merely as behaviours to be acquired or facts to be learned, but as a world view to be discovered in the language itself and in the interaction of interlocutors that use that language" (p. 237). Situating cultural interpretations at moments of discourse illuminates the socially constructed nature of cultural practices. Kramsch's (1991) view suggests that there are possible sociocultural forces behind interlocutors' language practices in cross-cultural settings, and understanding these forces is best done by investigating the spoken words. Kramsch's view of the relations between culture and discourse has formed the theoretical underpinnings of the current book.

There have been many attempts to define discourse. The authors here would like to take a sociocultural view and see discourse as the contextualized or situated use of language for social purposes and functions (Brown & Yule, 1983; Fairclough, 1992; Fasold, 1990). Candlin (1997, p. ix) summarizes lucidly the essence of discourse as

> a means of talking and writing about and acting upon worlds, a means which both constructs and is constructed by a set of social practices within these worlds, and in so doing

both reproduces and constructs afresh particular social-discursive practices, constrained or encouraged by more macro movements in the overarching social formation.

In this sense, discourse is more than just a grammatical string of words above sentence or clause level, but language in use that reflects social practices.

Scollon and Scollon (2001) also proposed a discourse approach to intercultural communication. Their approach provides a theoretical framework within which four aspects of culture[31] (that is, *ideology, socialization, forms of discourse,* and *face system*) contributing to meaning in intercultural communication can be interpreted. The discourse-based framework, according to Scollon and Scollon, is strongly influenced by the thinking of Edward Sapir, Gregory Bateson, Lev Vygotsky, Ludwig Wittgenstein, John Gumperz, Dell Hymes, Kenneth Burke, Mikhail Bakhtin, Kitaroo Nishida, and Pierre Bourdieu. It emphasizes the social constructivist nature, historical situatedness, and dialogicality (or conversational or practical inference) of cultural practices. It highlights the impact of the interlocutors' habitus (or accumulated experience of society), positioning (or identity claim), socialization, and othering experiences on the intercultural communication. Scollon and Scollon's (2001) framework has obviously avoided running into the danger of interpreting culture as essentialized fixed systems of behavior, but rather as processes of meaning with multiple social perspectives. The key constructs in their framework also prevail in the discussions in the present book.

Another study that attempts to approach culture through analyzing discourses is reported in Littlewood (2002) that investigates how cultural awareness in intercultural communication can be developed through *negotiations of meaning.* He proposed three tools to resolve problems in the process of intercultural communication, namely the concept of common ground (Clark, 1996a, 1996b), the principle of indexicality (Ochs, 1996), and the concept of cultural models (Shore, 1996; Strauss & Quinn, 1997). Although three different terms are proposed, they refer more or less to a body of knowledge and beliefs intersubjectively shared between two interlocutors, or among people descending from a social community. With interaction episodes collected from his personal experience, Littlewood (2002) showed how interlocutors tend to resort to their shared (partially or completely) or respective body of knowledge and belief systems to guide them in their intercultural communication. The results could be successful communication (when the systems concur) or miscommunication (when the systems differ). To facilitate intercultural communication, Littlewood indicated the need to develop awareness of cultural differences. He has also attempted to investigate culture from an "emic" (insider) perspective by trying to figure out what *mental* processes the interlocutors are going through in producing an utterance. Although on the whole in line with Littlewood's approach, our analyses in this book takes a sociocultural perspective that emphasizes the impacts of people's sociocultural resources and positionings on their mental processes in cross-cultural communication.

INVESTIGATING CLASSROOM INTERACTION

Most of the studies mentioned earlier investigated cross-cultural studies in noninstitutional social situations. The main thrust of the present book is to analyze cross-cultural contacts in classroom settings for learning English as an international language (EIL). It does not, however, render any of the perspectives discussed previously irrelevant to our purpose here because it has been fully acknowledged that as an institutional construct, the classroom is a minisociety with its own rules and regulations, routines, and rituals (Kumaravadivelu, 1999). Our concern, however, is not about explicit metalinguistic talk of culture in the process of teaching and learning a particular language, but about how the interactions between teachers and students are themselves cross-cultural events that encompass most of the cultural parameters previously mentioned. For example, culture is believed to be an active process of meaning construction. Effective participation in cross-cultural communication involves the understanding and negotiation of worldviews, systems of values and beliefs, and attitudes to knowledge beyond a "self and other" perspective. There is also a general acknowledgement that these potentially different, contesting, and conflicting worldviews and systems of beliefs and knowledge are subject to a macrocontext of sociohistorically constructed conventions. Besides, there is a crucial understanding that languages are the major *vehicles* of culture and *sites* for enactment of social and cultural practices.

In the rest of this chapter, we review literature on classroom interaction or discourse analysis that will form a useful background for readers to understand the theoretical framework presented in the next chapter, and the classroom data analysis in chapters 7 through 9. It must be mentioned that the body of research on classroom interaction studies is huge. Different research approaches often reflect cross-disciplinary traditions such as behaviorism, systemic grammar (e.g. Halliday, 1978), sociolinguistics (e.g., Bernstein, 1971; Searle, 1965), ethnography of speaking (e.g., Gumperz, 1982; Hymes, 1974), conversation analysis, and ethnomethodology (e.g., Garfinkel, 1967; Heap, 1985; Sacks, Schegloff, & Jefferson, 1974). For detailed overviews representing changing and developing focuses at different stages, readers may refer to Allwright (1988), Bloome and Willett (1991), Cazden (1988, 2001), Hall (1995, 2000), and Kumaravadivelu (1999).

In this book, the interpretive framework developed by the authors attempts to integrate theoretical underpinnings of the *discourse analysis approach,* the *sociocultural approach,* and the *critical approach.*

The Discourse Analysis Approach

The discourse analysis approach to classroom interaction emerged as a result of classroom researchers' realization of the limitations of the interaction coding approach[32] mainly developed by Flanders (1970). The interaction coding approach employs a finite set of preselected and predetermined categories of speech acts to identify and code the ongoing interaction (e.g., praising or encouraging, lecturing, responding) of the teachers and students. Although this approach no doubt could reveal the dominant patterns of teachers' and students' speech acts, it fails to account for *why* certain verbal acts dominated. Classroom researchers thus began to employ a qualitative discourse analysis approach to conduct classroom interaction studies. Acknowledgment was given to classroom discourse as "coproductions," as a result of the joint efforts of the teachers and students (Allwright, 1988). Emphasis was placed on contextual features of the actions and contributions of participants in the classroom (e.g., van Lier, 1988), and ethnography as a data collection method to capture the sociocultural effects on language use in the classroom (e.g., Mehan, 1979). Some significant outcomes of the analyses based on this approach are microanalysis of the linguistic labels (e.g., directive, informative, elicitation), interaction sequences (e.g., adjacency pairs), and participant structures (e.g., teacher–student or student–student) within a social context. A representative outcome of the discourse analysis approach is the three-part I(nitiation)—R(esponse)—E(valuation) or F(eedback) sequential discourse format with a dyadic participant structure identified by Mehan (1979) in his ethnomethodological work in a mainstream, mixed-ethnic third-grade classroom in America. A similar framework was first proposed by Sinclair and Coulthard in 1975.

The IRE/IRF model by Sinclair and Coulthard, and Mehan has been widely used for other classroom analyses, and found to contribute more to the *interpretation of the meanings* in the interactions than to the frequency count approach. For example, by looking at the sequential arrangement of the turns, Heap (1992) was able to explain how and why a student's attempt to act in a turn was considered to have been snubbed by the teacher due to the ambiguity in the communicative functions performed by the teacher's utterance. The student was considered a rule violator because he or she mistook the teacher's informative in the preceding turn as a directive and acted accordingly.

The typical IRF structure was, however, soon found to be restrictive in nature by some classroom researchers for its teacher centeredness (or teacher dominance) and lack of flexibility for the investigation of classroom scenarios that show students actively negotiating meaning and expressing their voices (Long, 1975; van Lier, 1996). Therefore, new focuses were developed on how variations on this default interaction sequence could open up learning potentials for the learners. For example, Wells (1993) argued that the conventional IRF triadic sequences can be conducive to the coconstruction of knowledge by the teacher and by the students through an extended feedback move to "extend the student's answer, to draw out its significance, or to make connections with other parts of the students' total experience" (p. 30). Poole and Patthey-Chavez (1994) found that negotiations of meaning, which are usually deficient in the default IRF pattern, exist in interactions with different student–teacher participant structures, and are conducted in a setting with peripheral institutional status, for example, in a computer lab. Hughes and Westgate (1998) found that even young children were capable of displaying talk skills such as interpretation and speculation when the teacher allowed the students to take up more initiating roles, avoided any direct evaluation of students' responses, and built upon students' previous contributions.

In L2 learning situations with language code alternations, a sequential analysis of interaction can also reveal how the switching of the codes is patterned and to what effects. Lin's (1990) study of language alternation in foreign language classrooms in Hong Kong is a representative example of such a study. Also drawing on the concepts of conversation analysis, Lin found that teachers (all Cantonese L1 speaking) followed a highly ordered pattern of switching between the L1 and L2 (English) when presenting grammar points and vocabulary items. The instructional sequences would normally start with the teacher using L2 to "illustrate or elicit," followed by "elaborate" and "supplement" in L1, followed by the teachers' L1 elaboration or the students' L1 responses, and finally concluded with the teachers' L2 summary of the teaching points or evaluation of the students' responses in L1 or L2. Lin argued that alternating between L1 and L2 in an L2 classroom reflects the teachers' sensitivity to the needs of the students, and proposed that the monolingual L2-only principle in the TESOL literature should not be translated rigidly into monolingual everyday classroom practices. Lin (1999) further illustrated how different bilingual classroom strategies might be used by teachers with differential consequences, for example, whether the students' habitus was reproduced or transformed. In the present study, it is shown that teachers and students' code alternation also reveals shifting sense of identities in addition to reflecting changing pedagogical purposes.

Bloome and Willett (1991) mentioned a British descent of ethnographic studies of classroom interaction that characterizes the classroom as "a site of actual or potential conflict, in which the participants engage in strategic interaction. Teachers and students are locked in a competitive struggle for legitimacy and control" (p. 213). This facet of classroom interaction seems to have found its representation in a body of research that not only focuses on the vertical and linear IRF structure of teacher–student interactions, but simultaneously on the existing and often contested speech frames by different parties in the classroom.

Analyzing classroom interactions through the concepts of frames (Goffman, 1986), or layers of talk, or on stage/back stage discursive performance in bilingual and multilingual classroom settings has enabled the researchers to capture layers of talk that are less institutional and teacher-directed in nature. These layers of talk often involve the issue of code choices that embody sociocultural meanings. Arthur (1996), for example, found that teachers in Malta oriented to Maltese and English as two systems of linguistic resources with different values. English was always used "on stage" to project an educated professional identity, whereas Maltese was employed to convey friendliness and warmth and to reduce the distance between the teacher and the learners.

The discourse analysis approach is highly relevant to the present book in that the classroom interaction practices are analyzed vertically (IRF) as well as horizontally (frames). Pennington (1999a, 1999b) was among the first to employ a frame approach to reveal the coexisting but often conflicting layers of classroom talk in a typical Hong Kong EFL classroom. It was found that apart from a lesson frame (characterized by the teachers' use of L2 as a dominant institutional form of discourse), and a lesson-support frame (comprising regulative moves by the teachers using mainly the students' L1, which aim at clarifying talk, repairing miscommunication, maintaining discipline, and generally supporting on-task behavior in the lesson frame), there exists side by side a commentary frame as the outer layer. The commentary frame features student-dominated discourse in which they usually employed L1 to move away from the set classroom roles and assert their comments and opinions on issues they found interesting. The students' commentary shows that they are trying to "reproduce the culture *outside* [emphasis added] the institution *within* [emphasis added] the institution" (Pennington, Lee, & Lau, 1996, p. 162). Pennington (1999b) suggested that opportunities for students' spontaneous commentary talk in their mother tongue could be "strategically planned and structured" (p.70) into the lesson frame and transformed into English so as to increase students' participation in the lesson. Whether students' interactive practices can be manipulated structurally needs further investigation, but Pennington's (1999b) findings point out the impact of the "outside" world on what happens inside the classroom, and this realization leads us naturally to the sociocultural contextual approach.

The Sociocultural Contextual Analysis Approach

The sociocultural approach to language use and meaning is relevant to the present study because of its emphasis on the role of *contexts,* or the spatiotemporally bounded moments, in understanding and interpreting interlocutors' interactive practices and resources. Unlike the coding and discourse analysis approaches that seek to tease out generalizable speech practices, the sociocultural approach establishes interactive practices as "locally created and negotiated among the group of interactants" (Hall, 1995, p. 210).

A sociocultural approach to classroom interaction has its roots ingrained in Vygotsky's sociocultural theory to learning. Vygotsky's (1986, 1994) perspectives on human cognitive development as socially situated activities have offered a breakthrough from the structuralists' and behaviourists' views toward language learning. One of the key constructs of the sociocultural theory that has been more widely researched is the zone of proximal development (ZPD). ZPD refers to the difference between what a person can achieve when acting alone and what the same person can accomplish when acting with support from someone else and/or cultural artefacts (Lantolf, 2000). As the concept was developed and applied in research, more concrete terms have been in use, for example, "assisted performance" (Poole & Patthey-Chavez, 1994; Tharp & Gallimore, 1988), "guided participation" (Rogoff, 1990), "learning apprenticeships" (Brown, Collins, & Duguid, 1989), "scaffolding" (Bruner, 1990; Donato, 1994), and "legitimate peripheral participation" (Lave & Wenger, 1992). Whereas some research on ZPD mainly focuses on expert–novice interactions in which the experts are supposed to play an important role in providing input for the novices' language development (e.g., Ellis, 1994; Long, 1996), some others lay emphasis on the collaborative and bidirectional nature of interactions that take place in the ZPD. For example, Donato (1994) found that scaffolded help should not be restricted to expert/novice configurations. During peer collaborative activities, learners are capable of providing guided support to their peers in ways analogous to expert scaffolding. These findings show the limitations of a "monolithic transfer of knowledge" and an underrepresented "instigating role of the novice" (Poole & Patthey-Chavez, 1994, p. 31) in interactional encounters.

Hall (1995) argued that the sociocultural approach to language use must also acknowledge the fact that an individual's ability to use interactive resources to create meanings is in fact subject to some larger political or historical constraints. Sociohistorical conventions and backgrounds are often determining factors in shaping all forms of human mental functioning, including discourse practice. Hall (1995), therefore, drew on Vygostky's contemporary, Mikhail Bakhtin's (1981) literary theory of voice and dialogism, and affirms the role of sociohistorical authority attached to linguistic resources. Therefore "every word comes to us already used, filled with the evaluation and perceptions of others, and their meanings are acquired from the arrangement of their uses against the predominant conventions" (Hall, 1995, p. 212). It is impossible to interpret meanings in discourse practices without attending to the sociopolitical and sociohistorical forces surrounding their uses. Hall (1995) also argued that our social identities, that is, who we are, and how we perceive our relationship with our interacting "others" also have a significant impact in shaping our voices in an interaction.

Another significant study on classroom discourse that makes frequent reference to Bakhtin's ideological constructions of voice and dialogism is that by Cazden (2001). Building on the 1988 edition of the same book, Cazden defined classroom life as *situated* use of "the language of curriculum, the language of control, and the language of personal identity" (p. 3). She highlighted four issues for teachers' and researchers' considerations in enacting and interpreting teaching and learning as cognitive and social activities (pp. 5–6). One of the issues highlights the need for teachers to acknowledge the difference in the form of discourse between formal schooling and informal talk of home and street. Students' "ways with words" often reflects their taking on new roles and expressing new identities.

Mediation is another key construct in Vygotsky's sociocultural perspectives. All forms of goal-directed activities have to be mediated by tools. In language learning, forms of discourse chosen can be used as mediation tools. In this regard, the effectiveness of the mediation tools relies on whether the semiotic mediation (e.g., discourse formats) can index the sociocultural backgrounds and worldviews of the participants. Sullivan (2000), for example, shows how playfulness in speech has mediated the interaction between participants (teacher and students) and the language being learned (English) in a Vietnamese classroom because this kind of oral language playfulness for verbal pleasure is part of Vietnamese cultural heritage. As a form of mediation, the playfulness of language provides a kind of local communicative reality to the ELT classroom that is usually not available in the Anglocentric communicative language teaching methodology. Set in the context of Hong Kong, Lin (2000) also looked at the sociocultural meaning of students' playful L1 in an L2 classroom. Unlike Pennington (1999a, 1999b), Lin found that students' use of L1 did not necessarily appear only in the outermost lesson commentary frame. The students in Lin's (2000) analysis manipulated their verbal play in L1 in a very creative and meaningful way. Their responses fit most relevantly in the IRF (occupying the R-move) discourse format.

Some current research with a sociocultural perspective on language learning focuses on the "affordances" of the ecology in enabling learning to take place. The word "ecology" is originally a biological concept that refers to an environment in which organisms come into contact (van Lier, 2000). Applied to the field of language learning, an ecological perspective examines how learners appropriate language as a system of "relations (of thought, action, power), rather than as objects (words, sentences, rules)" by being "immersed in an environment full of potential meaning" (p. 246). Such an environment can be understood in relation to the notion of "affordance," a term coined by the psychologist James Gibson. According to Gibson (as cited in van Lier, 2000, p. 252), affordance refers to "a reciprocal relationship between an organism and a particular feature of its environment." The notion of affordance draws our attention to whether an environment is full of language, and opportunities of interaction for participation by the active learner. It should be noted that one of the key reasons given by the authority about recruiting NETs in Hong Kong is to create an English-language rich environment in Hong Kong schools that were mostly monolingual.

The Critical Approach

The critical approach to classroom studies came into the limelight in the 1990s. We tend to see it as an extension of the sociocultural approach, although with some significant differences. Unlike other classroom discourse analytic approaches mentioned earlier that offer a method and theory to interpret classroom discourse features, critical classroom research seems to denote more an attitude, and a way of seeing and doing that is critically reflexive (Pennycook, 1999). The critical approach is felt to be of relevance to the present study because it seeks to "deconstruct dominant discourses as well as counter-discourses by posing questions at the boundaries of ideology, power, knowledge, class, race, and gender" (Kumaravadivelu, 1999, p. 476). CCDA has its theoretical source from the works of Foucault (poststruturalism), Said (postcolonialism), Bakhtin (dialogicality and voice), and Bourdieu (symbolic capital and symbolic violence). A common thread, which runs through these people's works, concerns the way "language is implicated in the reproduction of and resistance to inequitable relations of power in educational settings" (Norton, 1997a, p. 207).

Although the theoretical framework of CCDA and applied linguistics in general is beginning to crystallize with the work of scholars such as Norton (1997), Kumaravadivelu (1999) and Pennycook (1999, 2001), empirical studies in classroom settings illustrating CCDA remain scant. One such representative study that is highly relevant to the present study was done by Canagarajah (1993, 1999b).

Canagarajah (1993) conducted a critical and "politically motivated ethnography" (p. 605) on a Sri Lankan classroom. This new orientation in the field has enabled him to account for students' oppositional behaviors and paradoxical attitudes toward an ESOL program in which he was the head and the lecturer. On the one hand, the students highly valued the opportunity to learn English. On the other, their resistant behaviors were manifested in the dropping attendance rate, the abundant sexually oriented glosses against the discourse of the textbooks, and their strong desire to learn through the grammar approach rather than the communicative approach. They thought a western value-free program could come by with a more grammar-based pedagogical approach. It is only through examining the "conflicting pulls of socioeconomic mobility on the one hand and the cultural integrity on the other" (Canagarajah, 1993, p. 624) that students' attitudes could be understood. Their oppositional behaviors are responses to the conflicts and discomfort generated by the alienating English discourse and pedagogy from the communicative-oriented ESOL program with textbooks imported from America embodying foreign cultural values. The relevance of Canagarajah's (1993, 1999) work on the current book lies in its revelation of students' ambivalent attitudes toward learning English, which seemed to them a highly alienating language. Similar attitudes are also found with many students in Hong Kong. This is discussed in the next few chapters.

QUESTIONS FOR REFLECTION AND DISCUSSION

1. In your experience of cross-cultural social communication, were there frequent instances of miscommunication due to cultural differences, or mainly gaps in linguistic resources (e.g., unfamiliar speech accents, L1-based syntactical structures)? How did you resolve the "problems," or deal with the "challenges"?

2. In your opinion, how far is it possible for linguistic properties of a language (i.e., the phonological, syntactic, and morphological systems) to be mastered in isolation from the cultural conventions of the language and be employed for effective communication?

3. From your perspective as a prospective or practicing teacher, what features of classroom interaction (e.g., the IRF patterns and their variations, code mixing and switching, students' private talk) might reveal the most interesting nature of a second/foreign language classroom? Discuss your views in small groups.

5

Understanding Cross-Cultural Classroom Interaction—An Ideological Framework

A s mentioned in chapter 4, the theoretical framework for the interpretation of cross-cultural classroom interaction in this book attempts to integrate the discourse analysis, sociocultural, and critical classroom discourse analysis approaches. Figure 5.1 teases out the key elements of such an interpretive model based on the work of Hall (1993, 1995) for the analysis of oral practices and meanings in language use. Hall's 1993 model was influenced by Hymes' (1974) *SPEAKING* model that analyzed interactional events according to setting, participants, ends, act sequence, key, instrumentalities, norms of interactions and interpretation, and genre. Later in Hall (1995), after realizing that a sociocultural model failed to consider the "differentially weighted potential" (p. 206) in the interactive resources as well as the individual participants' freedom to use, modify, or transform the meanings attached to the language use, elements of a sociohistorical perspective that point to the need to take into account "the larger sociohistorical and political forces residing in both the meanings of the resources and the social identities of those who aim to use them" were added (Hall, 1995, p. 207). Hall drew heavily from Russian literary theorist and Vygotsky's contemporary, Bakhtin's (1986, 1990, 1994) works on genres, voice, ventriloquation [i.e., to (re)construct utterances for our own purposes from the resources available to us], and dialogicality. The present interpretive framework attempts to integrate these key elements and it also embodies major analytical foci of critical classroom discourse analysis (CCDA; Kumaravadivelu, 1999; Norton, 1997a) in the study of power structures, resistance and identity assertion as sociopolitical practices inside the classroom. Each element in the framework is explained later.

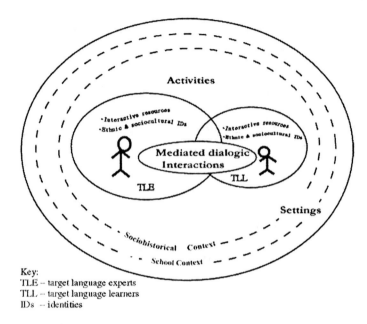

Key:
TLE — target language experts
TLL — target language learners
IDs — identities

FIG. 5.1. A cross-cultural model of classroom interaction.

SETTINGS—SOCIOHISTORICAL CONTEXT
AND SCHOOL CONTEXT

The outermost layer of the model is *settings* where activities and interactions are embedded in or bounded by a sociohistorically and socioculturally conventionalized context. In the present study, the English learning classrooms of the six participating teachers and their students were the immediate settings that were investigated. It should be noted, though, that setting here is not confined to physical or geographic locations where interactions take place. It also refers to the specific seating and grouping arrangements of the students. For example, Hong Kong students usually sit in rows. Sitting in rows thus gives students the idea that the lesson will be formal and routine. When students are arranged to sit around tables or in semi or full circles, they feel more relaxed and anticipate a freer learning environment. Sometimes, different settings may signify different types of learning activities. For example, in one of our cases, the NET preferred conducting oral activities such as language games in the English room where students sat around tables. Therefore, having lessons in the English room would immediately conjure up a relaxed and informal atmosphere in the students' mind. It was believed that different settings as perceived by different participants in the interactions and activities would frame different perceptions of the purposes, forms, roles, instruments, and act sequences that therefore shape different patterns of interaction (Kramsch, 1993).

Although classrooms constitute the immediate settings for our analysis, we do not overlook the position of schools as an integral part of the macrosocial community. As argued by Bloome and Willett (1991), much of what happens in the classrooms reflects and often is determined by multiple levels of reciprocal influence from the sociopolitical contexts in which the school forms a part. In the situation of Hong Kong, there used to be a great "social distance" (Gibbons, 1984) between foreigners and the average local people, especially those coming from the lower socioeconomic classes. Native English speaking foreigners in Hong Kong have been, and still are, leading a life toward the higher end of the socioeconomic scale. Students coming from low to lower middle classes thus have very little opportunity to have "direct social contact" (Gibbons, 1984, p. 70) with foreign people and are very often unfamiliar with foreign cultures. The "social distance" model (Gibbons, 1984) suggests a possible existence of incongruence or incompatibility in the ways of thinking between the NETs and the majority of HKSs. This incongruence may be reflected in their interaction practices.

The macrosociopolitical contexts where schools are situated also involve the education system, which in turn impacts on the curriculum cultures and teaching and learning styles in the classrooms. The status and perceived standards of English in Hong Kong during the sovereignty changeover period, and the language policies formulated in response to it (see chap. 2) all constitute significant parts of the macrocontext. More information about the education system of Hong Kong at the time of the study is presented in the next chapter.

ACTIVITIES

Institutional contexts such as classrooms are usually characterized by activities. Activity, as first developed by Leontiev (1978), is not merely doing something. It is doing something that is motivated by a biological need, such as hunger, or a culturally constructed need, such as the need to be literate in certain cultures. Needs become motives that are only realized in "specific *actions* that are goal directed (hence, intentional and meaningful) and carried out under particular spatial and temporal *conditions* (or what are also referred to as *operations*) and through appropriate *mediational means*" (Lantolf, 2000, p. 8). To put this concept in everyday language, activity in a classroom may refer to a reading comprehension task, a picture composition task, a student–teacher reading conference, a training session to prepare for the speech festival, a teacher-guided oral interview, and any goal-directed events involving a subject, an object, actions and operations (Leontiev, 1978), and where "collaborative interaction, intersubjectivity,[33] and assisted performance occur" (Donato & McCormick, 1994, p. 455).

In understanding activity theory, it is important to bear in mind that the same activity can be realized through different actions and with different forms of mediation, and that the same actions can be linked to a different motive and thus constitute different activities (Lantolf, 2000). In applying the activity theory in children's play and motivation, Hakkarainen (1999) pointed out the frequent coexistence of two activity systems; children's play and adults' educational work in day-care settings. If these activity systems do not have a common object (that is, same needs and motives), conflicts and problems will arise. It is shown in this book that tensions sometimes occurred between teachers and students because of the coexistence of conflicting activity systems without common goals and motives. The nature of an activity (could be pedagogical, managerial, or socializing) was occasionally perceived in different ways by the participants involved in it. For example, a well-structured lesson for extensive reading purposes (e.g., choosing books, reading, and conferencing) from the perspective of the teacher may be taken as a good opportunity by the students to have a rest and a free chat with peers by pretending to read and share views.

The macrocontexts, the history and expectations of a particular social community and institution like schools would have a deciding effect on what activities and practices can take place (Poole & Patthey-Chavez, 1994). In Hong Kong, the social and institutional realities in most schools such as large class size, traditional organization culture, exam-oriented mentality of most students, parents, teachers and principals will give rise to belief systems that conflict and compete with some educational philosophies. For example, it was mentioned in Johnson and Tang's (1993) study that some sorts of activities (e.g., popular film show) that might have generated language learning opportunities for students were banned because of opposing views from other influential institutional forces represented by people like principals, parents, and some local teachers. These conflicting perceptions of what makes a language learning activity useful and acceptable probably stem from different belief frameworks organized around different sociohistorical conventionalities.

THE PARTICIPANTS, THEIR IDENTITIES, AND INTERACTIVE RESOURCES

In this model, there are mainly two groups of interactants (the teacher and the students) forming the core part of the dialogic events. We label the teacher group as the "target[34] language experts" (TLE) and the student group as the "target language learners" (TLL) to signify the ultimate purpose of the activity as teaching and learning a "target" language, in this case, English. These groups of interactants were characterized by the type of interactive resources they had at their command and the ethnic and social identities they constructed in the macrosociohistorical context and in the process of interaction. These resources and sense of identity may or may not be shared or understood between or among the interactants (and hence are partially intersecting with one another), but are definitely playing significant roles in shaping the interaction patterns that arise. We discuss the participants' identities and interactive resources in the next few paragraphs.

Identities and Positionings.   According to Swann et al. (2004, p. 140), identity refers to "an individual's or group's sense of who they are, as defined by them and/or others." Identity can be expressed in a number of ways, for example, in terms of nationality, geographical location, ethnicity, gender, social class, occupation, and so forth (Hall, 1993). Ivanic (1998) provided a useful synthesis and elaboration of several related but different concepts of "identity" such as "self," "person," "role," "ethos," "subject position," and "subjectivity."[35] In her interpretation, "self" refers to "aspects of identity associated with an individual's feeling (or 'affect')" whereas words such as "person" and "role" seem to refer to the "public, institutionally defined aspect of identity" (Ivanic, 1998, p. 10). In this sense, the institutional roles of the TLE and TLL are "teachers" and "students" respectively. However, from the perspective of social theorists and social constructivists, "the use of 'role' serves to highlight static, formal and ritualistic aspects" (Davies & Harre, 1990, p. 43) that do not fully reflect the dynamic nature and multilayeredness of the term "identity." In this book, "identity" is used as the covering term for all these concepts because of its popular use in interdisciplinary studies. It is used interchangeably with "self," "subject position," and "subjectivity," to denote the kind of self-representations, conscious or unconscious, which are constructed and manifested through discursive practices in social contexts. Due to the multiplicity, hybridity and fluidity of identity performance shifting between different social settings, the terms "multiple identities" and "identities" are also used.

It should be noted that the term "identity" in the current book is used with a poststructuralist perspective. Along the line of social theorists, Ivanic (1998, p. 10) argued that identity is socially constructed from "a complex of interweaving positionings." A person's self-representation or positionings would not be meaningful and necessary without considering how he or she and other key players (e.g., significant others whose relations to the person makes the self-representations necessary) are situated in the sociocultural contexts. How a person "understands his or her relationship to the world, how that relationship is constructed across time and space, and how the person understands possibilities for the future" is what identity studies seek to answer (Norton, 2000, p. 5). The construction of self and identity is therefore often connected with a person's relationships with some significant "others," about how the inner self (or subjectivity) perceives its relationship with others and acts on it accordingly, often through use of language.

We therefore see a close relationship between "self/subjectivity" and the sociocultural notion of "voice" developed by Bakhtin (1981). On the intermental plane (i.e., the dialogic interactions between/among two or more people) and on the intramental plane (i.e., the psychological processes within a person), we perceive "self" usually as the primary source that gives meaning to the "voice," or "the speaking personality, the speaking consciousness" (Holquist & Emerson, 1981, p. 434, as cited in Wertsch, 1991, p. 51). "Voice" in Bakhtin's configuration is concerned with "the broader issues of a speaking subject's perspective, conceptual horizon, intention, and world view" (Wertsch, 1991, p. 51), implying that there is a presence of "self" of the interlocutors. However, a person's "voice" is never solely responsible for creating an utterance or its meaning because "every utterance must be regarded primarily as a *re-*

sponse to preceding utterances of the given sphere" (Bakhtin, 1986, p.91, as cited in Wertsch, 1991). Thus, an utterance carries with it not just the voice of the speaker, but also the voices of the addressees, and/or people in the sociohistorical contexts. In this sense Bakhtin's notion of the "dialogic self" precisely underlines our understanding of the social and dialogic nature of self, subjectivity, consciousness, and language. Under Bakhtin's sociocultural theories, both language and subjectivity are dialogic as they are first constituted on the social, intermental plane and then later become internalized as intramental psychological processes (e.g., the child internalizes the caretaker's regulatory practices and becomes self-regulatory). That is, the formation of self, subjectivity, language, and consciousness has always first taken on the social plane, in dialogues with others' voices as encoded in the language (utterances) we use to make sense to and of one another.

However, we contend that the relationship between identity and discourse practice is not linear (74). Being socially and discursively constructed, a person's identities are not "pre-given or assigned and static and consistent" (Bloome, Carter, Christian, Otto, & Shuart-Faris, 2005, p. 157), they are "in motion" (p. 158), as well as performed and situated in moments of talk (Pennycook, 2003). Drawing on Austin's (1962) performativity theory, Pennycook (2003, p. 528) claimed that "[i]t is not that people use language varieties because of who they are, but rather that we perform who we are by (among other things) using varieties of language." Pennycook's view has an important bearing on our understanding and interpretation of identities that tend to be essentialized by lay people such as male–female, native–nonnative speakers, teachers, and students. The idea that a person's identity is performed situationally rather than being pregiven is discussed in chapter 10.

In brief, due to its social and discursive constructedness, identity is now generally acknowledged to be highly fluid, sometimes incoherent, fragmented, multiple, and conflicting. As a person grows and moves across different social sectors, they may take up, resist, and shift between different identities or subject positions. This aspect of identity implies agency, conscious action, and authorship, and is best conveyed by the term "subjectivity," which is preferred in poststructuralist approaches to language and cultural studies. How different participants display agency (or an individual's capacities to act independently of structural constraints) through shifting identities and discursive practices is another key issue of this book.

Interactive Resources.   We believe that three key types of interactive or communicative resources are drawn on in the context of cross-cultural interactions (see chap. 7 for related discussions of the sense-making practices in Heap, 1976). The first type includes those linguistically (e.g., phonology, syntax, and lexis) and paralinguistically instantiated (e.g., gestures, facial expressions, volume of voice) meaning-making resorts available to the interactants in the process of interaction. Ochs (1996) adopted the term "linguistic index" to refer to the linguistic form or structure (e.g., interrogative form, sentential voice, emphatic stress, diminutive affixes, raised pitch, and the like) that is "used variably from one situation to another and becomes conventionally associated with particular situational dimensions such that when that structure is used, the form invokes those situational dimensions" (p. 411). This means that the situational meanings assigned to the linguistic forms are believed to be sociohistorically conventionalized. Following Bakhtin's (1986) ideas, interactants' linguistic utterances and paralinguistic features should not be assumed to all be created individually on the spot, but most of them are, in fact, sociohistorically conventionalized and culture specific. The presence, or absence of cognizance of, and the sharing, or lack of sharing of these sociocultural conventionalized interactive resources will have a great bearing on the abilities of the interactants to make meaning in the interaction process. According to Ochs (1996), cases of indexical breakdown occur when interlocutors project different contexts of situation from linguistic "contextualization cues" (Gumperz, 1982) that refer to any conventionalized linguistic features that contribute to the signaling of contextual presuppositions (p. 131). As argued by Ochs (1996),

[a] novice's understanding of linguistic forms entails an understanding of their indexical potential (i.e., the situational constellations of by whom, for what, when, where and to what ends forms are conventionally employed) in co-ordination with co-occurring linguistic forms and other symbolic dimensions of the situation at hand. (p. 414)

The symbolic dimensions may be what we mean in the following paragraphs—institutional and cultural resources.

By institutional resources, we refer to the interactive resources developed through the institutional roles of the teachers as the "teacher," and students as the "student," and part of such resources includes the consciousness of the status, power, responsibility, obligation, and accumulated experience of institutional practices that are associated with such roles. For example, the institutional identity of teachers allow them to solicit the assistance of another student to help in the sense-making processes, or allocate a speaking turn to a student who is more likely to provide an acceptable answer. Their professional knowledge of teaching, which is associated with their institutional identity, has also enabled them to employ a range of strategies (e.g., miming, drawing, using body language, visual aids) in making meanings to the students. The students' awareness and acknowledgment of their institutional identity as students may allow them to remain silent, or say "I don't know" when little sense could be made of the teacher's utterances or questions. Their general knowledge of doing lessons may also enable them to guess the meaning and purposes of teachers' utterances and actions even though they may not be able to make sense of every word they say. For example, on receiving a worksheet, they know that they have to work on it. If one worksheet is given to two students, they know that they are expected to do the worksheet with a partner.

When people come into contact in an interaction activity, they will inevitably interpret each other's behavior and messages based on a repertoire of recurrent episodes and routines from everyday life that reflects the regularity of life in a society with a particular social structure, culture, language, history, and ecology (Hundeide, 1985). This repertoire of recurrent episodes and routines is believed to form "a tacit background of expectancies" (Byram, 1989) that we tend to fall back on as one type of interactive resources, which we will label as "cultural resources." The most common type of repertoire of recurrent episodes is *cultural stereotypes*. According to O'Sullivan, Hartley, Saunders, Montgomery, and Fiske (1994), stereotyping is the process that "requires the simplification and organization of diverse and complex ranges of phenomena into general, labeled categories" (pp. 299–300). Stereotypes often carry assumptions and judgments concerning groups of people's behavior based on highly simplified and generalized signs. For example, Chinese social behavior is often interpreted as a reflection of Confucian ethics or ideological beliefs (see, e.g., Bond, 1996; Bond & Hwang, 1986). Thus, Chinese social interaction is generally believed to be built on harmony and hierarchy resulting in a stereotypical characterization of the Chinese as "collectivistic" (cooperative or harmonious) rather than "individualistic" (competitive, agonistic) as compared with the Americans in general. Chinese students were therefore traditionally characterized as displaying a lack of individualism and independent thought, feeling obliged to respect authority (e.g., parents and teachers), and adopt a more communal approach to things (also see Jin & Cortazzi, 1993).

However, due to historical circumstances, increased contacts among people and the changing value systems, some of these stereotypes may be oversimplistic. Biggs and Watkins (1996), for example, asserted that some of the cross-cultural comparisons were found to be misperceptions. For example, most Chinese learners do not necessarily learn through memorization without understanding, as many western cross-cultural studies have depicted. Gabrenya, Jr., and Hwang (1996) emphasized that Chinese also exhibit an "individualist" social interaction style in some contexts. Littlewood (2002) also reported survey findings that contradict western beliefs that Asian learners are largely passive learners showing unconditional obedience to authority. Most Asian students surveyed would like to be active and independent, and the results show much less difference between the European and Asian groups of students in this regard. Stephens (1997) boldly asserts that communication problems between people from different cultures (e.g., students from China and their English supervisors) may be "more economically explained in terms of aspects of language proficiency rather than cultural differences" (p. 113). As pointed out by Holliday, Hyde, and Kullman (2004), we should guard against cultural stereotypes because stereotypes are often "infected by *prejudice* which in turn leads to *otherization*" (p. 23). It will be shown in subsequent chapters that some of the NETs and their Hong Kong students brought with them different degrees of cultural stereotypes of the other party to the classroom, and it is the interest of this book to explore how these stereotypes may have an impact on their discursive practices.

Although cultural stereotypes label people with generalized categories, another construct to describe our images, or taken-for-granted assumptions about what are prototypical events around us is "cultural models" (Gee, 1996). According to Gee (1996), cultural models are people's simplified versions about the world that leave out many complexities. Part of the function of cultural models is to "set up what count as central, typical cases, and what count as marginal, non-typical cases" (p. 59). Shared cultural models in a speech community construct communicative norms and constraints shared by the community. For example, the cultural model for "bachelor" would normally exclude people like gay individuals and priests. People's configuration of cultural models arises from constant exposure to socially situated and discursively constructed use of related concepts. However, it should be noted that a person may claim membership in a number of speech communities (e.g., profession based, family based, religion based), which may in practice coincide with wider social boundaries such as ethnic, class, or national boundaries (Milroy, 1980). Therefore, it is essential to avoid essentializing our interpretations of cultural models and pigeonholing them into fixed categories.

It is shown in chapter 7 that cultural models often provide important resources for the teachers and students to make sense of the interaction practices and nonverbal behavior of each other. However, as argued by Gee (1996), cultural models tend to change over time and space, as well as with other new experiences. They can be partial, inconsistent, and sometimes in conflict with one another. Cross-cultural interaction informed by conflicting cultural models may result in misunderstandings.

In this book, the authors propose interpreting interaction as situated practices, the meanings of which can be more securely derived at moments of talk with due considerations given to the multilayers of sociocultural contexts. A person's knowledge of his language includes more than knowledge of syntactic, semantic, and phonological rules. Effective communicative performance involves knowledge of when to speak or be silent; how to speak on each occasion; how to communicate (and interpret) meanings of respect, seriousness, humor, politeness, or intimacy (Milroy, 1980). As argued by Gee (1999), meaning is not general and abstract; it is not something that resides in dictionaries, not even in general symbolic representations inside people's heads. Rather, it is "*situated* in specific social and cultural practices, and is continually transformed in those practices" (p. 63). In this sense, meanings are situated as well as changing across time and space. Different contexts of interaction may bring about different social and cultural practices. Successful communication in cross-cultural contexts requires the ability to interpret interaction practices as being positioned in relation to the social institutions and power relations that sustain them (Barton, Hamilton, & Ivanic, 2000). This ability forms a crucial part of "language socialization" that refers to "the process of internalization through which human beings become members of particular cultures, learning how to speak as well as how to act and think and feel" (Cazden, 1999, p. 63).

ASYMMETRICAL POWER RELATIONS

The difference in size of the two human figures and the circles they occupy in the model, apart from showing differences in the command of interactive resources, symbolizes a differential and asymmetrical power relation in typical educational settings in secondary schools in Hong Kong. The teacher, assuming the traditional and socially expected role of an expert knowledge possessor and giver, tends to take on a superordinate position in classroom activities where students will normally conform. When the teachers concerned are native speakers of the target language, it is normal to believe that the asymmetrical power relation would only be more conspicuous because of the societal status and power covertly enjoyed by the NETs in the field of ELT. It is of interest to see whether such a power relation will manifest itself (and perhaps become contested) in different forms (e.g., in reverse power relations) between teachers of different ethnic or cultural origins and in different activity contexts.

Interaction studies in the 1970s and early 1980s that involved a native target-language speaker (NS, may or may not be a teacher) and a nonnative learner (NNS) usually set the focus on the linguistic support rendered to the NNS by the NS. Researchers tended to accentuate how NSs adjusted their speech production, for example, in terms of the speech rate, the voice volume, the formality, the syntactic structures, and so forth to cater to the limited proficiency of the NNSs. Studies also reported how NSs performed their role in repairing miscommunications, recasting utterances, giving comments, and providing input to help NNSs formulate appropriate utterances to express themselves (e.g., Long, 1981; Tsui, 1985). Successful communications of this type usually attribute success to the contribution of the NS in terms of the provision of linguistic feedback/input and the use of communication strategies to guide the NNS in the negotiation of meanings [see the discussion of Tsui's (1985) and Tsang's (1994) studies in chap. 3].

Although investigations on expert–novice's interactions in the mid-1980s extended their concerns to include the role of NNSs in the negotiation of meaning and their output in the interaction, the focus was still on how the NSs enabled the NNSs to notice the gap of linguistic knowledge that existed between what he or she wants to convey and his or her ability to convey it. The focus of attention was seldom on the issue of culture and cultural practices and resources. However, in TESOL settings involving "native" English-speaker teachers and "nonnative" students with limited English proficiency in a former British colony, the cases of cross-cultural communication involve issues of power, ideological conflicts, and identity politics. It is shown in chapter 7 in particular that the asymmetrical command of target language linguistic and cultural resources between NETs and HKSs do not always favor the former in the process of intercultural communication.

MEDIATED DIALOGIC INTERACTIONS

Mediation is defined as the "instrument of cognitive change" (Donato & McCormick, 1994, p. 456). In a classroom setting, conventional instruments of mediation include those that bear a concrete physical entity such as textbooks, audio and visual materials, and aids prepared by the teacher (Donato & McCormick,

1994). Recent classroom researchers have identified other forms of mediation that put emphasis on the human effects. These forms of mediation include discourse patterns, types of direct instruction, or various kinds of teacher assistance (Ellis, 1996; Sullivan, 2000). In this book, we are going to show that interactions mediated by object- or human-based instruments, as induced, created, or manipulated by the NETs and LETs, may embody and encode different cultural perspectives. How students react to, and (dis)engage themselves in these mediated interactions is another point of interest.

In the dialogic process, we draw on Bakhtin's distinction of two modes for appropriation and transmission of other people's words (or a text, a rule, a model)—authoritative discourse and internally persuasive discourse (Bakhtin, 1981). Authoritative discourse is privileged discourse, the words "of a father, of adults, and of teachers," which demands our acknowledgment and adoption, our "reciting by heart." However, authoritative discourse is often met with resistance if it cannot be appropriated as "internally persuasive discourse," that is, by "re-accentuating" it in one's own words. To turn authoritative discourse into an internally persuasive one, the speaking personality (e.g., the teacher) must be able to practice addressivity (Bakhtin, 1981), which refers to the constant responding to utterances (including responding to and obtaining responses from) spoken by one's conversation partners. A response is not just a "reply"; a reply may occur in a sociocultural vacuum, lacking the proper mutual interpenetrations of meanings. Being able to obtain and formulate a response in making an utterance is essential because "[a]t the highest level of mental life, ... nothing means anything until it achieves a response" (Bakhtin, 1981, p. 48). A response not only addresses the current interlocutors' questions and assignments, but also the "former [interlocutors'] expectations and demands, to prior utterances heard or read, to imagined reactions of potential listeners or future readers" (Kramsch, 2000, p. 139). The ability to formulate a proper response thus lies in a considerable mastery of the linguistic and sociohistorical backgrounds of the interlocutors. In the data analysis chapters (chaps. 7 to 9), the authors show that for any interactions to be successful, dialogic moments displaying the process of interanimation and interpenetration are prerequisite. It is a kind of mutual ideological and linguistic crossover between or among the interactants that aims to promote appropriation of authoritative discourse in a way that will ultimately make it internally persuasive.

Why is the ability to respond appropriately so important in TESOL? Despite its many problems with implementation, the communicative approach to language teaching (CLT) has made a significant contribution in bringing to our attention the inadequacies of viewing classrooms as a place where teachers are mere providers of optimal linguistic input or reinforcers of good language strategies. As argued by CLT proponents (e.g., Breen, 1986; Breen & Candlin, 1980), if we present the learner with language only as an object, and reduce the act or experience of learning a language to linguistic or behavioral conditioning that were separable from the learner's relevant psychological and social experience, we are almost certainly postponing development of the learner's ability to communicate through the language. The underlying principles of CLT echo Vygotsky's (1986, 1994) sociocultural theory that presents learning as a high mental activity beginning with social interaction with people around us. Language learning research over the last 20 years, therefore, has focused on the role of talk and interaction as a means of language socialization, or "the process of internalization through which human beings become members of particular cultures, learning how to speak as well as how to act and think and feel" (Cazden, 1999, p. 63). The value of competent TESOL professionals does not lie in their ability to hand out a body of linguistic rules and patterns for learners to acquire and claim possession of, but in their ability to socialize learners into the target language community of practice through talk and interaction.

QUESTIONS FOR REFLECTION AND DISCUSSION

1. Based on one or two classroom excerpt(s) provided by the course facilitator, or taken from chapters 7, 8, or 9, analyze the discourse patterns of the chosen excerpts with the ideological framework elaborated in this chapter. In small groups, discuss and compare your findings.

2. How often do you resort to cultural stereotypes and/or cultural models when you are engaged in cross-cultural communication? To what extent does some knowledge of cultural stereotypes (or simplified generalizations or categories) of a culture enable you to achieve more successful intercultural communication?

3. Based on your everyday experience as a teacher or student teacher, discuss in small groups how far you would agree with the following observations mentioned in the chapter:

   • the power relation between teachers and students is asymmetrical
   • the macrosociopolitical contexts will influence the interaction practices inside classrooms
   • a person's identities are not pregiven, but are socially and discursively constructed

6

The Participants in Context

The key participants in our study reported in this book are six teachers (four NETs and two LETs) and their students. In our interpretation of the discursive practices of these teachers and students in interaction, a macrounderstanding of the education system and the institutional school contexts, and a microunderstanding of the participants' perceptions of teaching and learning of English in Hong Kong constitute important interpretive resources. In this chapter, we present significant features of the education system and school contexts where the teachers and students are situated, and the sociocultural backgrounds of the teacher participants that include their relevant academic histories and professional beliefs. The English learning practices of sampled groups of students is also discussed. All the information regarding the school contexts and the participants in this study was derived from interviews and observations during the first author's visits. We provide information about the education system and policies in Hong Kong at the time of this study in the next section, followed by the school contexts and the participants' profiles.

THE EDUCATION CONTEXT IN HONG KONG

As a social and political system, the education system in Hong Kong has recently undergone significant transformations and metamorphoses. What we are presenting in this section only represents the status quo of the system at the time of the data collection from 1998 to 2000. Due to this book's specific focus on classroom interactions, only issues considered to have an important bearing on the role perceptions, identity formation, and interaction practices of the participants in the English learning classrooms are discussed. Readers interested in knowing more about the Hong Kong school system and curriculum may refer to Adamson and Li (1999), Luk (1991), and Morris (1992, 1995). The current chapter covers the following issues:

- The banding, streaming, and evaluation systems.
- The medium of instruction policy.
- The education logistics, curriculum culture, and English language teaching (ELT) methodology.

The Banding, Streaming, and Evaluation Systems

The Hong Kong school system is mainly modeled on the British one, with 6 years of primary education (equivalent to Grades 1 to 6 in the North American system), 7 years of secondary schooling (equivalent to Grades 7 to 13), and 3 years of university. In 1978, Hong Kong initiated a 9-year compulsory education system (6 years of primary plus 3 years of lower secondary), thus abolishing the Secondary School Place Entrance Examination. Up until 2001, secondary school place allocation was based on a proportion of results each primary pupil received from a standardized aptitude test[36] and their respective internal primary school results. All school-leaving primary students were roughly categorized into five bands, with band one as the highest in academic ability and band five the lowest.[37] An average secondary school in Hong Kong would receive students mainly from band three, with a minority from band two and band four. To reduce the problems of mixed-ability teaching, most schools practiced a streaming policy by placing students of similar academic abilities into the same class. In one particular year level, there may be one or two so-called good classes and three to four average classes. Some particularly weak students would be pulled out to do the major academic subjects (Chinese, math, & English) in smaller groups (around 20) and these classes are usually labeled "remedial classes." Most students are aware of the standard of the class they are in and this awareness often exerts an impact on the self-image of the students concerned.

At the end of the 9-year compulsory schooling, most Form 3 students are eligible to proceed to Form 4. They then need to choose between arts and science streams[38] of study. English is compulsory for both streams. Hong Kong people are well known for their pragmatic and utilitarian attitude toward work and study. Students are no different. Even though English is important, only a pass is required for entering most of the disciplines in the majority of the universities. Therefore many advanced level (A-level) students (especially science stream students) only give English low priority in their study plans and put much greater effort in studying the content subjects. To most students, their goal for studying English at A-level is to pass the Use of English examination and enter university.

Although tertiary education places have increased markedly in the 1990s, currently only about 17% of the relevant age group (ages 17–20) can receive university education.[39] Therefore, most upper secondary students put great effort in passing the two competitive public examinations, one at the end of Form 5 and one at the end of Form 7, if they wish to enter one of the eight local universities. It is no exaggeration to say that to many secondary students, all educational goals are subsumed under the sole objective of passing these two public examinations. Such mentality is often reinforced and supported by their teachers' teaching orientations (see later sections).

The Medium of Instruction (MOI) Policy

Before September 1998, almost 90% of secondary schools in Hong Kong (usually labelled as Anglo-Chinese schools) claimed to be practicing an English immersion education by adopting English medium textbooks for all subjects other than Chinese and Chinese history, whereas actual classroom delivery was usually in both Cantonese and English (see Boyle, 1995; Lin, 1996a, 1997, 2001 for a review). This situation has changed since 1998 with the strong enforcement of mother tongue education policy by the first HKSAR Government (see Lin & Man, in press; Morrison & Lui, 2000, for critical discussions). All except 114 secondary schools in Hong Kong have to teach through Cantonese (the mother tongue of most Hong Kong students) at lower secondary levels in all subjects except English. However, because most prestigious universities in Hong Kong are still adopting English as the major medium of instruction, many schools would switch to English in selected subjects at senior secondary levels.

The MOI policy of Hong Kong, whether old or new, has long been an object of public criticism. As early as 1988, Yu and Atkinson (1988) pointed out that "English medium education in Hong Kong adversely affects many students' educational attainment" (p. 283). Students learned little English because English was generally irrelevant to their daily lives and they learned inadequate subject matter because of the learning difficulties posed by a foreign language (see Lin, 1996a, 1999; Pennycook, 1998, for more discussion). The bilingual delivery of the actual teaching was scapegoated by the government as jeopardizing students' development of both English and Chinese. The "new" MOI policy, however, has met with even greater public outcry. As pointed out by Morrison and Lui (2000), the mother-tongue MOI policy has resulted in acute social stratification of schools in Hong Kong. "CMI [Chinese medium of instruction] schools would become second-class institutions, recruiting less able children from less educated parents. Students from EMI [English medium of instruction] schools would constitute the elite" (p. 477). There was widespread press coverage when the policy was enforced in 1998 reporting how students, teachers, and even parents cried upon knowing that their school lost in an appeal to maintain their EMI status. Some students even condemned the government of depriving them of any chance of success because high English proficiency is required everywhere. This vociferous desire for English-medium education by parents and by many school personnel, and the consequent language-based social stratification would inevitably impact on the students' self-image building, their subject constitution,[40] or identity construction. It is shown in later sections of this chapter and the classroom data chapters (chaps. 7 to 9) that this MOI policy has produced an impact on some teachers' pedagogical orientations and discourse practices as well.

The Education Logistics, Curriculum Culture, and English Language Teaching (ELT) Methodology

Hong Kong has practiced the communicative approach to language teaching (CLT) since the early 1980s. The revised Hong Kong English syllabus (Forms I–V) emphasizes the importance of providing learners with plenty of opportunities for "meaningful use of the language for purposes of communication" (Curriculum Development Council, 1983, p. 15). Until recently, the principal theories of the communicative approach still underpin the latest English Language Syllabus (Forms I–V; Curriculum Development Council, 1999) even though the main thrust of the syllabus lies in its introduction of the task-based approach (TBL).[41] It can be said that at the time of data collection for this study, the ELT curriculum and methodology was in a transition from the communicative language teaching to the task-based approach. As perceived by some Hong Kong-based curriculum researchers such as Carless (2003) and Mok (2001), CLT and TBL share some common pedagogical principles, for example, both emphasize learner centeredness, or the need to engage learners in active participation to fulfil curriculum tasks that are close to the daily experience of the learners. However, most of the teacher participants in the present study quoted CLT as the principal method they used in their everyday teaching. Because of this, we focus mainly on discussing the recommended methodology and actual practice in Hong Kong classrooms under the CLT flag.

The advent of the communicative language teaching was seen by many as an important breakthrough from the traditional view that took learners as an empty receptacle who must learn a new language by means of a new set of stimulus–response behavior traits (Holliday, 1994). CLT methodology argues that communicative competence involves more than knowledge of linguistic rules and phonological representations. The development of communicative competence can best be done by actively engaging learners in negotiation of meaning in which the target language (or the language to be learned) can be used in an authentic way. CLT methodology is characterized by student–student interaction in the form of pair or group work. Therefore, CLT methodology is said to be learner centered,[42] that is, the teacher should no longer dominate the turns of talk during lessons. Rather, learners should be given the power to exercise choice and autonomy in their learning, and be actively involved in communicative tasks that call for problem-solving, information exchange, expression of opinions, and so froth [see Breen & Candlin, 1980; Holliday, 1994; Savignon, 1991 for the essentials of CLT].

Although the CLT approach has been implemented in Hong Kong for almost 20 years, it does not seem to have yielded the desired effects on the development of learners' communicative competence. Talks of declining English standards of Hong Kong's younger generations prevail in public and academic discourses (Evans, 1996). A survey study of over 400 secondary school students conducted by Lai (1994) established learners' confidence level and self-esteem as major factors undermining a successful implementation of CLT. Her findings also revealed that insufficient provision of communication opportunities by the teachers was also a crucial factor. Similar findings showing a close relationship between teachers' perceptions of language teaching and the implementation of CLT have been reported by Evans (1997) using similar research methods. His study indicates that the communicative curriculum has had a minimal impact on the Hong Kong English language classroom because

> [p]ower, authority and control continue to be in the hands of the teacher. Teachers still appear to favour a didactic, transmission and text-book based type of teaching, while the students' main classroom role seems to involve listening to the teacher and working individually on examination-focused exercises. (p. 43).

Lai (1994) and Evans (1996) seem to be suggesting that some teachers' pedagogical mindsets might have formed obstacles to the effective implementation of CLT methodology. Although this may be true, readers should not overlook the possible impact of contextual factors on teachers' teaching approaches in Hong Kong.

The education system in Hong Kong has traditionally been featured by a heavily examination-oriented curriculum (see previous sections), as well as a large class size. Most secondary classes in Hong Kong contain an average of 40 students, crammed in a small classroom of 56m2 in size.[43] A large class size and the juxtaposition of several classrooms wall-to-wall on one floor make many teachers feel hesitant to conduct teaching activities that involve a lot of student–student interaction because of the noise problems. These physical constraints have been identified as the major culprits for a teacher-centered transmission-style teaching method in local classrooms by many teachers including the NET participants in this study.

Although teachers in Hong Kong rank high in the world in terms of their monthly salary, their workload is also on the top of the list. Most teachers have to teach up to 32 lessons on a 6-day cycle system. On individual days, a teacher may have to teach up to seven out of eight 40-minute periods. To cope with constraints generated from the large class size, the exam-oriented curriculum, and the heavy teaching and marking load, most teachers resort to textbook-based teaching, with little motivation to practice curriculum tailoring and innovations to cater to the special needs of their students (Lin, 2000). Teachers of the public examination classes spend a considerable amount of the class time drilling students on past examination questions to prepare them for the high-stake public examinations. Anything unrelated to the public examinations is usually not taken seriously by either teachers or students.

Apart from practical constraints arising from education logistics, students' limited English proficiency has also been identified as a factor affecting an effective implementation of CLT in Hong Kong. As observed by Carless (2003), in situations where the students are believed to lack linguistic resources, or have limited English proficiency (such as primary classes), a "weak" approach to task-based learning (TBL) as described by Skehan (1996) is usually implemented. This is roughly comparable to the production stage of a presentation-practice-production method. In this weak approach, tasks are "the prime organisational focus and the language to be transacted emerges from these tasks" (Carless, 2003, p. 487). Skehan's (1996) weak version of TBL parallels a weak version of the CLT approach (see, for example, Howatt, 2004) that also emphasizes structured linguistic input from teachers and output from students. As interpreted by Holliday (1994), the weak version of CLT focuses on "the practice of language use, with the basic lesson input as presentation of language models" (p. 170). While the weak version of TBL is felt by Carless (2003) to be more appropriate in EFL situations where students do not possess a high command of the target language resources, the weak version of CLT is considered by Holliday (1994) to be too dependent on teacher–student interactions (difficult in large-class settings) and lacking in elements that are culture-sensitive, or easily adaptable to any social situation.

The classroom scenarios described in Lai (1994) and Evans (1996) seem to be resonated in Tsui (1996), which raises concerns over great student anxiety and reticence, with little student initiation and responses in the target language. However, some recent classroom studies reveal a rather different type of classroom scenario that is characterized by students' lively, but often impish verbal play in their L1, Cantonese (Kwan, 2000; Lin, 2000; Pennington, 1999a, 1999b). Such discourse practices of the students in the English classrooms, while expressing their agency and creativity, do not however seem to help them master the L2, and might further reproduce their social disadvantage. Classroom data and discussions related to this issue are presented in the subsequent chapters.

Reasons for these oppositional classroom practices are manifold. Some people ascribe the reasons to the lack of a favorable language environment to support the implementation of the communicative approach in the classroom. It is well known that although English is one of Hong Kong's official languages and enjoys second language status in Hong Kong, up to 95% (Hong Kong Yearbook, 2002) of the population in Hong Kong is predominantly of Chinese descent. Cantonese remains the dominant language at home, in the street, and in the school corridor. English is seldom used for intracommunity communication. As pointed out by Lin (2000), the majority of students in Hong Kong inhabit a Cantonese sociocultural life world, where there is little access to English and where English is largely irrelevant to their daily lives.

The Hong Kong government introduced the NET scheme with a major underlying purpose to create "opportunities for students to interact with non-Chinese, non-Cantonese-speaking members of staff outside as well as inside the classroom" (Johnson & Tang, 1993, p. 206). It is also believed that teachers from a western cultural background may be less transmission oriented in their pedagogy than local Hong Kong teachers (Evans, 1997). Have these NETs all brought with them the appropriate methodology to implement CLT successfully in Hong Kong?

In the rest of this chapter, we show how the teachers and students in this study conceptualized their everyday classroom positionings and practices under the macroeducational contexts and curriculum cultures described earlier. For convenience of presentation, the focal unit of each section is the teacher participant. Due to the highly similar nature of students' perspectives of English learning, their views are presented together in the last section of this chapter.

Six teachers, four NETs and two LETs, are addressed in their pseudonyms. The following criteria have been adopted in the identification of teacher participants:

- The NETs in this study are those who do not normally speak the L1 (i.e., Cantonese) of the Hong Kong students and have, for most of their lives, been living in an English speaking country such as the United Kingdom and the United States.
- The LETs are those who are as proficient in English as the NETs, at least with respect to the functional classroom English. This criterion reduces the possibility that any observable differences in discourse practices between the two types of teachers are the result of the differences in the teachers' English proficiency.

Each teacher case is presented under the same headings; (a) academic and professional history, (b) the school context, and (c) professional beliefs. The source of the data is the in-depth interviews done at three stages; preobservation (In1), during-observation (In2), and postobservation (In3).

MS. BERNER

Academic and Professional History

Ms. Berner was in her earlier 40s at the time of the study. She came from the United Kingdom and was an experienced NET in Hong Kong. She joined the Expatriate English Language Teacher scheme (a precedent of the NET Scheme) in 1989, served for 2 years, went home, and later came to Hong Kong again to join the revised scheme in 1996. Ms. Berner has got a BEd degree in teaching German and French. The qualification she has in teaching English as a foreign language was a certificate issued by the Royal Society of Arts specially organized by the British Council for the native English teachers in Hong Kong.

Back home, Ms. Berner mainly taught German and French. She has also had some experience in teaching German students English. Even though she did not have a very strong background in ELT, she felt that her training and experience in teaching other modern languages were great assets in her present job because of her experience as a second language learner.

Among our participants, Ms. Berner was the most experienced NET. Her commitment to the job is seen in her taking the initiative to propose to the school principal a series of suggestions to improve students' English. The key suggestions included setting up an English corner in the school, requesting all English teachers to use English to communicate with students all the time within the school premise, and assigning NETs[44] to teach junior forms only because younger students might benefit more from NET teaching than the exam-pressured senior students. For a couple of years, she volunteered to be the teacher mentor of student teachers from local universities. She agreed to participate in both the pilot and main study of this project almost immediately. She told the first author that she had lots of experience in similar research projects, for example, the evaluation project for the previous NET scheme. This may be the reason why she was very relaxed about the presence of the first author in her classrooms, although at times she would look tired and moody on a "seven-up"[45] day. In general, she seemed a highly confident teacher who felt that she understood the needs and interests of her students very well.

The School Context

Ms. Berner was working in a government school, which used to have mainly Band 2 students before mother tongue education was enforced in 1998. After the school was "forced" to adopt Chinese as the medium of instruction, the bands of the students dropped a little bit. According to Ms. Berner, the principal was very disappointed about not being able to maintain the EMI (English medium of instruction) status.

The school was situated in a public housing estate in the New Territories. Because Hong Kong is practicing district-based secondary school place allocation, most students in the school came from the nearby public housing estates built for the low income working-class citizens. However, there are also some private premises for higher income families nearby. The socioeconomic backgrounds of the students were thus quite mixed, although the majority were from low to lower middle classes.

Like most other schools in Hong Kong, the students in Ms. Berner's school were very mixed in ability and motivation to learn English. Students were streamed into good classes, average classes, and remedial classes. Remedial classes (one in each junior form) are considered weaker in academic performance. Therefore the classes would split into two smaller groups (around 20 each) for the language subjects and mathematics so that they would have more teacher attention during these lessons. Even before the territorywide enforcement of CMI, the remedial classes in Ms. Berner's school used Chinese as the medium of instruction for all subjects except English. Two of Ms. Berner's classes (1E and 3E) were remedial classes.

> [Compared to students in the United Kingdom,] students here are more motivated to work. They seem to understand at an early age that they have to work in order to get a job. Parents here push their children much harder than those in the UK. My Chinese colleagues told me if you don't work, you don't eat. There is no social security in Hong Kong. (In1)

However, although most Hong Kong students "are interested in learning a foreign language, … they are shy about asking help in the classroom. Because they kept all the problems to themselves, their learning progressed slowly" (In1). Despite that, Ms. Berner found most of the students in her school more friendly and respectful than those in the United Kingdom.

Professional Beliefs

At the time of the study, Ms. Berner was mainly teaching all junior classes. She used to teach some certificate-level examination classes as well, but the year before she participated in this study, she requested to concentrate on teaching junior forms because from her experience, junior forms worked better with NETs.

Ms. Berner was the only NET in this study who had a great interest in Cantonese. At the time of the study, she just joined a Cantonese course. To be in the same situation (learning a foreign language) as her students created a kind of "mutual sympathy" (In3) with her students. On a few occasions during the visits, she provided students with the Cantonese equivalents of some English vocabulary items. To strengthen the relationship with the students, she said she deliberately displayed her knowledge of Cantonese in explaining vocabulary even though she understood there could be other means of getting meanings across. She felt that some knowledge of the students' L1 gave her an advantage as a NET. She could understand the students better and shorten the psychological distance between them. She also admitted that giving an L1 equivalent was sometimes more effective and time-saving judging from her personal experiences in learning second languages.

Ms. Berner was well aware of the current approaches recommended for English language teaching such as the communicative approach and TOC,[46] which she considered a follow-up of the CLT. However, she felt that these approaches were very often difficult to implement because of practical constraints. In Ms. Berner's words,

> The education system is much less pupil-centered in Hong Kong. Students are used to sitting there, listening. Less teaching activities focused on pupils' finding out knowledge for themselves. Due to large class size, it's easier for the teacher to stand in front of the class and deliver. (In1)

Ms. Berner mentioned two elements in designing her favorite teaching activities. "Basically, ... it should be fun, and it should involve real use of the language, and at the end of the day, I have to make sure that the students have learnt something." (In2). From the first author's observation, Ms. Berner was sometimes the first one to laugh over some funny comments made by the students. "I'd like to have a relaxed atmosphere. I'd like to encourage people to speak, to talk to me. The more they talk to me in English the happier I am" (In3). "In the west," Ms. Berner went on, "teachers were used to making a fool of themselves to arouse students' interest in the language lessons." Ms. Berner felt that the Chinese teachers might feel more "inhibited" in this aspect (In3). Ms. Berner told the first author that some students called her "Mrs. Bean."[47]

However how much fun the class could enjoy still depends on the nature of the class. If some classes got too hysterical and noisy during games, Ms. Berner admitted that she would stop the games and assign some grammar exercises to the students. That happened once during a lesson with 1A, which Ms. Berner described as a "headache" because they always talked at the same time and often in Cantonese. However, "1A is the quietest when they've got a grammar worksheet," said Ms. Berner in the postobservation interview.

Ms. Berner was given the task to promote the English standard of the school through setting up an English room[48] of the school. She took great pride in her work. With the assistance of one local teacher, Ms. Berner had taken charge of the setting up, resourcing, and day-to-day management of the room. Ms. Berner mentioned to the first author in an informal chat the rather indifferent attitudes of most local English teachers in her school about the setting up and running of the English room. It made her wonder if these local English teachers really loved teaching English.

MR. WILLIAMS

Academic and Professional History

Like Ms. Berner, Mr. Williams was in his early 40s during the study. He came from Britain and has a degree in English and education and a diploma in TESOL. He has ample experience in teaching English to foreign learners in Eastern Europe. Back in the United Kingdom, he taught English to immigrant children with language problems. He also has some experience in teaching adult learners from Hong Kong.

The School Context

Mr. Williams was highly positive about his work context. "I really enjoy the experience of being here. This is the best school I have worked in" (In1). The school was situated in an old urban district surrounded by low-rent public housing estates. The school also turned CMI after 1998 but according to the English panel head, this change has not resulted in a very big difference in the student intake of the school. It may be because there were not many EMI schools around.

Mr. Williams' school was actually quite similar to Ms. Berner's in terms of student background. Before he came, Mr. Williams got an impression from the media in the west that "all students in the Asian countries are hard-working, serious, quiet, and passive" (In1). This was only partially true. "In this school, there is a real mixture. There are some nice students, very well motivated; but there are some naughty ones" but in general, they are "friendly, cheerful, outward going, just a pleasure to be with" (In1). Compared with his experience in the United Kingdom, Mr. Williams found it "refreshing" to see how education is valued here. He also believed that the strong family values in Hong Kong have helped to foster "well-balanced individuals." For example, his 2E class was at times badly behaved and lacked concentration, but they were friendly and interested in his teaching. He thought he was lucky because some of his NET friends had had a bad time in schools with Band 5 students. "It's not the quality of the students that matter, it's the relationship between the staff and the students" (In1). In his school, there was a good teacher–student relationship.

Mr. Williams of course also felt upset about practical constraints universal to most Hong Kong schools. "I nearly pulled out after the interview because they [the recruitment team] told me you are going to have 40 kids in the class, tiny classroom, it's really hot. A lot of the students are not academic and you are going to have thousands and thousands of marking to do" (In1). In this respect, education in Hong Kong is "underresourced" because "in England, they are very large school I worked in, nice carpets on the floor, whiteboards and two computers in every classroom, lovely furniture, 25 children in each class … that was very shocking in Hong Kong, still using chalk and blackboards, no computers" (In1).

Professional Beliefs

The ideal ELT methodology for Mr. Williams was "communicative activities, ones where language is used for genuine communication" (In1). However, like Ms. Berner, Mr. Williams identified a list of problems in implementing CLT in his school—"the size of the classes, small classrooms, difficult to get another space other than the classroom, … unless the kids are doing something they think will be assessed, otherwise they won't be doing it seriously, it's very hard to do freer activities because they think you are wasting their time" (In2). He ascribed the reason to the phenomenon that English was usually taught in Hong Kong as an academic subject with overemphasis on language forms and mistakes. "They said they want to do more grammar practice as they would do in the exam. But if you do more grammar and exam practice, they will complain, it's boring. You can't win" (In2). Therefore, despite the many good virtues of the students (such as being generally friendly to the teachers and placing high value on education), Mr. Williams was upset to notice that students "are not interested in learning English for communicative purposes. They are interested in passing exams and they see those things as being separate" (In2). "It's very frustrating to see practices which research has proved not workable" (In1).

Nevertheless, Mr. Williams was still satisfied with the impact he was creating as a NET. Like Ms. Berner, he stressed real use of the language as the most effective teaching strategy and real use of the language can best be promoted through increased interactions between teachers and students. He believed that he and the local English teachers were probably doing more or less the same things in terms of pedagogical design. However, "if you are speaking to a native speaker, the interaction would be more valid" (In1). He quoted instances on how his students communicated with him for real needs (about studying overseas) whereas the classroom tasks in which the students had to communicate with their classmates in English were comparatively artificial.

Like Ms. Berner, Mr. Williams told the first author he was interested in learning Cantonese. But unlike Ms. Berner, he was not paying to join a course and he was not observed to have used any Cantonese in his lessons. In fact, lots of students and minor staff in the school were making an effort to teach him Cantonese. Like Ms. Berner, Mr. Williams has developed a kind of "mutual sympathy" with the students from his experience of learning a foreign language. "The staff here [in the school canteen] insist that I speak in Cantonese. I understand how the students feel. I go and ask for **wai ta nai** <soya bean milk>, **sui** <water>. I have learned that hard, but they want more now. They try to teach a bit more Cantonese, but they do it by coming out with a stream of Cantonese. They don't demonstrate. I'm just paralyzed. I don't understand a word they say. This may be the same thing that I'm doing to my students" (In2). In this sense, his experience in learning Cantonese also helped him understand better the students' difficulties in mastering a foreign language.

MR. NELSON

Academic and Professional History

Mr. Nelson is an American who was around 30 years old at the time of the study. He first came to Hong Kong after university as a volunteer worker. Later, the project was canceled and he became a teacher and has since then developed an interest in it. His first degree was international studies. That might have explained why he was more interested in working overseas. To equip himself to be a teacher, he obtained a certificate in education in Hong Kong and earned a Master of Arts degree in TESL (Teaching English as a Second Language) at a local university. Mr. Nelson later acquired an MPhil in TESL at the same university.

The School Context

Before Mr. Nelson joined the school that the first author visited, he worked in two others. He left the previous one (after working there for 4 years) because the English panel head was so restrictive that he did not have any freedom in his teaching. As for the school he was working in during this study, he was given comparatively more freedom to use his own materials instead of sticking to the textbooks. There were two English panel heads in that school. As described by Mr. Nelson, the junior form head, Ms. Hung, who was another participant in this research, was more receptive and supportive to innovative teaching ideas whereas the senior form one was more conservative. The first author was introduced to Ms. Hung through Mr. Nelson.

The school was the only EMI, and unisex (all boys) school in the sample of this study. Because only about one fourth of all secondary schools in Hong Kong can maintain their EMI status after 1998 (as opposed to 90% before that), students in that school were among the top 30% of secondary school-age boys in that district. To maintain the EMI status, all students were required to use English as much as possible on campus. During her visits, the first author heard announcements from the head prefect in English. She was once approached by a Form One pupil who told her in broken but understandable English that he could not attend the interview because of some other engagements (fieldnotes).

The school itself has been established for more than 50 years and was well known in the district for its public exam results and university entrance rate. The geographical surroundings of the school were rather the same as Ms. Berner's. There was a mixture of students coming from lower and middle classes. From the first author's observation, some students in the school were very vocal and some spoke English very well. However, compared to other elite schools in the more well-off areas, most students' English (at least in the classes observed) was by no means outstanding. For example, some students' English was characterized by a distinct Cantonese accent and Chinese grammatical structures. The students' discourse and behavior during the lessons observed showed that they were displaying a kind of culture that was very local and Cantonese oriented.

Mr. Nelson did not think that students in his school liked English.

> Students see English as something they need to learn, but English is not taught in an interesting way. Students have negative views towards learning it even though they know it's important. Some students' attitude is 'I'm a Chinese man. I don't need English.' (In1)

Being a Catholic missionary school, there was a native English-speaking Father residing in the school. The first author met the Father once and not surprisingly, he told her he thought he was benefiting more from the students' Cantonese than the students were benefiting from his English. That might be implying that he and the students interacted more in Cantonese than in English.

According to Mr. Nelson, most students in his school were very exam focused in their study. "Students expect me to help them through the exams" (In2). This mentality may have been induced by some local teachers who spent most of their lessons drilling students on exam-oriented practice tasks. Mr. Nelson told the first author that one of the teachers worked at an exam school and he taught his class the way he did in the exam school. "[T]here is in fact a sort of indirect influence. If the school allows teachers to give exam papers to students every day, it may affect my students because they may make the same demand on me" (In2). Like Mr. Williams, Mr. Nelson has observed the same contradiction in students' expectations. "They would say they want exam practice but if you gave them a lot of such practice, they would say it's boring. I don't think they have the skills to identify their needs" (In2).

Concerning his relationships with the students, Mr. Nelson said that students liked "playing tricks" on him and speaking foul language. "Discipline can be a problem, but the more freedom I have in what I taught, the students' behaviour became better because I can adapt to their interest … Students won't challenge you if you can make the lesson interesting" (In1).

Professional Beliefs

Mr. Nelson strongly believed in a learner-centered and activity-based approach to ELT, "not the traditional teacher-fronted teaching" (In3). Learner-centered teaching was the topic Mr. Nelson had chosen for his MPhil research. Actually, Mr. Nelson practiced a research-informed teaching design. He conducted a survey at the beginning of the year to find out what students would like to do. Project work, drama, and debate were the three most favored activities indicated by the students. During the first author's visit, Mr. Nelson's class was at the final stage of their project work. They then began their drama activity (classroom excerpts available in the next three chapters). Of course, not every student liked these activities. "Some students told me that they cannot adapt to my method. They just want to be spoon-fed grammar every day" (In3). However, Mr. Nelson had strong faith in his approach and he believed students would finally see the value of this approach to learning a language. "In some ways, the teacher knows better than the students how to learn a language" (In3).

Compared with his last school, he was given more freedom in this school to try out new ideas. However, he felt that he was "working like an island" (In2). Nobody else in the school shared his perceptions nor cared what he was doing unless something had gone wrong. "Most local teachers are just teaching to their textbooks, they don't have time to find extra materials"[49] (In2). He was the only teacher who would turn up to help students in the lunch club meeting. This experience echoed Ms. Berner's views about local teachers' indifference toward the English room. Mr. Nelson said that he sometimes felt very frustrated having to follow some undesirable practices passed down from the traditional practices. For example, he was instructed to deduct one mark for every grammatical error in composition marking. Some creative students therefore got very low marks in examinations because they attempted to express themselves through complex structures that they had not yet mastered. The low marks thus weakened their desire to be innovative and creative.

Mr. Nelson had no plan to learn Cantonese.[50] However, after staying in Hong Kong for 6 years, he understood most of what the students were saying, especially the foul language. Still, he admitted that a knowledge of Cantonese would help him understand their common problems, "but there are enough resources that will help a teacher to understand students' problems with learning English" (In2). For example, he could talk with other teachers or obtain relevant input by reading academic articles, newspapers, and magazines. Besides, "the school is English medium. Students are expected to use English" (In2). Nevertheless, he expressed the same view as Ms. Berner and Mr. Williams that sharing the students' L1 would have an affective impact on his relationship with the students. "Knowing their L1 may make them like me better" (In2).

MS. HUNG

Academic and Professional History

Ms. Hung is a local teacher participant working in the same school as Mr. Nelson at the time of this study. She was in her late 30s and had been an English teacher in the same school for more than 15 years. She received her undergraduate studies at the University of Hong Kong, majoring in English linguistics, and obtained a Master's degree in education in a university in the United Kingdom, specializing in TESOL. Having received university education in the most prestigious English medium university in Hong Kong studying English linguistics, and having spent a whole year's time living in an English-speaking country, Ms. Hung said that her English proficiency was more than sufficient for her job as a teacher and she would describe herself as "comfortably bilingual" (In1). Although acknowledging the inextricable link between language and culture, she declined to admit that her English-related cultural knowledge was comparable to her proficiency. "I do not have a strong feeling toward western culture; all knowledge comes from reading books. I am not integrated into their [English-related] culture. I'm very Hong Kong oriented" (In1).

Professional Beliefs

Even though Ms. Hung agreed that it was impossible to avoid touching on cultural issues in the process of learning a language and some cultural knowledge of the target language would help learners understand why people behave in a certain way, she asserted that she would not intentionally transmit cultural knowledge of English to her students. "What I could do is to bring western films or TV series like *Mr. Bean* to the students. What I could not do is to nurture the kind of cultural knowledge in the students through myself as a model" (In1). She believed that culture could not be "learned" in the classroom. Nevertheless, whenever the situation warranted it, she would discuss matters about culture during her lessons.

Ms. Hung openly identified herself as adopting a more or less teacher-centered approach in teaching. "I think I'm under the influence of past experience in schools, a very teacher-centered environment" (In1). Although she agreed in principle to the rationales of some of the current teaching approaches such as communicative and task-based learning, she thought that "successful implementation of these approaches depends on whether the environment is appropriate, whether the teacher is ready to do it, and whether the students are mature enough and have mastered the necessary skills to do it well" (In1). She felt the need to change her own perspectives of these approaches first before actually using them in her classroom. In Ms. Hung's words, "I need more input to 'wash' my brain" (In1, translated from Cantonese).

Ms. Hung identified three elements of her favorite teaching activities. First, they should be tasks and activities that were well liked by the students. Second, they should be activities that were challenging. "If it is challenging, even a traditional reading comprehension task could turn out to be very enjoyable and effective" (In1). Third, they should be activities in which the students saw relevance to their everyday experience and future needs of English. Concerning the future needs of English, Ms. Hung argued that in Hong Kong, English was mainly used for utilitarian purposes such as further study and finding jobs with good prospects. To many students, "English as a communication vehicle is only confined to classroom situations. English is a subject they need to pass" (In1). She felt that the skills assessed in public examinations reflected what students need in their future career and it was the teacher's responsibility to enable students to cope with these requirements in the exams. On a couple of occasions during the first author's observations, evidence emerged showing Ms. Hung's explicit effort to link up students' language performance in class with their anticipated performance in the public examinations even though the class had 2½ years to go before any such examinations. For example, she once asked the class "How many of you think that you would get a pass if this is Paper 3?" immediately after the class had listened to a recorded text (3E, 17 March 1999). In the final interview, Ms. Hung explained her practice: "Maybe I have used it as a motivation. Sometimes, if I relate the task to exam, students will see the relevance, otherwise, what's the point of sitting there and listening?"

Even though Ms. Hung is Chinese-English bilingual, she has never used any Cantonese in her English lessons. Outside the classrooms, English was also used as much as possible. "It is our responsibility to maintain an EMI school status, in which students are supposed to immerse in English as much as possible" (In2). Basically, Ms. Hung agreed with Mr. Nelson in thinking that the majority of students in her school did not need Cantonese to assist in their learning of English. With more able students, she would even use English to inculcate moral values because "they are too used to hearing it in Cantonese, and begin to feel numb" (In3). Only under circumstances when the students had emotional and psychological problems would she employ Cantonese to communicate with them.

Talking about the major differences in roles between a NET like Mr. Nelson and a local teacher like her, she first showed her appreciation of Mr. Nelson because he had brought in a number of innovative ideas. However, she further maintained that to be an all-around teacher, she had to take care of students' personal growth. "A teacher has to take care of other things of the students, like their family, in addition to helping them with exams and imparting knowledge" (In1). That means she sometimes had to play the role of a counselor. In those situations, knowledge of the students' L1 would be a definite asset.

MISS LOGAN

Academic and Professional History

Miss Logan was from London. She was in her late 30s. Her first degree was in languages (German and French). After getting tired with her job in finance back home, she looked for opportunities abroad and became an English teacher on the Japan Exchange and Teaching (JET) program, a program quite similar to the NET scheme in Hong Kong (see relevant discussions in chap. 2). She then began to develop an interest in teaching and went back to Britain to do a certificate course in teaching English to foreigners, then a PGDE in education before she came to Hong Kong to join the NET scheme. Miss Logan took part in this study as part of a larger Hong Kong government-funded evaluation[51] of the NET Scheme. Unlike other NET participants who agreed to join the study almost immediately, it took Miss Logan several days to consider before consenting to take part. Perhaps due to the sensitive nature of the evaluation element of the project, Miss Logan seemed to be under great pressure throughout the study, and on a few occasions she declined the first author's requests to observe some of her lessons because, in her opinion, the students behaved too badly during some previous lessons. From the first author's observation, Miss Logan was very gentle and soft-spoken. Some students might have taken advantage of her gentleness.

The School Context

Like all other participants, Miss Logan was working in a school situated in a working-class district. The district was believed to be heavily populated by new arrivals from mainland China. According to Mr. Sze (the other LET participant teaching in the same school), the school was one of the 20 schools in Hong Kong with the highest number of students having financial difficulties. Therefore it could be imagined that students there had very limited English capital from home. However, as pointed out by Mr. Sze, some students' academic abilities were not necessarily weak. Like many medium-band schools in Hong Kong, the school was very mixed in terms of pupil abilities. After turning CMI, the school has also inevitably experienced a drop in students' bands.

In Miss Logan's opinion, the students were "quite nice, quite friendly, and reasonably well behaved. Not all classes are well behaved, but generally quite good"

(In1). As for students' attitude toward English, "I think they quite like it, even though they don't want to work seriously" (In2). Very often students would come up to her and speak to her in English. "I can see that they enjoy using English" (In2). But she thought that some students were very passive and not working hard enough. "They'll just do what they are led to do, or told to do. Some of them do read the South China Morning Post, but I don't think they do much for themselves" (In2). She admitted that she had discipline problems with the weaker classes (see the streaming policy in earlier sections of this chapter).[52] "Being a foreigner, if the students are going to play anybody up, it's going to be the foreign teacher because I'm different" (In3). On two occasions, she requested not to be observed in those classes because she felt that her performance would be affected.

Professional Beliefs

When the first author asked about her favorite ELT activities, instead of answering the question directly, Miss Logan prefaced her responses by saying that she could not actually do what she liked to do there because they did not work with large classes of 40 students (the same problem mentioned by Ms. Berner and Mr. Williams).

> My favourite type of activities are where students are really involved and they are generating. First of all you have to drill, controlled practice and drilling. But when it gets on to freer practice stage, when they are generating language for themselves, manipulating what they know, and it's really theirs, they own the language, it's more meaningful. (In2)

However, when students were given the freedom to practice freely, some of them would take that as a time "to put their feet up, to talk Cantonese, and have a laugh" (In2). Under these practical constraints, she very often had to do something she did not enjoy, for example, very teacher-controlled practice. "I gave them a prompt and they all had to give me the same answer which is not their answer" (In2). It was also due to this reason that she did not have high hopes that task-based learning, an ELT methodology recommended in the current English syllabus of Hong Kong, would be successful if the classes remained so large.

Miss Logan's attitude toward students' use of Cantonese in class was quite similar to Ms. Berner's and Mr. Williams'. She thought it was just natural for a monolingual group of students to revert to their home language when unmonitored. But she would "keep nagging, encouraging them to speak in English" (In2). Contrary to Ms. Berner and Mr. Williams, her personal experience in learning second languages supported a target-language immersion environment. "That was much better to develop the four skills simultaneously" (In1).

Even though she would like to learn Cantonese, she had no time to do it. She agreed that some Cantonese might help the students to understand her teaching better, and cope with classroom discipline. "When I'm scolding them, it will be in a foreign language. Sometimes they just don't know I'm scolding them" (In3). At the beginning of the term, she enlisted the help of her colleagues to write down Chinese characters for some presumably unfamiliar English words to the students so that she could show the Chinese in class to aid students' understanding, but basically she believed there were other ways of producing the same effect and she did not want to bother her colleagues too much.

MR. SZE

Academic and Professional History

Mr. Sze was Miss Logan's colleague. He was the youngest among our teacher participants. Despite his relatively short experience in teaching (4 years), Mr. Sze appeared to be very confident and to have a strong conviction about the virtues of the principles he had been upholding in his profession. That might be due to the fact that he had not stopped pursuing higher degrees after undergraduate studies. After obtaining a BA in teaching English as a second language, he got an MA in language studies, and at the time of the data collection, Mr. Sze was doing a Doctor of education affiliated with a university in Britain. He had also received more than 1½ years' overseas education experience in high school and colleges in Canada.

Probably due to his education background, he was very open to research and to his strengths and weaknesses in comparison to a NET such as Miss Logan. Right from the beginning, he welcomed the idea of recruiting NETs in local secondary schools. He believed motivated students would benefit. Besides, he himself also benefited from the NET because he could seek editorial comments from Miss Logan on his written productions very conveniently. "Whenever formal handouts are produced, I will ask Miss Logan to take a look to see if there are any mistakes" (In1). He did not consider it a loss of face. "It's a natural thing that my English is not good. I'm not a native speaker [of English]" (In1). However, he did not think it was a problem as long as his English was good enough to function as an English teacher at secondary level. On the other hand, he would be happy to share his experience in handling problem students and public examination requirements with Miss Logan.

Professional Beliefs

Mr. Sze quoted composition as his favorite ELT activity because he was given the freedom to play with some innovative ideas of his creation. The effect was good as students were taught how to write on traditional topics such as schools, picnics, and festivals from some interesting and new perspectives. Basically the activities he liked the least were those that were forced on the teachers by the school. One example he quoted was one that required students to copy sentences mechanically under the disguise of sentence making. According to Mr. Sze, this practice was long-standing, but nobody had ever challenged it.

As for students' favorite activities, Mr. Sze thought that it all "depends on the level of difficulty of the tasks. They should be set at the level of the students, perhaps a little bit beyond" (In2). Mr. Sze reported that his students did not like pair and group work because "boys never want to discuss with girls" (In2). Comparatively speaking, Mr. Sze found that his students generally preferred "receptive skills practice" (such as listening and reading) to "productive skills practice" (such as speaking and listening). Basically, Mr. Sze felt that "teacher's personality" plays a much greater role in producing an effective lesson than task formats and topic choice. "Even if the topic is not that interesting, if the teacher can cultivate a friendly atmosphere, ask them some interesting questions, or if the teacher can link the topic to things students like, it can still be successful" (In3).

Mr. Sze overtly supported an interplay of Cantonese and English during lessons. He believed that students' L1 had an important cognitive role to play in assisting them to acquire a second language. "When students' quality is not so good, using all English is a very boring thing to the students. It may weaken their motivation to learn. I support a bilingual mode" (In2). Using Cantonese at an interval with English could reduce the stress the students experienced for having to concentrate for a long time. Cantonese could "keep them awake, and help to sustain their interest in learning, student–teacher relationship will be much closer" (In3). Nevertheless, Mr. Sze agreed that there should be a progression of the amount of English input from the teachers and output from students when they proceed from the lower forms to higher forms. According to Mr. Sze, even though Cantonese would still be used with senior form students, it should only be used when necessary, for example, to obtain information from an editorial in a Chinese newspaper to write a composition in English. "I think it's a shame to make Cantonese a taboo in the English classes" (In3).

THE STUDENTS

To obtain a balanced picture of both types of interactants in the classroom, the teacher participants were requested to sample six students of high, mid, and low proficiency in English from each of their classes for an interview with the first author.[53] Some students of the NETs were very worried at the beginning about whether they needed to use English to do the interviews. When the first author told them the interviews would be done in Cantonese, many sighed with relief. Therefore, all student quotations are verbatim accounts translated from Cantonese.

In the following paragraphs, we report findings from these interviews under two key aspects; (a) their views about learning English; and (b) their views about their English teachers. Like any socially constructed labels, the term "students" should not be understood as a fixed and static entity. Views from the "students" the first author interviewed were inevitably diversified, contrastive, and unstable. Sometimes, the same students could display ambivalent attitudes toward the same issue.

Views About Learning English

Students' views were sought with regard to their attitude toward learning and using English, their English-learning experience, and their learning strategies.

Attitudes Toward Learning and Using English.   As expected, almost all students said English was important. They would learn it whether it was compulsory or not. A few low-proficiency students would usually take the opposite stance at the beginning because to them, English was difficult. But most of them tended to change their mind and followed the majority. In general, almost all students wanted to learn English for one major reason—English is important; it is an international language. They heard everybody everywhere (their parents, teachers, the mass media) say that English is important for finding a job with better prospects and for international communication. One said that his parents wanted him to learn good English. One said that he learned English to meet the needs of the society. Both students were from Ms. Hung's classes.

However, even though all these students realized the importance of English, the use of the language was mainly confined to the English language classroom. To most of these students, Chinese remained the language for their everyday life. It was almost always the language they would use when chatting with friends, watching movies (reading the Chinese subtitles when watching English movies), singing songs and reading for pleasure (mainly fictions by local writers). Interestingly, most of them liked Euro-American based festivals (such as Christmas, Easter, and Halloween) more than Chinese ones (except Chinese New Year because of the red packet money). Some told the first author that they liked "western[54] festivals" because there seemed to be more holidays with more activities and more fun for young people.

It is interesting to note that a few high English proficiency students from Ms. Berner's and Mr. Williams' classes said they would choose something else more interesting to study if English were not compulsory. The first author later found out that these students were returning emigrants from English-speaking countries such as Australia and Canada.[55] Most had received primary level basic education abroad and therefore spoke fluent English. Their high English proficiency may not be due to an interest in learning the subject.

English Learning Experience.   In response to whether they liked having English lessons, most said "quite," or just "a little bit," or "sometimes." In general students said that they liked activities that would give them "freedom," and "freedom" meant they could do what they liked, unsupervised. Initially, the first author felt a bit surprised to hear that some low proficiency students said they liked extensive reading lessons. Then she found out the reason was because in such lessons, the teacher was not directing any activities and they did not need to listen to the teachers. Therefore they could have a rest while pretending to read.

The favorite English lesson activities quoted included games (almost all junior classes), and discussion (Mr. Williams' 4E). Some junior students looked really happy when they described the games to the first author. Once or twice, the first author asked the students if they had learned more English from their favorite activities. Some of them would say no. They liked the activities only because they were easy and fun. To learn grammar, they should study the textbook and do exercises (Ms. Hung's 3E).

Most students showed an ambivalent attitude toward what they liked to do during the lessons and what they perceived to be effective English learning tasks. The exam classes particularly exhibited this attitude. For example, a 4E female student has this comment on Mr. Williams' teaching approach—"He doesn't know how to teach us. He thought that we could learn English through playing, but we all learnt English since childhood through drillings and exercises. Every 'missie'[56] did the same. Then all of a sudden we are made to look so lazy and lax this year [by not doing enough exercises]." Another Year 4 student from Mr. Nelson's class also felt that the teacher had done them a disservice, although with a very good will—

> Mr. Nelson wants to have a balance between some traditional methods of teaching, in which the teacher will teach you everything, and some more modern approach he brought from America in which students are encouraged to take the initiatives to discover knowledge by themselves. But I think Mr. Nelson has not been able to strike a good balance. Very often, his approach to facilitate students' learning depends very much on whether the students are willing to take the initiative, but we are not that kind of students. We may not learn much from him and he may not know.

This student's view represents some general passive attitude toward learning English among most students in Hong Kong including these top-notch students. This point is picked up again in the next section.

The students' least favorite activities included dictations and any activity that they had to listen to the teacher talking for extended periods. Several students mentioned that it was extremely boring to do **"fo man"** <text> (課文 in Cantonese). It refers to the reading comprehension text that usually begins a unit of study in many textbooks and the concept **"fo man"** is probably borrowed from the Chinese language subject. When they studied **"fo man,"** they usually had to sit quietly and listen to the teacher. However, although most students interviewed did not like listening to the teacher talking about **"fo man,"** unconsciously, they seemed to consider this teaching activity as related to the examinations. This is probably because internal school examinations usually assess what has been covered in the textbook. For example, several students from different teachers said that the teacher should **gaau sju** <teach the book> (教書 in Cantonese) in order to prepare them for the examinations. He or she should not just **zou wud dong** <do activities[57]> (做活動 in Cantonese) with them.

When the first author asked the students to rate their current English proficiency level, only a minority (basically the returnees) said that they were satisfied with their English standard. A couple of the returnees said that their English had shown signs of regression after coming back to Hong Kong. The rest of the students (often including those considered to be high ability by the teacher concerned) generally were not satisfied with their current English standard.

English Learning Strategies.   Apart from a few low proficiency students, most of them were able to come up with a list of strategies to improve their English. The most popular ones were read more books and newspapers, do more exercises, pay more attention in class,[58] and talk more with the NETs. Most students, however, admitted that they were not paying sufficient attention in class and they were not working hard enough, for example in doing exercises and reading books. When asked if they would do those immediately, most said they had to see. Some said English was difficult and some confessed it was their own problem—they often daydreamed in class, were shy to ask questions in public, and spent too much time watching television at home. It seems that very few students, not even the high proficiency ones, were taking an active role in learning English outside the classroom.

Inside the classrooms, most of these students would follow the teachers' instructions to do pair work in English. Several students from the NETs' classes reported their interesting feeling of being "forced" to use English to talk with the NETs. "I didn't know what I said but Miss Logan understood me," said a Year 2 girl. However, they seldom, or never, took the initiative to speak English to their peers in unsupervised situations. They said that they felt very uneasy speaking English to their Cantonese-speaking friends and teachers because such behavior would be interpreted as attempts to show off. An exceptional case happened in Mr. Nelson's 4E. The students being interviewed told the first author delightfully that the teacher set up a penalty system to fine students who did not speak to others in English to prepare for her visits. Although the mechanism involved penalty, they ended up feeling more natural speaking English. An interesting comment from one of Mr. Nelson's students stated that some of his classmates had gone so "crazy" that they began to speak English in Chinese lessons. A similar comment was made by Ms. Hung's 3E—"Some classmates have been 'contaminated' by western culture recently and they only spoke English." This might somewhat represent the culture of students in EMI schools.

Again, students (particularly junior form students) seldom spoke to their local English teachers in English outside the classroom except for students in Mr. Nelson and Ms. Hung's school. Ms. Hung's students said that they were made to do it by the teacher because she would not respond to them if they spoke in Cantonese.[59]

Interestingly, Mr. Williams' 4E class was particularly pessimistic about the prospect of learning good English in Hong Kong. A girl, for example, boldly asserted that "nobody here can speak English well." Four out of six students in that group believed that the only way to learn proper English was to stay overseas in an English-speaking country.

Views About Their English Teachers

Students taught by the NETs gave interesting comments on the arrangement. The most frequently heard terms (translated from Cantonese) are "special, quite good, quite novel, happy." Although the general feeling seemed positive (some in Ms. Berner's classes said they felt proud), there were individual students who reported feeling "anxious" and "inferior" because they feared that they would not be able to communicate with the NETs. No matter what, to most students, an ability to communicate with the NETs has become their English proficiency benchmark. A Year 4 student of Mr. Williams said the class activity that really helped him learn English was talking to the NET one on one. "His oral English is of course better than the local teachers' because he is a **gwai lou** <*foreigner*>." Similar views have been expressed by several students from Ms. Berner's 1E, 3A, and Miss Logan's 2B—"Their [the NET's] English is more standard and accurate." Most students interviewed also welcomed the kind of "freedom" they enjoyed during the NETs' lessons. Because the NETs did not understand Cantonese, they were freer to joke in Cantonese.

When students were asked to compare the NETs and local teachers, most of them from the NET classes tended to depict the LETs as looking more serious and being very strict with discipline. Students in Mr. Williams' 4E told the first author that the NET seemed more tolerant of students' errors. The same male student in Mr. Williams' Year 4 class mentioned earlier made this comment about their local teachers—"If you make mistakes when talking to a **gwai lou** <*foreigner*>, they won't laugh at you. But if you make mistakes when talking to a Chinese, they will laugh at you until you blow up (**siu dou nei baau** 笑到你爆 in Cantonese)."

About half of the students interviewed admitted it was sometimes difficult to understand the NETs, but the situation improved once they had adapted to the speed and accents of the teachers. Some students reported gaily how the NETs (e.g., Miss Logan and Ms. Berner) used body language and drawings to convey meanings. These students seemed to enjoy these paralinguistic means of communication. One female student from Miss Logan's 2B described with smiles how funny Miss Logan's drawings were. Nevertheless, according to the students, it was good to have a NET because they could be "forced" to use English. However, the majority thought that if the NETs could understand Cantonese (not necessarily to speak it), the situation would be "perfect" (Miss Logan's 2E). These students' remarks about the NETs align to a great extent with the findings reported in Luk (2001).

Interestingly, those students who were taught by the LETs also liked their teachers a great deal (particularly Mr. Sze's 1B). Most of them said that their teachers were kind and the English lessons were quite fun sometimes. Ms. Hung's 3E said that Ms. Hung spoke good English. When asked if they would want a NET to teach them, most students first said they did not have a special preference. Some of the high proficiency ones expressed the desire to have some of the English lessons taught by the NETs so that they could benefit from the more accurate pronunciation whereas the lower proficiency students usually preferred local teachers because they could communicate in Cantonese. One student from Mr. Nelson's 4E made an interesting point about what students go best with the LET:

> For long-term purpose, those of us who are lacking in initiative can try a local teacher. There are many good local teachers, for example, they will prepare a lot of notes and teach students, not just distribute the notes. Some local teachers have in-depth knowledge of some aspects for which the natives may not be comparable.

To the authors, the underlying meaning of this student's viewpoint is that only local teachers could help students obtain good results in the high-stake examinations.

SUMMARY

In this chapter, we present key issues of the macroeducation context of Hong Kong at the time of our study, and introduce the backgrounds and views about learning and teaching English of the teachers and students.

In general, all the teacher participants in this study gave us the impression that they were operating under different degrees of practical constraints generated by the macroeducation system and learning culture prevalent in Hong Kong schools, for example, large class size, exam-oriented curriculum culture. Despite all of these constraints, they were trying hard to bring about changes with different degrees of persistence and perhaps success. Of the four NETs, Mr. Nelson, in particular, persisted in implementing a more student-centered approach, despite the indifferent attitude of other teachers toward his efforts. Ms. Berner and Mr. Williams were confident that their unique contributions lie in necessitating students to use English for genuine communication and developing students' English competence. Comparatively speaking, Miss Logan seemed to be more submissive to the existing system, or pessimistic about what she could do to change the whole culture of teaching and learning. As the first author observed, she got along well with the good class (2B), but experienced discipline problems with the weaker ones (e.g., 2D and 2E), and therefore could not practice what she believed to be effective TESOL methodology.

As for the two LETs, they seemed to be rather certain about their differential roles and capital in the face of the NETs. Mr. Sze, in particular, was highly confident in code-switching practices, which obviously went against suggestions made in the official English language syllabus (Secondary 1–5; Curriculum Development Council, 1999) that teachers of English "must speak and use English as frequently as possible" (p. 37).[60] Ms. Hung, on the other hand, was aware of her own value and contribution as a local teacher who understands the long-standing traditions of the education and examination culture, while highly appreciative of the potential contributions of the NETs.

As for the students, most of them interviewed were rather ambivalent in their attitudes toward their English teachers and learning English. On the one hand, they preferred NETs because they felt that NETs could make the boring task of learning English fun and perhaps more effective. NETs are native speakers of English and therefore, the students surmised, their English must be "better." In this respect, the students seemed to be living exemplifications of the effects of the hegemony of "native speaker fallacy." They also looked forward to the greater degree of freedom they believed stereotypical NETs would provide. However, they somehow believed that to learn English in a fun way is one thing, to get good results in English in the public examinations was another. To achieve the latter, they needed to learn grammar and examination skills. In these aspects, most of them did not think the NETs were doing the job properly because they thought the latter lacked firsthand experience to share with them.

In general, findings presented in this chapter show that the NETs, LETs, and their students were harboring different desires, ideologies, and agendas about how English should be taught and learned. It is likely that these differences would result in conflicts and tensions, or intriguing "cultural chemical effects" if we believe that practices reflect ideologies.

QUESTIONS FOR REFLECTION AND DISCUSSION

1. Discuss in small groups how the educational or institutional contexts in which you are situated affect your work as a teacher, with particular reference to your choice of pedagogical approaches, activity design, and lesson arrangements.

2. How far do you agree or disagree with the views expressed by Ms. Hung and Mr. Sze (under "Professional Beliefs") concerning the differences between NETs and LETs (e.g., in terms of language proficiency, cultural knowledge, and modeling, and the provision of a natural environment for language use, etc.)?

3. Talking from your personal experience, how far do you agree with the 4E student's comments on local teachers' attitude toward student errors (i.e., they will laugh at you until you blow up)?

7

Making Sense in the Lessons

B eginning with this chapter, we present classroom episodes unfolding cross-cultural encounters under three themes. We begin in this chapter with data showing how teachers and students made sense to and of each other during the lessons.

TUNING-IN DISCUSSION

1. Consider from the point of view of NETs/LETs,

   - what are the usual key factors causing difficulties in communication between teachers and students in a foreign language classroom?
   - what strategies would teachers usually use to make sense *of* and *to* students in a foreign language classroom?

2. Considering the point of view of students, what strategies do you think students would use to make sense of and to NETs/LETs in a foreign language classroom?

The study of "sense making practices" has been a topic of interest in ethnomethodological studies since the 1970s. Sense making is often used interchangeably with terms such as "practical reasoning," "concept formation," and "interpretive procedures" (Cicourel, as cited in Heap, 1976). In any face-to-face interaction, sense making is a procedure that is believed to be engaged in by both the interlocutors. Like any other institutional context where interaction takes place, the classroom is a place where a lot of sense making needs to be done both by the teacher and the students. Making sense *to* and making sense *of* is a circular route between the teacher and the students. The purpose of this chapter is to present and discuss classroom data showing how practical reasoning and interpretive procedures are organized, what interactive resources (see chap. 5) are activated in the process, and to what extent the patterns reflect the linguistic and cultural limits and potentials of the sense-making resources of teachers and students.

SENSE-MAKING RESOURCES

Heap (1976) reported Cicourel's (1970) attempt to answer the question "What are sense making practices?" and concluded that the search for universally invariant properties of sense-making practices is misguided by trying to presuppose, rather than discover, the "possibilities of ordinary use" of the concept. As the term "making sense" seems very widely used by laypeople, instead of attempting to define what are sense-making practices, we would like to explore in the present book "what makes sense making possible." In chapter 5, we mention three major types of interactive resources that interlocutors often access when interacting, namely linguistic resources, cultural resources, and institutional resources. From the data of the present study, these resources are found to be asymmetrical in terms of quantity and quality between the teachers and students, and between NETs and LETs. In this chapter, we illustrate with classroom excerpts how teachers and students employed these resources in their sense-making processes, and to what effects. Before that, we would like to give an overview of the three types of interactive resources for sense-making purposes in the light of the present study.

In this study, the linguistic resources in focus include the language systems of both Cantonese and English (including different styles and varieties). The distribution or mastery of these linguistic resources are by no means identical, or symmetrical, among the teachers and between the teachers and student participants. Mr.. Sze, for example, explicitly compared his mastery of English unfavorably to that of his colleague, Miss Logan (see chap. 6). However, Mr. Sze did not show any sense of inferiority as an English teacher perhaps because of his mastery of the students' L1, a type of resource highly valued by Mr. Sze. The knowledge of students' L1 also seems to be the major distinguishing factor between NETs and LETs. The two LETs are apparently proficient in the students' L1 and English. As mentioned before, Mr. Sze consistently employed both English and Cantonese in his interactions with the students. As for Ms. Hung, even though she did not use a single word of Cantonese with the students in our data, her ability to understand students' Cantonese seemed to have played an important role in her interactions with them.

The four NETs, on the other hand, could only function in English most of the time. Ms. Berner was the only NET participant in this study who could claim to have some knowledge of Cantonese. Ms. Berner was rather efficient in her Cantonese learning, but at the time of the first author's observation, she had just been learning Cantonese for 6 months. Her Cantonese proficiency was not sufficient to understand most of what the students said. However, it would be interesting to note here that in some situations (e.g., excerpts 7.3 & 7.10), some students used Cantonese to answer Ms. Berner's questions, probably out of the belief that the teacher could understand it.

Our data show that most students relied heavily on Cantonese in the process of sense making. Except when the teachers were absolutely unable to speak Cantonese (such as Miss Logan and Mr. Williams), or the teachers had made it a rule for them to speak in English (such as Mr. Nelson and Ms. Hung), in most cases, they would take advantage of any situations to respond to the teachers in Cantonese.

Given the English learning background of the classroom interactions under study, it seems that a richer body of cultural resources associated with English (generally believed to be an attribute of the NETs) would have a distinct advantage. LETs such as Ms. Hung has explicitly admitted the difficulty for her to model English cultural practices because of her local Hong Kong upbringing, which resulted in limited command of English-related cultural resources. As for the students, they often made use of the Cantonese linguistic resources or of local Hong Kong cultural models to make sense of and to the teachers. A gap or conflict in the mastery of linguistic and cultural resources between the teachers and students seem to be the basic factor causing some of the communication breakdown.

Lastly, institutional resources are institutional role related. Even though both the teachers and the students were situated in the same institutional contexts, they did not necessarily share the same amount of institutional resources. For example, new teachers may not be fully aware of the particular practices of the institution (e.g., whether compositions should be handed in during lessons). Like linguistic and cultural resources, institutional resources are often conventionalized and situational, developed and constructed through repeated contacts with other members of the community.

As can be imagined, in every moment of day-to-day interactions between teachers and students, the three major types of meaning making resources previously mentioned have to be used in an intertwining way (or used simultaneously). For example, when a NET does not have the appropriate linguistic resources to make sense of a student's L1-based utterances, he or she might utilize institutional resources to request translation service from other students. Sometimes, the students' sense-making strategies are subject to the sanction and discipline of the teachers, as when the latter demands the use of English from students on some occasions. It follows that the sense-making practices of the teachers and the students are in constant negotiation and reconfiguration. They sometimes do not occur in harmony and may create tensions due to a partial mastery of different types of resources and asymmetrical power relations between the teachers and students.

In the rest of this chapter, we show how the teachers and the students made sense by employing a variety of sense-making resources. We present representative instances showing how the two parties succeeded or did not succeed in mutual communication, and explore the reasons why different degrees of success or failure of communication took place.

EXPLORING SUCCESSFUL SENSE-MAKING PRACTICES

We begin this section with examples showing socioculturally significant features of successful sense-making practices. These features include the teachers' ability to comfortably travel between the L1 and L2 linguistic and cultural borders, to capitalize on some students' bilingual proficiency as linguistic "brokers," and to initiate repair in cases of miscommunication.

An Ability to Travel Between L1 & L2 Linguistic and Cultural Borders

Ellis (1996) discussed how teachers should act as "cultural mediator" and demonstrate an "awareness of other culture identities" (p. 217) for the communicative approach to be culturally appropriate in "Far Eastern" countries. The mediator role, of course, should not be confined to cultural aspects only, but should also include linguistic or discursive aspects. On several occasions from our data, the teachers succeeded in making sense to the students, and of the students' reactions, due to their ability, or at least awareness of the differences between the cultural models (Gee, 1996; see related discussion in chap. 5), and linguistic and cognitive frameworks associated with the L2, and those brought to the communication task by the students.

However, it should be noted that teachers' mediator role would not be effective without the corresponding effort on the part of the students to respond to the teachers and test out hypotheses in the negotiation of meaning. In the following excerpts, we show how teachers and students engage themselves in coconstructing meaning.

Excerpt 7.1.   #Sze (1B, 25/03/99).

In this excerpt, Mr. Sze is preteaching some vocabulary items taken from a text that the students are expected to read.

1. LET: What does it mean by (..) invent?
2. B1: **Faat-ming** <*To invent.*>
3. LET: **Faat-ming** <*To invent*>. That's right.
4. B2: [in anglicized tone] **Faat^-ming^**
5. LET: **Tung bin jat-go zi hai hou m-tung gaa** <*Which word is it very different from?*>. Start with 'D', (.) D-I-S^ (..) Dis^
6. Ss: (??)

7. LET: Discover, that's right. Marco Polo discovered that Chinese started to use paper money okay, in the seventh century. (.) Okay, but he didn't invent paper money.

As has been mentioned in chapter 6, Mr. Sze overtly supported the use of L1 to assist students' learning of L2. Two dominant code alternation patterns can be found in Excerpt 7.1:

Type 1 (turns 1-3):	T-initiation (I) in English
	P-response (R) in Cantonese
	T-feedback (F) in Cantonese
Type 2 (turns 5-7):	T-initiation (I) in Cantonese
	P-response (R) in English
	T-feedback (F) in English

These two different types of IRF patterns recurred frequently in Mr. Sze's lessons. Of course, to achieve the same purpose, Mr. Sze could have avoided Cantonese by using other strategies, for example, giving the definitions, or illustrations of the two words, just like Ms. Hung who never used a single Cantonese word in her teaching in our data. However, Mr. Sze's and his students' code-alternation practices seemed to be concise and effective in the mutual process of sense making. In the latter part of the lesson, Mr. Sze checked students' understanding of these two words and they were able to produce both words in English. From the first author's observation, Mr. Sze's students did not seem to resist answering in English. Even though Cantonese seemed to just come to them first in all situations, when requested by the teacher, they could and would switch to English actively and naturally.

One thing that should be noted about Mr. Sze's use of students' L1 as communicative resources is that he seldom used it to annotate his previously said L2 utterance, like one of the types of code alternation analyzed in Lin (1996b) and Pennington (1997). Mr. Sze told the first author that annotating L2 with L1 would be an ineffective code-switching pattern because it wasted time and students would be conditioned to tune out from the L2. Rather, he switched between the two languages to express different meanings. This is to make sure that students listen to his L2 utterances, whereas the L1 utterances were used to allow some space for students to digest or process the L2 utterances, which he believed to be a heavy cognitive task for young students with limited English proficiency.

As mentioned before, although Ms. Hung did not use Cantonese in her lessons in our data, her knowledge of students' L1 still had a role in her teaching. The following excerpt shows how Ms. Hung attempts initially to assist a Year 1 (Grade 7) boy to translate his Cantonese into English, but later ends up disapproving of the sense-making practice of the student.

Excerpt 7.2.   #Hung (1E, 12/10/98)

Ms. Hung is having a reading conference with a student during an extensive reading lesson (see footnote 60).

    1. B: She've (..) ehh, she:: ehh (.) they ver::y em ehh (…)ehh (..)
       Hou can-oi dim gong aa jing-man <*How do you say they love each other in English?*>
    2. LET: They love each other very much? Do they love each other?
    3. B: Yes.
    4. LET: So they love each other very much, so what do they want to do?
    5. B: (…) Uhm, **gong keoi-dei //git-fan** <*It talks about they got married.*>
    6. LET: //yes
    7. B: **Gong keoi-dei zik-hai** <*It says they, that means they …*> Ehh
    8. LET: You speak in English, you try to.

The frequent and lengthy hesitations of B in turn 1 shows that he is struggling hard for English words, and the subsequent use of the Cantonese in line 2, turn 1 could be taken as a self-inquisition, or private talk, which is quite common among Hong Kong students as a kind of pre-L2 production L1 processing. However, it could also be a request for the teacher's assistance. Ms. Hung's English annotation of B's Cantonese in turn 2 in the form of a comprehension or confirmation check (rather than intended as a direct translation as evident from the rising intonation) is a strategy to introduce the L2 version to the student, probably hoping that he would pick up the English utterance. This seems, however, to have been taken by B to be a tacit permission to use Cantonese. When B uses Cantonese again in turn 5, the teacher only acknowledges her understanding but stops annotating. Her explicit expression of disapproval (turn 8) of B's using Cantonese the third time reflects her limits in indulging the student's use of L1. Ms. Hung probably understands the paradox of being a bilingual teacher. Although she has the advantage of being better able to understand students' difficulties than a NET and to provide relevant assistance by virtue of sharing their first language, students might take advantage of her bilingual competence and overly rely on Cantonese, something she did not encourage in class.

    Although nobody would deny the good intention of teachers in disciplining students' code choice in sense making, this authority of the teachers has reflected the power differentiation between teachers and students. The students were sometimes not free to employ sense-making strategies that they felt were most effective and with which they were most comfortable. This situation seems to be the case in all of our data. Even Mr. Sze, who allowed students to respond in Cantonese, would at times request students to answer in English. The NETs, who seemed to be very open-minded about using Cantonese, had on many occasions demanded that the students stop talking in Cantonese, or reasserted the rule that they must use English. Mr. Nelson even set up a penalty system to fine students for speaking Cantonese even among peers. The students told the first author joyfully that Mr. Nelson's practice was to prepare them for her visits. Mr. Nelson told them that the visitor wanted to see them use more English. From the students' tone of voice, they did not feel any resentment at all. As mentioned in chapter 6, some thought that they benefited from this penalty system because they really had spoken more English. As for the other students who were interviewed, almost all of them showed their understanding of the need for and benefits of using English in class. It seemed that they wanted to be disciplined or helped to use more English (many students expressed the view that the availability of the NETs had forced them to use more English), even though they might sometimes prefer using Cantonese especially when they had difficulties expressing themselves in English.

Whereas there is nothing new about a local Hong Kong teacher using Cantonese in English lessons, a native English-speaking teacher using Cantonese in English lessons may raise a few eyebrows. There was actually more than one such instance in Ms. Berner's lessons in the study. More straightforward instances include the provision of a Cantonese annotation of an English vocabulary item; for example, "wine" means **"zau"** (1A, 05/03/99). With the next excerpt, we would like to show a more intriguing example in greater detail.

Excerpt 7.3.   #Berner (1E, 24/10/97)

This excerpt takes place at the beginning of the lesson. The students were given a questionnaire to complete. A group of girls sitting close to the teacher's desk[61] finishes early and initiates a casual conversation with the teacher. After the teacher has chatted with them about her favorite cartoon character, Garfield, G2 initiates the following exchange about a famous children's movie, "101 Dalmatians."

1. G2: Ms Berner, **jat-baak ling jat** *<One hundred and one>*.
2. NET: One hundred, yeah, **jat-baak** *<One hundred>*. I know that, yeah.
3. G2: **Jat-baak ling jat** *<One hundred and one>*.
4. NET: [following the student, with a slightly anglicized tone] **jat^-baak ling jat^** *<One hundred and one>*. One two one.
5. G1: One oh one.
6. NET: [repeating the phrase with a slightly anglicized tone] **Jat^-baak ling jat^, jat^-baak ling jat^, jat^-baak ling jat^** *<One hundred and one, one hundred and one, one hundred and one>*. [begins to laugh]
7. G2: **Jat ling jat** *<One hundred and one>*, **jat ling jat baan-dim-gau** *<One hundred and one Dalmatians>*.
8. [Some Ss begin to bark like dogs.]
9. NET: What? **Gau** *<Dog>?* It's **gau** *<Dog>*? What did you say before?
10. G1: **Gau** *<Dog>*. **Jat ling jat baan-dim-gau** *<One hundred and one Dalmatians>*, one hundred and one=

11. NET: [excitedly] =DALMATIANS! White dogs with black spots. Dalmatians, RIGHT, have you seen that film? Very GOOD.

12. Gs: [very happily] Yes, yes.

13. NET: [laughing and continues to repeat in Cantonese with her Anglo accent] **Jat^-baak ling jat^** <*One hundred and one*>.

Excerpt 7.3 best illustrates that sense making is a joint endeavor. The students' limited English proficiency has prevented them from expressing in fully well-formed English utterances what they wanted to say. They try their best to employ both linguistic resources [by correcting Ms. Berner's wrong translation of one hundred and one (turns 4-5) and paralinguistic resources (by barking to enable the teacher to associate the Cantonese word with dogs, turn 9]. Here the teacher's knowledge of Cantonese, and more importantly, her positive attitude toward the Cantonese clues offered by the students, play a key role in achieving common understanding in this interaction. Perhaps Ms. Berner's attempts to use Cantonese in her teaching could be best described as featuring "code crossing" rather than simply code-alternation. According to Rampton (1995), code crossing denotes "code-alternation by people who are not accepted members of the group associated with the second language they employ" (p. 280). Ms. Berner has established herself as a native English-speaking teacher in Hong Kong and this label carries a lot of status that local English teachers do not enjoy. Nobody, not even Ms. Berner herself perhaps, expects a "NET" to claim any membership of the local Cantonese community, not to say using Cantonese to communicate. However, nobody could deny the unique value of such occasional crossings on the part of the teacher in facilitating communication and in showing a genuine interest in the students' language and culture (see Luk, 2004). In the postobservation interview, Ms. Berner said that she sometimes used Cantonese intentionally to shorten the psychological distance from the students, in addition to enhancing communication. She hoped to establish a sense of solidarity with the students. However, she would take care not to allow students to take advantage of her knowledge of Cantonese to avoid using English. That is, she would only maintain a minimum working knowledge of Cantonese so that students basically still needed to use English to make sense to her.

Sometimes, the need to cross borders springs from cultural and pragmatic differences in ways of thinking and expressing between people coming from different linguistic and cultural backgrounds. Excerpt 7.4 illustrates one such instance that happened to Ms. Berner.

Excerpt 7.4.   #Berner (1E, 25/02/98)

At the beginning of the ERS lesson[62] Ms. Berner asks B1 to check whether the whole class has finished reading books of a certain grade level.

1. B1: [asking the whole class] **Jau bin-go mei-tai G gaa** <*Who hasn't read G?*>[63]

2. B2: **Mou aa** *<None>*.

3. B1: **Mou aa** *<None>*? **Tai-sai laa maa go-go dou** *<Everybody has read them>*?

4. B2: Hai aa *<Yes>*.

5. B1: [to the teacher] Eh, everyone read stock G=

6. NET: =em, who is still on level G put your hand up, level G, nobody?

7. Ss: Yes yes.

8. NET: (...) So you me:an yes, nobody, is on level G, so when I say nobody? Yes, just no, nobody is on level G okay (.) Nobody?

9. Ss: No.

10. NET: Okay, nobody then, thank you. So we just need D, E and F.

Perhaps the fact that only B2 responded to B1's enquiry made to the whole class prompted the teacher to check by asking again. Being Cantonese ourselves, the authors also sometimes have confusion about the English positive–negative linguistic structures. As observed by Littlewood (2002, p. 29), "when a Cantonese native speaker is answering a negative question in English, we have no sure way of knowing whether he or she is using the communal common ground of the Cantonese community or that of the community of English speakers (L1 and L2)." It requires sensitive cultural awareness on the parts of the non-Cantonese interlocutors to decipher the actual meanings. It seems that Ms. Berner has demonstrated some such kind of awareness. The 3-sec pause in turn 8 shows that the teacher was wondering whether the "yes" (turn 7) meant "everybody has finished" or "there is still somebody." As Cantonese speakers, the authors have reason to believe that the students' "yes" in turn 7 reflects their processing of the question in the Chinese way of thinking. The "yes" probably meant **"hai aa"** *<yes, it is true>*. Of course, "yes" may also mean **"jau aa"** *<yes, there is still somebody>*. But in this situation, if somebody has not finished reading grade G texts, the number of students would not be big and individual students would probably raise their hands to tell the teacher. Ms. Berner might have experienced similar confusion before and she decided to clarify by elaborating her question. Although there is no way to prove this, we believe the students' response in turn 9 reveals their final understanding of the English way of speaking. Semantically, this "no" also matches our interpretation of the "yes" as "Yes, it is true that nobody is on level G." Here, the source of the potential miscommunication did not seem to be totally linguistically related, and the teacher's awareness of the contrastive features of the consensual pragmatic practices of the two language systems has effectively prevented indexical breakdown.

An Ability to Capitalize on Students as Linguistic "Brokers"

Lin (1996b) reported how local teachers of English often have to act as "linguistic brokers" (p. 130) to annotate L2 texts or verbal input with L1 translation. However, when the teachers are themselves not L1-speaking, just like the NETs in the present study, the job of a linguistic broker has very often had to be taken up by some of the students.

From our data, Mr. Williams and Miss Logan provided evidence of soliciting assistance from higher English proficiency students in the class to help them make sense to less proficient students. In most cases, successful sense making has been achieved. The following excerpts illustrate how that happens.

Excerpt 7.5.   #Williams (2E, 20/04/99)

In this excerpt, the teacher seeks help from Nancy (N; a returnee from Canada) to help him make sense of the problem of another student. A boy, Raymond (R), has forgotten to bring his ERS book.

1. NET: Nancy, Nancy, Raymond's got a problem here I can't understand.
2. R: **Ji-gaa hai-mai m-bei lok** locker **lo je** <*Are we not allowed to take things from the locker now?*>
3. N: **M bei aa** <*Yes, not allowed.*>
4. R: **Hai laa nei tung keoi kong //nei bong ngo-** <*Yes, so you tell him, you help me to->*
5. NET: //Nancy Nancy can you tell me what the problem is here?
6. N: [to R] **Nei seung lok-heoi lo di mut-je** <*What do you want to go down and get?*>
7. R: Eh..**lo** <*to take*> ERS book.
8. N: [to the teacher] He wants to bring the ERS book, em, and he bring it in his locker.
9. NET: Why can't he take it from his locker now?
10. N: Em.., he want to go down to the locker.
11. NET: Yes, he CAN go down to his locker.
12. N: **Heoi lo aa, heoi lo aa** <*Go and get it, go and get it.*>
13. R: **Ah** Sir **m-bei wo** <*Sir (Mr. Williams) didn't allow me to.*>
14. N: **Keoi waa bei aa, keoi bei aa** <*He said you could. He allowed you to.*>

The role of Nancy in Excerpt 7.5 is like that of an interpreter. Nancy moved across the L1 and L2 linguistic border effectively and confidently. She performed this role professionally. For example, to clarify the problem, she asked Raymond questions that were not directed by the teacher. In this sense, she was not just a mechanical interpreter, but an effective interlocutor. Later in the same lesson, the teacher again sought help from Nancy to translate the content of a storybook to a less proficient student.

Like Mr. Williams, Miss Logan has been observed soliciting help from more proficient students in her lessons. The incident presented in Excerpt 7.6 is, however, not as smooth in its operation as the one shown in Excerpt 7.5.

Excerpt 7.6. #Logan (2B, 30/03/99)

The teacher is giving feedback on students' compositions and commenting on the differences in the usage of the words "shade" and "shadow." When some students show difficulty understanding the differences of the two words, she invites a student, Sally (Sa), to provide the Cantonese version of the word "shade."

1. NET: There was a^ (.) shadow, it should be, okay (.) A shade is, for example, if the sun is shin-? shhh, if it's a sunny day, and you are too hot, you can say to your friend, oh let's go and go under the shade. If you stand under a tree, a big tree, with lots of branches, the sun cannot reach you, so the shade is there under the trees.

   The place where the sun cannot reach is the shade. Do you understand? (.) So if it is too hot and you're in a country park with your friends, you're too hot, say you want to be cooler, you go under a big tree and you have some shade. Yes? Do you understand?
2. B: No.
3. NET: So shade, I can understand-what's the word in Cantonese Sally?
4. Sa: [in small voice] **Jam-jing aa** *<A shade.>*
5. NET: You say in a loud voice.
6. Sa: **//Jam-jing aa** *<A shade.>*
7. G: **//Jing** *<Shadow?>*
8. B: **Jing za-maa** *<Just shadow, isn't it?>*, **me-je jam-jing** *<What shade?>*
9. NET: //okay
10. G: **//Hai bin-zung jam-jing aa** *<What kind of shade is it?>*
    Sam leoi-min go-di aa *<That which is inside our heart?>*
11. [Some students laugh.]
12. G: **Zik hai bin-di aa** *<What is it actually?>*
13. Sa: **Taai-jeong saai lok-lei jau-go jing lo** *<What we have when the sun shines down.>*
14. [Ss laugh briefly]
15. G: **Ngoh:::** [a Cantonese particle showing understanding]
16. NET: Is that clear?

Even though G shows her understanding in turn 15, we actually find Sally's last explanation rather confusing (we usually get a shadow under the sun). Her first annotation **"jam jing"** 陰影 <*shade*>, in our opinion, is not totally accurate because the meaning of "shade" as elaborated by the teacher should be **"jam deng"** 陰頂 <*a sheltered area*>. G's metaphorical association of the abstract meaning of **"jam jing"** in our heart is interesting. The kind of **"jam jing"** in our heart mentioned by G refers to traces of memories left by some unpleasant experiences. Even though G's association raises some laughter, it is totally justified. This incident shows the potential problem with requesting direct translation of a term from L2 into L1 due to the possible existence of different shades of meanings of a word that may not be directly translatable by the students.

Nevertheless, soliciting such language service from students may be an effective strategy when communication problems arise. It is interesting to note how such incidents temporarily reconfigure the power structure between the teacher and the students in the classroom. Those students whose language broker services were required by the teachers seemed to enjoy a higher status than other students in the class. In these cases, their status and expertise might even be felt to be above those of the teachers concerned (although only temporarily) due to the latter's lack of linguistic or cultural resources to mediate between the two languages. Note how Miss Logan's attempt to end the student–student interaction on line 9 was ignored by the whole class when they still saw the need for further clarification. This proves that genuine communication would take place naturally when interlocutors see personally relevant meanings in the discourse.

Similar instances in which the NETs took the initiative to capitalize on other students as linguistic brokers have not appeared in the data collected from Ms. Berner's and Mr. Nelson's classes. However, there were a couple of occasions in Ms. Berner's classes that some eager students provided such service as linguistic brokers of their own accord, or at the request of their classmates, but in all cases unsolicited by the teacher. Excerpt 7.7 shows a peer-solicited, then a self-initiated linguistic broker service in a reading conference activity in Ms. Berner's 1E.

Excerpt 7.7.   #Berner (1E, 24/02/98)

Ms. Berner is doing reading conferencing with a female student. She is checking if the student has any difficulty with the book.

1. NET: Were there too many new words? Or-
2. G1: [asking her classmate sitting near the teacher's desk] **Di zi ho-naan dim gong** <*How do we say the words are difficult?*>
3. G2: More difficult.
4. G1: [to the teacher] Ehh, this word very difficult.
5. NET: The words are very difficult, okay? So you didn't understand a lot of words, yeah? Tell me what the story's about.

6. G2: [translating T's utterance to G1] **Man nei ni-go gwu-si gong mat-je**
   <*Ask you what the story is about.*>

In Excerpt 7.7, G2 first provides an annotation for G1 at her request in Cantonese (turn 2). Then in turn 6, G2 annotates the teacher's request for G1 even without
a verbal request from G1. Because the reading conference was done in the front of
the classroom around the teacher's desk, it is not possible to see if G1 expresses
any need for broker service with body language or eye contact in the second case.
It is interesting to compare G1's request for broker service in Excerpt 7.7 with that
of Ms. Hung's 1E boy in Excerpt 7.2. Requesting such service from classmates,
rather than from the teacher, seems to be more institutionally acceptable. As teachers, we often emphasize the importance of mutual assistance among students as
long as they do not become overreliant.

On the other hand, in the cases of Mr. Nelson and Ms. Hung, who taught in the
same school, they both held the view that inviting language broker service from
students was not necessary because they believed most students in that school (a
prestigious EMI school in that district) were capable of making sense of the English lessons in English.

An Ability to Repair in the Face of Communication Breakdown

When miscommunication appears, appropriate and timely repair strategies may
help to solve the problem. Excerpt 7.8 shows how Ms. Berner employed repair[64] as a
sense-making strategy in the face of miscommunication.

Excerpt 7.8.   #Berner (1E, 24/10/97)

To teach comparatives, Ms. Berner asked two students, Larry (L) and Dick, to stand
in front of the class to serve as subjects for comparision. She first tries to compare
some personal particulars of the two students.

1. NET: Okay, Larry is fatter. How much do you weigh?
2. G1[65]: [to Larry who is standing in front of the class] **Man nei jau gei-do
   cin aa** <*Ask you how much money you have.*> **Ji-gaa jau gei-do cin**
   <*How much money do you have now?*>
3. L: Me?
4. NET: Yeah.
5. G1: **Ji-gaa jau gei-do aa** <*How much do you have now?*>
6. L: Ehhh (..) I have two thousand.
7. NET: Two thousand what?
8. L: What?

9. G1: **Ji-sap man aa** <*Twenty dollars?*> Twenty dollar.

10. NET: Do you know how much you weigh?

11. L: [in playful tone] Ehhhhh …

12. NET: Forty? Forty kilo, Forty? How much do you weigh? Do you know?

13. L: **Jau aa** <Yes, I have>, **jau m-sap** < *I have fifty.*>

14. Ss: Five, fivety [sic], fifty.

15. NET: You weigh (.) you weigh fifty.

16. [Other students are discussing and helping Larry in Cantonese. Not clear on the tape.]

17. B: **Jat-baak** <*One hundred?*>

18. L: **Mou** <*No*>, **mou jat-baak** <*I don't have one hundred*>. (…) Eight.

19. NET: [sounds very surprised] You're eighty?

20. L: No no no no, **hai-** <*It's ->*

21. NET: Eighty pounds?

22. L: **Mou aa** <*No*>, **mou aa** <*No*>. **Ngo mou bong gwo cung m zi gei-do** <*I haven't weighed myself, don't know how much*>, **M zi gei-do** <*Don't know how much.*>

23. G1: **Man nei gei-do cin** <*Ask you how much money.*>

24. L: **Man ngo gei-do cin aa** <*Ask me how much money?*>
    [L begins counting some coins in his hand.]

25. NET: English English (.) No, how much-how heavy are you?

26. G1: [talking to herself, sounds a bit doubtful] Heavy?

27. L: Se::ven, se:ven

28. B: **Nei dak cat-sap bong** <*You have only seventy pounds?*>

29. NET: [referring to Dick] Do you know how heavy you are?

When a logical response does not come forward, Ms. Berner first uses repetition (turns 10 & 12) as a type of repair strategy. Then she tries to suggest possible answers (turns 12 & 21). Actually at this stage, Larry begins to understand what is required if not being misinformed by G1 who thinks the teacher is asking about money. When Ms. Berner wants to ask the question for the third time, she realizes the problem (upon seeing Larry counting his coins) and does not repeat but reformulates her question using a word probably more familiar to the students, "heavy," instead of "weigh" (turn 25). Even though Larry's response (turn 27) sounds confusing, from his earlier Cantonese utterances (turn 22), it seems that he knows what is happening.

One interesting point about Excerpt 7.8 is the problem created by G1's unsolicited broker service that has resulted in her misannotation of the teacher's question and some confusion between Larry and the teacher. Her misannotation probably came from her limited knowledge of the phrase "how much" that is frequently used when asking about prices, a popular topic in the primary English curriculum. It is therefore natural for G1 to interpret "how much" with her existing schema. It is not until the teacher rephrases her question using the word "heavy" that G1 perhaps begins to realize her own misunderstanding.

EXPLORING UNSUCCESSFUL SENSE-MAKING PRACTICES

Even though three types of sense-making resources are available to the teachers and students in this study, they did not always succeed in making accurate sense of what was going on, often without the awareness of the interaction participants. As analysts and observers of the interactions, we sometimes found it arbitrary to decide whether certain discourse practices of the teachers and students had succeeded in making meaning or not. Some people may argue that only the participants should know whether the other side has made accurate sense of what they mean. However, as fluent bilingual Cantonese and English speakers, we are able to identify a few instances of unsuccessful sense-making instances of which the participants themselves (e.g., due to insufficient bilingual linguistic resources) might not be aware. This generally happens in the NETs' classes (as compared to the LETs' classes). Interestingly, intriguing communication disruptions were not captured between the LETs and their students in our data even though we believe that miscommunication may also happen to interlocutors sharing the same L1. All other classes, including Mr. Nelson's 4E students, whose English standard was the highest in our sample, have experienced problems of communication, although of a comparatively minor nature.

Most of the instances of miscommunication stemmed from unequal or incompatible linguistic resources. In these cases, the linguistic cues provided by the teachers or the students somehow led to misinterpretations. However, some of these miscommunication cases, as we will show in Excerpts 7.10 and 7.12, although spawned by a linguistic problem, actually involved cultural issues (Excerpt 7.10) and institutional issues (Excerpt 7.12). On a few other occasions, the problems seemed to be more culturally oriented than linguistically oriented. Instances of miscommunication due to incongruent mastery of institutional resources do not appear often in our data but we show one such instance in Excerpt 7.15 in addition to Excerpt 7.12.

Linguistic-Based Interaction Breakdown

Unsuccessful use of sense-making resources of a linguistic nature resulting in interaction breakdown arose from lexical misinterpretations (Excerpt 7.9), lexical deficiencies (Excerpt 7.10), syntactic and pronunciation inaccuracies (Excerpts 7.11, 7.12 and 7.13).

Excerpt 7.9.   #Berner (1E, 24/10/98)

The teacher is chatting with some girls near her who have finished a questionnaire more quickly than the others. A boy at a table nearby shouts out a question.

1. B: [asking the teacher] Ehhh, how many do you have one month?
2. NET: How much money do I earn?
3. B: Yes, one month.
4. NET: [in laughing voice] Five million Hong Kong dollars.
5. Ss: [shouting out, sounding very surprised] **WAAAH, gei-maan man** <*Several tens of thousands of dollars*>, **m-maan man** <*Fifty thousand dollars*>, **jat-go jyut m-maan** <*Each month fifty thousand.*>
6. NET: Every month I buy a new house. [laughs]
7. Ss: **WAAAH** [shouting out in surprise while NET laughs]

Most students in this class obviously did not know the meaning of the money unit "million." Otherwise, some of them should have shouted out a different version. To them, earning $50,000 a month was already a huge sum of money. Because Ms. Berner did not understand Cantonese well enough, she was not able to realize the misunderstanding of the students. In this case, the misunderstanding is linguistically or lexically based.

Another excerpt related to lexical problems also appeared in Ms. Berner's classes. However, the nature of the problem is rather different. Apart from revealing lexical gaps on the part of the students, Excerpt 7.10 also shows unsuccessful sense-making practices due to phonological interference (on the NET's side) as well as sociocultural distance between the teacher and the students.

Excerpt 7.10.   #Berner (1A, 05/03/99)

Excerpt 7.10 happens at the beginning of the lesson in which the teacher initiated a question with a view to establishing the students' schemata of fast food restaurants in Hong Kong. This is supposed to form part of the preparation for a textbook-based reading comprehension task.

1. NET: Right, [clearing her throat] fast food restaurant. What is a fast food restaurant?
2. B1: **Mak-dong //-nou** <*McDonald.*>
3. Ss: **//Faai-caan dim, faai-caan dim** <*Fast food restaurant.*>
4. NET: //McDonald's for example.
5. [other Ss are making suggestions]
6. B2: **Daai-faai-wud** <*Fairwood*> [name of a local fast food shop],

[in anglicized tone] **daai-^ faai-^ wud-^. Daai^** [literally meaning "big"]-Big **faai^-wud^** [literally meaning "happy"] Big happy.

7. [many Ss laugh]

8. B3: [anglicized] **daai-^ gaa-^ lok-^** <*Café de Coral*> [name of another local fast food shop]

9. [many Ss talking at the same time]

10. B2: Big happ::y [chuckling at the end]

11. B4: [rather softly] Pizza Hut.

12. NET: Okay okay. Shh shh shh, it's easier?
    // shhhhh=

13. B2: [chuckling] //Big happy

14. G: //Wendy, Wendy

15. NET: =shhhhh it's easier I think, if you put your hand up and I can hear one (??) instead of forty. Okay? So we've got McDonald, Wendy's, thank you?

16. B5: Hardee's

17. B6: [loudly] **HAA-DIK-SEE** <*Hardee's*>

18. B7: [anglicized] **Hang-^ dak-^ gei-^ gaa-^ heung^ gai^** <*Kentucky Fried Chicken.*> [laughter]

19. [T gestures, shushes and writes on the blackboard]

20. NET: What is it about big firework?

21. B: [laughs] Big FIREwork!

22. B: **Daai-gaa-lok** <*Café de Coral*>, [anglicized] **Daai^ gaa^ lok^,** big happy.

23. B: **Daai-faai-wud** <*Fairwood*>

24. NET: Tell me what it is in Chinese, and I'll find out.

25. B: [loudly] **Daai-gaa-lok aa** <*It's Café de Carol*>

26. NET: How about? Shh, a place where you can get chicken?

To make sense to their teacher who is a non-Cantonese speaker, students in Excerpt 7.10 are observed to have adopted what the authors would call a "multilevel speech adjustment mechanism":

1. Level 1—L1-only (**daai-faai-wud**; e.g., turn 6, line 1)

2. Level 2—L1 in an anglicized tone (**daai^faai^wud^**; e.g., turn 6, line 2)

3. Level 3— literal L2 translation-cum-anglicized L1 (big **faai^wud^**; e.g., turn 6, line 3)

4. Level 4—literal L2 translation (big happy; e.g., turn 6, line 4)

This multilevel speech adjustment mechanism appeared several times in Ms. Berner's lessons. It reflects students' creativity and efforts in getting meanings across to the teacher. The code-alternation or code-mixing elements in the students' discourse reflect systematic metalinguistic knowledge of the students. Canagarajah (1999b) argued that students' ability to switch codes displays their "development of meta-linguistic and meta-cognitive competence" (p. 140). They need to be aware of the boundaries of two distinct syntactic, lexical, and phonological systems when putting them in juxtaposition. In Excerpt 7.10, apart from demonstrating the more common intersentential code switch for L1-L2 annotation (turns 6, 16 & 17), the students also display a distinct type of code-alternation practice that we call "intralexical code mixing" (big **faai^ wud^**). In turn 6, line 3, when B2 offers "big **faai^ wud^**" as an improved answer of the anglicized one **"daai^ faai^ wud^,"** he has demonstrated his knowledge of some linguistic features of both Chinese and English. He certainly understands that the name **"daai faai wud"** consists of three syllables and therefore three stand-alone characters of Chinese. At the same time, **"faai wud"** in Chinese constitutes a compound word with one unified meaning that could be translated into the English word "happy." Therefore, instead of offering a strictly word-for-word translation (which would be "big quick live"; or randomly translating any two words of the name (which could be "big quick **wud**"), the student offers "big happy" that caters to both form and meaning. This kind of intralexical code mixing reflects creative and rule-governed manipulation of both the L1 and L2 by the student. In the later part of the lesson, another student has employed a similar strategy and put forward "potato **jung^** <*a mashed mass*>" to refer to "mashed potatoes." Even though such a hybrid use of language caused quite a bit of laughter from others, students like B2 actually fulfilled their institutional role to answer in English as well as they displayed a rudimentary form of bilingual proficiency.

Although we appreciate the creativity and metalinguistic awareness displayed in this speech adjustment mechanism, we should not overlook the fact that students of limited English knowledge were seen to be relying heavily on their L1 for cognitive processing and communicating among themselves and even with the non-Cantonese-speaking teacher. This communication strategy shows striking similarities to the L1-based achievement strategies demonstrated by NNS learners during communication disruptions when interacting with native speakers as reported in Haastrup and Phillipson (1983). But also similar to the findings in Haastrup and Phillipson's study, the L1-based communication strategies used by B2 in Excerpt 7.10 did not lead to successful communication of messages, as evident in Ms. Berner's query in turn 20 when she misheard the students' anglicized Cantonese word **(faai^ wud^)** as the English word "firework."

The causes for the ultimate failure of communication in Excerpt 7.10 are manifold, and both the students and the teacher should bear some responsibility. For the students, their problem seems to be a lack of sensitivity to the real meaning of being bilingual, or learning English in addition to knowing Cantonese. The inability of the students to tell the NET the English versions of **"daai faai wud"** and **"daai gaa lok"** reflects the stark reality that the culture of the students is so much Cantonese-based. Knowing **"daai faai wud"** and **"daai gaa lok"** is already sufficient for them to function well in most contexts in Hong Kong. Therefore, even though the English versions of **"daai faai wud"** and **"daai gaa lok"** always appear beside the Chinese ones, they seldom notice or pay attention to them. The English versions of these two restaurants have never entered into the students' sociocultural worlds.[66] The need to also know the English names of these two popular local fast food restaurants seems never to have occurred to them until this lesson.

On the teacher's side, being a non-Cantonese speaker, Ms. Berner actually has potential in motivating some students to try to communicate with her in the target language. However, due to insufficient, if not total lack of, sociocultural knowledge of the local community and its common local fast food restaurants, Ms. Berner failed to understand the students' messages, and so could not take them across the cultural and linguistic borders by providing the L2 versions they needed. She seemed to be aware only of the globalized (if not Americanized) fast food restaurants such as McDonald's, Wendy's, and Kentucky Fried Chicken but not the local ones. In this incident, the teacher failed to be an effective linguistic and cultural mediator.

Because of the linguistic and cultural resources gap between the teacher and the students, despite the efforts of the students to appropriate the English version and the reciprocal efforts of the teacher to test hypotheses (turn 20) and invite students to use Cantonese (turn 24), mutual understanding had not been established.

In contrast, the next excerpt that shows pronunciation-based miscommunication in Mr. Nelson's class seems to be more straightforward, but at a deep level, it might also reveal some common features of student cultures in Hong Kong.

Excerpt 7.11.   #Nelson (4E, 17/03/99)

Mr. Nelson is organizing the students into groups to do a drama script production activity. According to the teacher, this drama activity was organized because many students indicated in a survey (designed by Mr. Nelson) that drama was their most preferred lesson activity. However, some students refused to admit that they put down this preference when they learn that they have to write their own drama scripts.

1. NET: I thought it was your group yeh?
2. B1: Our group?
3. NET: I remember you all said you wanted to do drama in class, so now it's a big chance.
4. B1: Won't be our group.
5. B2: In next group ("group" is pronounced as /gwʊp/)
6. NET: (mix scope)?

7. B2: Yeah.

8. NET: What is a (mix scope)?

9. B2: (??)'s [seems to be a student's name] group (pronounced as /gwʊp/)

The root of the problem seems to be B2's failure to say the consonant clusters /gr/ and /kst/ clearly (replacing /r/ with /w/, and deleting /k/ and /t/ in /kst/). These are all common pronunciation features of Cantonese English speakers. Apart from this, the adding of the preposition "in" before "next group"[67] has also confused the teacher. B2's affirmative response ("yeah") to the teacher's wrong repetition is a point of interest. From our experience of lesson observation as teacher educators, Hong Kong students have a tendency to give affirmative responses toward teacher's initiation that they do not really understand. Several occasions have been captured in Ms. Hung and Miss Logan's lessons in which students usually responded with "yes" (sometimes not very assertively) to the teachers' questions of "yes or no?" for checking understanding. Students seem to be aware of the appeasing effects of a "yes" on the teacher. It is perhaps a good strategy to get themselves off the hook from further inquisition by the teacher. After B2's expression in turn 9, Mr. Nelson just dropped the topic and moved on to another group.

So far, instances of miscommunication previously mentioned have not resulted in any serious consequences apart from minor pedagogical hiccups. However, the phonology-based miscommunication in the next excerpt that happened in Mr. Williams' 2E class may have produced a far-reaching impact on the relationship between the teacher and the student concerned. We show how it happened in Excerpt 7.12.

Excerpt 7.12.   #Williams (2E, 20/04/99)

This happens in an ERS lesson. Mr. Williams found that Zero[68] (a student who had a reputation of being lazy) has got all correct answers to some preset questions on a story that he has not finished reading. Mr. Williams suspected that Zero had copied answers from the answer cards.

1. NET: Zero, so you've answered all the questions, you've got them alright, very good, but you haven't finished reading the book, (..) this is strange, isn't it, this is very strange, how can you answer the questions if you haven't read the book?

2. Z: (??)

3. NET: Mhm? (…) How can you answer the questions if you haven't read the book?

4. Z: Found [dropping the final consonant, sounding like "foun"] it [also dropping the ending consonant /t/ in "it"]

5. NET: Mhm?

6. Z: found [dropping the final consonant, sounding like "foun"] it [also dropping the ending consonant /t/ in "it"]

7. NET: Funny book? Lovely, magic trick, thank you (..) Have you read the book? Finished. (…) Now we had a long talk about this book, didn't we? Do you remember? We both went together to choose this book, you, d'you remember? We chose this book together, do you remember (…) No. Okay, I think what's happened here is is that you've got the question cards, and you've written down the questions, and then you got the answer cards, and you've written down the answers and you haven't read the book.

8. Z: (??) [seems to be protesting against what the teacher has accused him of, but indistinct on the tape]

9. NET: Okay, I can ask you some questions then. Do you remember the answers? (..) Mmm [sound like singing] What's th::e, what's the name of the man in the book (..) Shuuuuuu [the teacher then moved on to discipline some other students]

Zero happened to be sitting at the back of the classroom just next to the first author. Therefore, the first author observed how the whole incident happened. Zero talked in a small and flat voice and his answers to the teacher's queries were always one or two words. Even when the first author talked to him in Cantonese later, he answered with the same small and monotonous voice. That might have reinforced the teacher's suspicion that Zero had done something wrong. As experienced teachers, we have seen many poorly set reading comprehension questions that could be answered without having to read the text (e.g., by locating the key words in the text).[69] The grading of the storybooks also allows slower students to stay at a lower level longer before they proceed to the next level. Therefore, the storybook that Zero was reading could be very short and simple. The authors are uncertain if Mr. Williams had checked the quality of the comprehension tasks and the awareness of the existence of some poorly designed reading tasks as part of his institutional resources. What seems to be clear is that he did not catch Zero's attempt to explain in turns 4 and 6, and mistook it as something else ("funny" which sounds like Zero's pronunciation of "found it"). The causes of misunderstanding could be Zero's muttering voice and imprecise articulation. The first author talked to Zero (in Cantonese) after Mr. Williams went away to handle some other students. Zero told the first author that he had not "read" the book, but he did answer the questions by simply flipping through the pages. When the first author asked him why he did not explain again, he did not say anything, and the first author seemed to sense a shade of hatred in his eyes. After Mr. Williams had disciplined some other students, he came back to Zero and demanded Zero to go out to choose another book with him. When he found that Zero might have difficulties understanding English, he asked Nancy (the same Nancy in Excerpt 7.5) to help translate the content of some storybooks to Zero so that he could choose one that he liked to read. Although Zero did not seem to appreciate this offer for help from the teacher, Mr. Williams had actually done all he could to help Zero. However, by lacking knowledge of the students' L1 to negotiate and explore, he missed the chance of understanding the students better. The behavior of Zero and probably his friend, Jerry, in a subsequent lesson showed that Mr. Williams' misunderstanding of Zero's explanation might have planted some seeds of resentment in the students' minds. (See the discussion after Excerpt 9.14, chap. 9.)

Culture-Based Interaction Breakdown

Culture-based breakdowns in sense-making practices are often more complex and intriguing than purely linguistic based. We begin by presenting a case from Mr. Nelson's 4E. This incident also shows that miscommunication often results from the incompatible or mutually insulated sociocultural life worlds of the teacher and the students as previously mentioned.

Excerpt 7.13. #Nelson (4E, 17/03/99)

This excerpt comes from the drama writing lesson. The students are working on their drama scripts in groups while the teacher is walking around to monitor their work. In this excerpt, the students seek help from the teacher concerning the English name of a building that has appeared in a TV commercial on mobile phones.

1. B1: [asking the teacher] The the the building, what's the name of the building?
2. NET: What have you chosen?
3. B1: Sunday[70] independent's day.
4. NET: Okay.
5. B1: It was the advertisement.
6. NET: Aah.
7. B1: What is the name of the place, the the the, the big place, the building.
8. B2: White in colour.
9. B3: White house.
10. NET: You mean the house with the president?
11. B: White house.
12. NET: The White House?
13. B: Sunday? it doesn't look like.
14. NET: I haven't seen it. [NET chuckles]
15. B: [sounding a bit disappointed] Och.
16. NET: I think it's the White House.
17. B: Okay.

The student's description of the building as being white in color (turn 8) has led the teacher to provide "White House" (different from "white house") as the possible answer. Obviously, that was not what the students have in mind.[71] The fact that the teacher was not a frequent TV viewer (not to say a viewer of local Hong Kong programs) and not somebody interested in local mobile phone commercials (confirmed by Mr. Nelson) has rendered the teacher's native speaker resources rather ineffective in achieving mutual understanding in this situation. Even the authors ourselves who are familiar with the local cultures are not able to decipher completely what the students were referring to; however, we did not think the students were referring to the White House of the U.S. president. As somebody belonging to a different generation from the students, middle-aged local teachers like the authors often find it difficult to understand what is popular among young people. The same difficulty may be exacerbated with a non-Cantonese speaker who is unfamiliar with the local cultures.

The most intriguing incident in our data showing culture-based sense-making problems took place in Ms. Berner's third-year class. This incident, apart from further reinforcing the far and deep-reaching impact of popular youth culture on the students' everyday life world, also shows how the students might naturally marginalize or exclude the NET in the communication process by refashioning the semantic reference of some mundane expressions. Such in-group peer talk with indexicality of meaning inclusive to the distinct student group naturally excludes the teacher as an outsider. The interaction is presented in Excerpt 7.14.

Excerpt 7.14. #Berner (3E, 02/03/99)

The class is doing English activities in the English room. Ms. Berner and an English Language Teaching Assistant[72] (ELTA) are each taking care of about 10 students[73] of the class. Due to the smaller group size, the students are sitting close to one another around two large tables. The activity reported in Excerpt 7.14 is the second activity. The teacher is trying to motivate the students to fill in some speech bubbles on some cartoons with creative speech. On that particular picture, one of the cartoon characters looks like the then U.S. president Bill Clinton whereas the other one looks like the then president of China, Jiang Ze Min.

1. NET: You first, you start here, [T sounds a bit angry] come on (..) okay, here, they got a picture of Mr. Jiang and Mr. Clinton, =
2. B1: =**Ngooh! Hak-zai aa?**= <*Oh! "Clink-boy"?*> [Clink-boy is the nickname of Bill Clinton used by HK people]
3. NET: =shaking hands?=
4. B1: =**Hak-jam-deon aa?** <*"Clink-sleazy-ton"?*> [the nickname of Bill Clinton used in Hong Kong media, referring to his indecent sexual behavior with his female subordinate] [B1 chuckles]
5. NET: So what is Mr. Clinton saying?

6. B1:: **Kei-wan-si-lei** ("Kate Winslett," the female lead character of *Titanic,* but B1 probably means Lewinsky, the female intern of Bill Clinton)

7. B2: Hello!

8. NET: Okay hello, Mr. Jiang, that's not really exciting, okay, hello, Mr. Jiang, what's Mr. Jiang saying?

9. [some are making suggestions in English, inaudible on the tape]

10. B2: Your hand is very big

11. NET: Your head is very big [other boys broke into laughter on hearing this]

12. B: **Zek sau hou-daai !** <*The hand is very big!*> [laughing]

13. NET: [in an amused tone] Okay, Mr. Clinton says, hello Mr. Jiang, and Mr. Jiang says, your head is very big (.)

    [Ss are talking and joking among themselves all along while the T is talking, indistinct on the tape]

    (..) Alright, let's have a look at yours, what have you got (.) right, two men whispering and laughing together, what do you think one is saying?

14. B: Kiss you^

15. B: Hello, where are you boy? [Ss laugh]

16. NET: Alright, he said [Ss laugh], //shh! shh!

17. B: //**Bin-dou aa lei**? <*Where are you?*>

18. NET: He says, have a look at this picture, yeah, one man is saying, can I give you a kiss, the other one saying, okay, be quick, yeah? what do you think, they are saying?

19. [many Ss are laughing and chatting, indistinct on the recorder]

20. B: Hello, where are you?

21. NET: Hello, who- who are //you?

22. B: //where are you

23. NET: [rising tone over "you," sounds doubtful] Where are YOU?

24. B: Yeah! [chuckles]

25. NET: [in a different tone, rising over "are"] Hello, where ARE^ you?

26. B1: I'm forty.

27. B: Where do you come from?

28. NET: I'm what?

29. B1: I'm forty. [others laugh]

30. NET: [sounds confused] Forty?

31. B: [laughs] Chai Wan forty [Chai Wan is a place near the students' school]

32. B: **Caai^ waan^** [anglicized Cantonese of Chai Wan] forty, of Chai Wan

33. NET: [asking another boy sitting on the other side] What have you got over there?

Throughout this interaction that involves multiple dialogues among the students and between the students and the teacher, something that mainstream adults might regard as obscene seems to prevail in the students' speech. The sex scandal that Mr. Clinton was involved in was well known to the whole world. This group of students, all boys at an age when having fantasies about sex is common, immediately conjured up the sexual image of Mr. Clinton. The nicknames of Clinton in turns 2 and 4 were widely known in Hong Kong at the time of the study. The one in turn 4 is coined creatively by changing the middle character, **"lam"** (literally meaning "a forest"), of the three-word official Chinese translation of "Clinton," **"haak-lam-deon,"** into a rhyming counterpart **"jam"** (literally meaning "obscene"). This has immediately given Mr. Clinton a sleazy image. It is obvious that Ms. Berner's Cantonese proficiency level was not yet up to scratch to pick that one up.

Then the reference to the big hands of Mr. Clinton is again suspected by us to be sexually related. The sex scandal of Mr. Clinton had given most people the impression that Mr. Clinton was a person with strong sexual desires. It could be very natural for the students who were interested in sex according to their teacher, to think of "masturbation," which is about deriving sexual pleasure with hands. As the picture shows the two men shaking hands, it is highly likely that the image of "hands" has aroused their association with sex.

When the first author presented the case to a young female teacher currently teaching Year 3 secondary students, what the teacher spotted was not the image of "hands," but "head." She told the first author many male students coming from the working class often joked about the male sex organs and one such organ involves the use of the Cantonese word for "head." Ms. Berner's mishearing of the students' "hand" as "head" (turn 11) may have unexpectedly instigated some more sexual insinuations from the students, as evident in their laughter.

The questions "where are you" (first appears in turn 15) and "Where do you come from?" (turn 27) suggested by the student(s) in a playful manner caused another indexical breakdown on the part of the teacher. Taking the question literally would make it difficult to understand the meaning of asking this question. However, the authors' very limited experience about gang culture in Hong Kong has enabled us to arrive at a highly possible speculation. Asking others "Where are you from?" (你邊度㗎?) is a way to "state their allegiance" (繿朵) among triad gangs (Bolton & Hutton, 2002, p. 159). Such a practice of the triad societies in Hong Kong often appears in local Cantonese films. The mentioning of "Chai Wan forty" further confirms our speculation. There is a well-known triad gang called "14K" that has branches in different districts. "Chai Wan" (a pseudonym) is the district in which the school was located, which also means the place where most of the students lived and hung around. It is also a common pronunciation feature of many Cantonese students to mix up "fourteen" and "forty." Therefore, B's "I'm forty" (turn 29) might actually mean "I'm from the fourteen K."

Ms. Berner's failure to make sense of what was going on among the students is understandable. At several points in the interaction, the teacher was naturally excluded from the students' interaction even though on the surface, she seemed to be monitoring. She could not understand why such things were said and could not join in the fun and laughter of the students. The students have marginalized her participation in this activity. It seems that the students have created such texts as an enactment of social and cultural strategies in a network of power relations to estrange the teacher. Although they were expressing in English, their crossing over to English may only be a tactic to avoid the possible sanctions from the teacher if Cantonese were used. It seems that English has provided an effective camouflage for these working-class students to assert their class-specific "common culture" (Epstein, 1998), which is usually taboo in schools. Their structurally well-formed English, however, is not intelligible to a native English teacher because of her culturally "out-group" status. The students' English, ironically, could only be understood among their peers who share the same L1 and more importantly, the same class-specific subculture. They could have conducted the talk in Cantonese if not for the presence of a NET and the latter's inability to make sense of their English utterances, despite her English expert identity, might have added to the fun of the whole process. This event also exemplifies the importance of developing cross-cultural resources in interactions of this type.

Institution-Based Interaction Breakdown

In the following excerpt, a deep-level analysis of the reasons causing the breakdown reveals that the teacher lacked some kind of institutional resources to enable her to understand the institutional student culture properly.

Excerpt 7.15.   #Logan (2B, 30/03/99)

This takes place in the last few minutes of the lesson. Miss Logan is reminding the students of a project they need to do during the holiday.

1. NET: Don't forget to do your project, also shhhh, read your story, "Babe the Sheep Pig," and write a report, a summary of the story, what happens in the story, about half a page, okay, about half a page
2. B1: //Half a page?
3. Ss: //**Haah** <*What?*>
4. NET: One page maximum, okay?
5. B: **Gei-do jip aa zik-hai** <*How many pages that is?*>
6. NET: What else, I will announce the winners when we come back because I said that I would give prizes this time for the most scary story and the best stories, so I haven't got time to announce it about, when we come back, I will //do that, okay?
7. B1: //How page have we-
8. NET: Sorry?
9. B1: How page-

10. NET: How^
11. B1: Page we (??)
12. NET: How^
13. B1: How many page?
14. NET: How many pages? For what?
15. B1: (??)
16. NET: Project?
17. B1: Project, yes.
18. NET: O::h, at least twenty.
19. Ss: **HAAAAH** <*WHAT!?*>
20. NET: No, I think about (..) six, about five or six, between five and ten, I think will be very good, okay? More if you want to. Okay let's say good-bye. Stand up.
21. B: **Mou-dak waan aa** <*No time to play.*>

It is clear from the context that the students are uncertain about the requirements and expect the teacher to clarify (as is evident from B1's repetition of the teacher's utterance "half a page" in rising intonation as a confirmation check or a request for clarification, and some students' Cantonese particle "**HAAH** <*What*>?" to show comprehension problems). The teacher's attempt to provide extra information has clearly confused the students even more with the mentioning of a contradictory piece of information "one page" followed by probably an unfamiliar word to the students—"maximum." B's query in Cantonese in turn 5 of course could not be understood by the teacher and she actually shifted the topic to something else that she probably considers more motivating to the students—giving prizes to the best story writer. However, the students are still obsessed with the homework requirements. The students' earnestness to sort this out has prompted B1 to do something rarely done by Hong Kong students—to interrupt the teacher and initiate a question (turn 7). The teacher, however, did not immediately understand the broken English of B1. It has taken a few turns for sense to be made on both sides. Actually, as an outsider, the authors cannot tell for sure whether B1's initiation in turn 7 is related to the book summary or to the project. The only thing we can be sure is hard-working or institutional requirements-oriented students in Hong Kong are very concerned about homework requirements. Therefore, although B1 might be thinking of the book report on making that initiation, he certainly also has the project in mind.

A postlesson informal discussion with Miss Logan revealed that she actually had not prepared for such details about the length requirement of the book report and the project. The answers were made up on the spot. Like many teachers in Hong Kong, Miss Logan agreed that Hong Kong students were particularly concerned about the length requirement of their homework. From the authors' experience, length would usually be the first question students would ask in public concerning homework, followed by the date of submission. These concerns have already formed part of the institutional student culture in Hong Kong. class 2B was one of the best classes in the year and their concerns about these issues were understandable. Before this incident, however, Miss Logan was not aware of this student culture in Hong Kong. In other words, she had not yet mastered sufficient local institutional resources to get herself prepared for her students' concerns.

One thing that makes Excerpt 7.15 different from other excerpts in this section is the final achievement, at least on the surface, of understanding between the teacher and the students. It also seems that an occasional negligence by the teacher, plus her NET identity, has unexpectedly afforded an opportunity for the students to initiate in English. Given the students' English proficiency and their desire for absolute clarity of such issues, they would have initiated the questions in Cantonese if the teacher concerned were Cantonese speaking. B1's reformulation of the question (turn 13) following the broken ones (turns 9 & 11) is, after all, a significant attempt to move toward the proper linguistic form needed. It seems that the communicative value (both in terms of language and culture) of the sense-making hiccups in Excerpt 7.15 should not be overlooked.

SUMMARY

In this chapter, we present and discuss different types of sense-making resources available to the NETs and LETs, and their students, and how they sometimes differ in their possession, mastery, and employment of these resources as sense-making strategies. As is shown in this chapter, the NETs and LETs, apart from using English as a major type of linguistic sense-making resource, always found themselves challenged by situations that called for other types of sense- making resources or strategies. LETs such as Mr. Sze would actively employ students' L1 to facilitate communication. As for Ms. Hung, even though she intentionally avoided using students' L1 for sense making, her ability to comprehend it is a definite asset when miscommunication occurred. The NETs, on the other hand, due to their general lack of resources in the students' L1, had to employ other resources and strategies such as inviting language broker service from more able students, making hypotheses, and attempting to repair. However, the effectiveness of these strategies seems to be situational. Sometimes, it may take several turns of negotiations but without achieving the understanding. It seems that the higher the sensitivity on the part of the teachers of the linguistic and cultural differences between the L1 and L2, the higher the opportunity for sense making to be successful. By being proficient in both the L1 and L2, it seems that the LETs are in possession of a wider repository of sense-making resources and strategies compared to most NETs.

On the other hand, we should not overlook the role of the students' efforts and their local cultural resources in the sense-making processes. The data in this chapter seem to reveal that in situations when the use of L1 is not possible, the students could actually demonstrate a high degree of linguistic creativity in their attempts to make sense. Although sometimes not very successful, their attempts to cross the linguistic boundary from L1 to L2 are intriguing and significant. In this aspect, the NETs seem to be playing a particularly significant instigative role due to their lack of resources in the students' L1. For example, we show in Excerpts 7.10, 7.11, and 7.15 how students attempted, with varying degrees of success, to communicate their ideas to the NETs. These experiences might have furnished students who are motivated to learn English a positive image of themselves as second language users.

However, it should also be noted that some students (like those in Excerpt 7.14) would take advantage of and manipulate the NET's lack of L1 linguistic and cultural (often working-class specific) knowledge to have fun during the lesson among themselves with the exclusion of the teacher. Even though they may be expressing themselves in English, their utterances are so locally culture-specific that only some of their peers could understand. Their intention seems not to be on making sense *to* the NET, but on the joy of not being made sense *of* by the NET. Similar situations might of course also be experienced by a LET who may not share the class-specific subcultures of the students.

The class-specific subcultures of students also manifest most prominently in students' attempts to make fun out of the lesson content and joke with the teachers. We look at how these happen in the next chapter.

QUESTIONS FOR REFLECTION AND DISCUSSION

1. How could NETs/LETs and students develop their ability to mediate between the L1 and L2 linguistic and cultural borders?
2. What are the pros and cons of inviting students to be "linguistic brokers"? Should teachers themselves play the role of a linguistic broker? Why and why not?
3. Under what circumstances and to what extent would you discipline your own as well as your students' sense-making practices (e.g., forbidding them from using L1)?
4. Among the three types of sense-making resources (linguistic, cultural, and institutional), which type seems to you to be more conducive to solving communication problems in a foreign language classroom with NETs/LETs?
5. Choose one to two excerpts from this chapter in which you think something could have been done to prevent the interaction breakdown from happening and share your suggestions with other people.

8

Having Fun in the Lessons

TUNING-IN DISCUSSION

What kind(s) of students do you often have? Quiet and shy? Playful and lively? Which type do you like better? How far do you agree that a lively atmosphere in the classrooms is conducive to language teaching? Do you think NETs and LETs would employ different methods to create a pleasurable learning environment, or display different responses to students' playful behaviors?

For some time, Hong Kong students' reticence and anxiety in second language classrooms has been a cause for concern. Getting oral responses from students has been identified as one of the major problems in ESL classes (Tsui, 1996). However, there has recently been a growing body of research on local ESL classroom interaction that reveals increasing student responses and lively interaction in the form of verbal play (Kwan, 2000; Lin, 2000; Pennington, 1999a). It has been discussed in chapter 4 that such verbal play not only appeared in the outermost layer of the lesson frame (Pennington, 1999a) but also in the student-response slots in the institutional IRF interaction sequences (Kwan, 2000; Lin, 2000). Such verbal play that is often realized in students' L1, while being creative, can be disruptive to the teacher's lesson agenda.

Instances of language play pervade in our classroom data, varying in degrees of frequency in different classes. The kind of language play or verbal play presented in this chapter falls mainly under the category of *mimicry* in Caillois' (1955/1969) classification of games[74] that involves the playing of sounds.

The increasingly frequent playful and sometimes disruptive L1 verbal play of the students mentioned earlier is perhaps a response in the form of opposition, or resistance, to the uninteresting and unstimulating classroom activities (Kwan, 2000; Lin, 2000, 2005), or to the kind of unequal power structure between the teacher and students common in Hong Kong classrooms. Critical classroom researchers such as Canagarajah (2000) tend to take simple acts of false compliance, parody, pretense, and mimicking as "the weapons of the weak ..., the strategies by which the marginalized detach themselves from the ideologies of the powerful, retain a measure of critical thinking, and gain some sense of control over their life in an oppressive situation" (p.122). How far does Canagarajah's argument apply to students in the present study is explored in the coming sections.

The playful and sometimes roguish verbal practices of the students in the classrooms also coincide in many ways with adolescents' discourse practices in the streets. In a study to investigate how adolescents at risk of joining gangs in Hong Kong use discursive devices to negotiate and construct identities, Candlin, Lin, and Lo (2000) found that the adolescents were using a rich and dynamic variety of discourse features that would not normally be allowed in Hong Kong classrooms such as ignoring the authorities' instructions, talking among themselves, and self-selecting to speak. It seems that more and more Hong Kong adolescents are trying to assert their identities constructed in noninstitutional social settings in the more institutional school and classroom settings (Pennington, 1999a). This is exactly the kind of discrepancy and connection existing between home-school discourses (or primary and secondary discourses) of which teachers must be aware (see Cazden, 2001; Gee, 1996).

Although students' verbal play practices in our data share some of the characteristics with those Hong Kong-based studies previously mentioned, they reveal some other interesting features. For example, in addition to the playful commentary talk mentioned in Lin's (2000) and Pennington's (1999a) works, there are data in this study showing how students created laughter in the classrooms through social talk, teasing, and taboo talk. We show that these moments are not always mischievous and peripheral to the lesson agenda, but sometimes embrace intriguing communicative values. The teachers involved also evoked some of these fun-making practices. In the following sections, we present different types of playful discourses of the students, and sometimes of the teachers, available in our data, including phonological play, social talk, teases, and taboos.

PHONOLOGICAL PLAY

The biggest category of fun-making linguistic play reveals students' nonsensical but often adept word play based on phonological properties of the utterances. In chapter 7, Excerpt 7.10, we present and discuss how some students' anglicized Cantonese and word-for-word direct literal translation of L1 to L2 as an attempt to make sense to the NET resulted in roars of laughter from the whole class. It is obvious that the students derived great fun from the phonological and semantic manipulations of the two languages. As argued by Lin (2000), anglicized L1 is a way of mocking "**Gwai-Lou**'s" (a colloquial Cantonese term for "foreigners") way of speaking Cantonese. Such an attempt to mock the foreigner's Anglo-accented Cantonese perhaps makes the students feel less ashamed when they cannot pronounce English properly and are laughed at by other students.

Apart from Anglo-accented Cantonese, we illustrate how students made funny and nonsensical analogies between an L2 utterance and a totally unrelated L1 utterance based on their phonological similarities in the three following excerpts (all coming from the same lesson).

Excerpt 8.1. #Berner (3E, 05/03/99)

Under the guidance of the teacher, this all-boys group is interviewing the ELTA (see note 10, chap. 6), Elsa (E). To add to the fun of the interview, the teacher sometimes encourages the students to ask rather personal questions such as the following one about whether Elsa has a boyfriend.

1. E: Yes I do.
2. B1: **Eih**? [Cantonese particle showing interest]
   [Ss become quiet] Sorry?
3. NET: How about his name?
4. B1: Terry? ["Terry" is the name of a male ELTA working with Elsa.]
5. E: [laughs]
6. B2: [laughs] No way!
7. E: No, his name's Jonathan.
8. B3: Geo-? John?
9. B2: **Dai-nang** <*Low ability*>? [some Ss laugh]
10. B3: (.) Elephant **aa**? [Cantonese particle in rising tone for seeking confirmation]
11. Ss/E: [laugh loudly]

Excerpt 8.2. #Berner (3E, 05/03/99)

This takes place at the end of the interview.

1. NET: Any more questions?
2. B1: No.
3. NET: Thank you Elsa.
4. E: It's my pleasure. [Elsa leaves the room]
5. Ss: By:::e (Ss go on talking about the vital statistics of Elsa, making a lot of noise.)

6. NET: Shhhhhh, shhh, boys, there is lesson going on in school, (.) Gentlemen.
7. B2: **Zu-tau** <*Pig-headed*>**man** [a common Chinese word; used in this
   context, it could refer to an unidentifiable person] **aa** [Cantonese particle].
   [The whole phrase "**zu-tau man**" sounds like 'gentlemen'.]
8. [many Ss laugh]

Excerpt 8.3.   #Berner (3E, 05/03/99)

After Elsa has left, the teacher revises some of the answers with the students and
teaches them how to put together the answers into a coherent composition.

1. NET: ... and her mother's name is?
2. [Many Ss are laughing at the interesting pronunciation of Elsa's father's
   name while T is writing on the board.]
3. NET: Mother's name is?
4. B1: Err, //R-
5. B2: //Ru-
6. B: Ruby
7. NET: Ruby
8. B: Rugby [laughs]
9. B: Snoopy [chuckling, others laugh too]
10. B: **Si-lou-bei** <*Snoopy*>

These three excerpts show how these students have taken every possible opportunity to make fun of anything they heard in the lesson. They particularly enjoyed
making L1 associations with the sounds of the L2 utterances. These associations, although basically nonsensical, are at times ironically relevant to the situation and created with wit. For example, the phonological similarities between "Jonathan,"
"elephant," and **"daai nang"** <*low-ability*>; and "gentlemen" and **"zu tau man"**
<*pig-headed man*> make whimsical associations between the L1 and L2 terms. De-
scribing somebody's friend as having "low ability" and a gentleman as being
"pig-headed" is malicious but not totally irrelevant. These discursive practices of the
students remind us of a piece of comment from Candlin et al.'s (2000) study on the
everyday discourse of Hong Kong adolescents that to a certain extent, "the adolescents enjoy joking about how decadent they are" (p. 79). Here in our data, adolescents of a similar age group seem to be enjoying the denigration of others as well,
and they also seemed to enjoy joking about decadent things in general. This may be
the result of a desire to display an identity opposite to and transgressive of what is
deemed appropriate by mainstream adults. Or it may be their "weapon" to counteract the alienating discourse of English. Or it may only be a reflex action to something

that did not make sense in the first place. Because we did not conduct postobservation interviews with the student groups, all our interpretations can only be based on existing literature findings and our own experience as a teacher and teacher educator. The authors personally do not think the students had any intention of insulting Elsa's boyfriend, but the readiness with which these pejorative terms came to mind of the students certainly reflects something about the nature of their verbal repertoire, and the popular youth culture[75] they were immersed in every day.

In Excerpt 8.3, "Snoopy" and "Ruby" share the same vowel in both syllables. Although putting them together does not create that satirical effect found in the other examples, associating somebody's mother with this cartoon character is cute and cool. The student who put forward "rugby" has demonstrated his letter-sound awareness. "Ruby" and "rugby" are worlds apart in terms of meaning, but the student put them together as fun-making subjects based on their similarities in shape, alliterating beginning sounds, and identical final syllables. These examples show that as language users, the students were actually rather creative and resourceful and skillful in playing with linguistic sounds.

Whereas the instances of linguistic play presented in the earlier excerpts that were created at the moments of the talk seem rather ad hoc, there may be some playful creations that have already been "institutionalized." We show what we mean by this with the following excerpt from Mr. Nelson's 4E.

Excerpt 8.4. #Nelson (4E, 17/03/99)

This takes place in the middle of a lesson during which the students were writing a drama script for performance in the next lesson.

1. B1: [responding to some other students' dialogue about HSG]
   No way, dirty, too dirty. [laughs]
2. B2: [asking the T when he walks near] Do you know what is H-S-G?
3. NET: Yes, handsome guy.
4. B2: Handsome guy, no, another meaning.
5. B1: No other meaning, no another meaning.
6. B2: It is a Chinese translation **aa** [a Cantonese particle]
   [some Ss laugh]

It is mentioned in chapter 7 (e.g., Excerpt 7.14) that some students would take advantage of the NETs' lack of Cantonese resources and joke about things that do not make sense to the NET. They seemed to relish showing off their insiders' knowledge of some culture-specific jokes and seeing how the NETs reacted to them. Excerpt 8.4 shows one such incident where students intentionally presented to the native English teacher a challenge imbued with cross-cultural linguistic and cultural delicacies.

The first author later checked with Mr. Nelson to see if he understood the implied meaning of the term "handsome guy." He told the first author that he knew it was something indecent, although why the term "handsome guy" was used was not clear to him. For the benefit of the readers who do not know Cantonese, we would like to note here that the pronunciation of the word "handsome" sounds similar to the Cantonese phrase **"haam sup"** (literally meaning "salty and wet") that is used to describe somebody, usually a man, who has a dirty mind. This extended use of "handsome" is so popular among adolescents in Hong Kong that it seems to have been institutionalized. It should be noted that the word "handsome" comes up again in a later excerpt (8.11) in this chapter and this background information will help readers understand the students' discourse better.

Instances of phonology-based linguistic play have been captured in other teacher participants' classes except Ms. Hung's. Most of the cases were very situational and rather nonsensical, but most students in the class seemed able to share the fun, with or without the understanding and involvement of the teachers. For example, in one of Miss Logan's lessons with 2B, her students laughed on hearing the teacher saying the word "kitchen" after addressing a girl whose name is "Kit Ching." In a lesson on names of countries and their people, Mr. Sze's students shouted out "Tyson" on hearing "Thailand."

Although no instances of phonological play of this type have been captured in Ms. Hung's lessons, it does not mean that students in Ms. Hung's lessons had no fun at all. During the first author's visits, Ms. Hung's classes had several fun activities that students enjoyed very much. For example, in one activity, the class worked in pairs to formulate a list of questions that they would use to interview a well-respected Chinese history teacher in the school who had fought in the Sino-Japanese War. On another occasion, the students were asked to formulate a dialogue to show off what their father possessed. The students followed the teacher's example and prefaced their utterances with "So what!" in response to the previous boastful statements of their peers. Two boys working in pairs were heard on the audiorecording to be making up exaggerated statements ridiculing people they know, for example, "XXX is very clever. He knows one plus one equals two"; or "XXX is very beautiful, just like Wong X Wai."[76] However, when pairs of students were invited to perform their dialogues in front of the whole class, they did it seriously. Most performances invited some laughter as well as hands clapping as prompted by the teacher. In general, students in Ms. Hung's lessons did play with language, but the play was more of an ideological nature than nonsensical sound manipulations as what the phonological play examples show in this section. They were also done mainly in private talks among peers and never involved the teacher (see more discussion of Ms. Hung in the second paragraph after Excerpt 8.14). This is interesting evidence showing how students were able to display multiple identities based on changing circumstances.

SOCIAL TALK

Social talk refers to the light-hearted and casual communication between students and teachers not directly related to the lesson agenda. Excerpt 8.4 can also be considered an example of social talk initiated by the students. The appearance of social talk in the classroom is revealing about the relationship between the teacher and the students. On the one hand, the interaction that results from this type of talk usually contributes to a better interpersonal rapport between the teachers and students concerned. Social talk establishes mutual trust and respect between students and teachers and a friendly nonthreatening atmosphere in which to work (Biggs & Edwards, 1994, p. 86). On the other hand, an already good rapport between the teachers and students also tends to prompt more interactions of this kind. As is shown in the next few excerpts, the teachers and students seemed to derive pleasure from this kind of talk.

Apart from Miss Logan and Ms. Hung, instances of social talk have been found in other teacher participants' lessons.[77] All these instances occurred in more private interactions between the teachers and the students, but not necessarily one-on-one. They also seemed to take place only when the tasks were more learner independent such as ERS and writing. Several instances of student-initiated social talk were observed in Ms. Berner's 1E class. Two of these instances are presented in Excerpts 7.3 and 7.9. Those excerpts and the next one all came from the same lesson, and the whole thing actually begins with Excerpt 8.5.

Excerpt 8.5.   #Berner (1E, 24/10/97)

This excerpt takes place before Excerpt 7.3. Ms. Berner is reading a newspaper while waiting for the class to complete the questionnaire.

1. G1: [talking to her classmates] **Jau hou-do jan tai gan bou-zi** <*Many people are reading newspaper*>.
2. G2: [in anglicized tone, to the teacher] **Tai^ bou^-zi^** <*Read newspaper*>.
3. G1: [to the teacher] We read newspaper.
4. NET: You read the English newspaper?
5. Gs: Yes.
6. NET: Fine. Very good. Do you read the cartoons? I'll show you my favorite bit. [flipping through the newspaper]
7. G1: Fa- favorite **dim-gaai** <*What's meant by-* >
8. NET: My favorite bit.
9. G2: **Zeoi zung-ji tai** <*Likes to read most*>.
10. NET: The bit I like best.

11. G1: This?
12. NET: No. (..)
13. [Gs talking in Cantonese while the T flips through the pages of the newspaper]
14. NET: It's Garfield . Garfield? No Garfield? Oh, no Garfield, (.) cat for Garfield, (.) cat.
15. G1: Pets?
16. NET: There's a cat and you find him on pictures, on birthday cards.
17. G1: Birthday card? //Cat?
18. NET: //Yes. He's a cat and he's called Garfield.
19. G1: On the birthday card?
20. NET: Uhuh, and also on pens and pencils and, Garfield. [T keeps flipping through the pages.]
21. G3: **Hai mai go-di me ju aa** *<Isn't it a kind of fish>?*
22. G2: Birthday card? **Saang-jat-kaat** *<Birthday card>?*
23. NET: On Monday on Monday I'll bring you a picture of Garfield.
24. G1: OH! *<GAA-FEI> <GARFIELD>!*
25. G2: [talking to her classmate, sounding very annoyed] **M HAI gaa-fei aa** *<It ISN'T Garfield>!*
26. G1: [addressing NET] Garfield cat?
27. NET: Garfield, that's a Garfield.
28. G1: It's a cat, //orange.
29. NET: //Yes, and looks like this.
    [T makes a funny facial expression and Ss laugh.]
    [with amused voice] It's very naughty, **hou-jai** *<Very naughty>!*

This interesting piece of casual talk in which the NET shares with the students her favorite cartoon character begins with an informative statement by the students about the current behavior of other students, and this statement was first done in Anglo-accented Cantonese, then in English. Although the utterance looks like a plain statement (turns 1–3), the illocutionary[78] meanings and perlocutionary force of the statement may vary. It could be a request for permission to read the newspaper, or an indirect invitation for the teacher to join in the talk. The latter meaning seems to have been picked up by the teacher who shows her interest in continuing the conversation, not so much in the capacity of an authority figure in the classroom, but as an ordinary conversation partner. The feedback of the teacher in turn 6 to the girls' positive response is, however, highly evaluative in nature. It shows that the teacher is still eager to fulfill her institutional role as an English teacher, and acknowledging good practice of students is part of her role. However, her initiation in turn 6 (Do you read the cartoons?) and her almost immediate response with an informative statement (I'll show you my favorite bit.) reflects that she is not expecting any student's language response. The teacher's intention seems to be more of sharing information than of teaching from this turn onward. Similar to Excerpt 6.3, the final achievement of common understanding (turns 26–29) causes considerable pleasure on both sides, as evident from the teacher's funny Cantonese expressions (**hou-jai**) and the students' laughter.

This incidental piece of small talk between the teacher and the students shows dynamic interaction patterns. As pointed out by Coupland (2000), small talk is sociolinguistically significant in that it highlights the centrality of the relational function of talk, and it often reveals the changing orientations, framings and footings of the speakers. Unlike the conventional IRF pattern, all pupil turns in Excerpt 7.5 are self-selected by the students. The NET also amuses herself and the students by self-annotating the L2 term "naughty" with the Cantonese version (turn 29). All these observations reinforce what we have discussed about the impact of Ms. Berner's ability to cross between the L1 and L2 linguistic codes under Excerpt 7.3. Apart from contributing to the sense-making effects of the interaction, Ms. Berner's eagerness to use and learn the students' L1 (e.g., practicing the Cantonese term for "one hundred and one" after the students) has shortened the distance between herself and the students. As evident in Excerpts 7.3, 7.9 and 8.5, these young students enjoy initiating casual conversation with the NET perhaps because the latter had not projected an alienating image by pouncing on the use of L1 by the students. On the other hand, Ms. Berner also seems to have derived pleasure from practicing her Cantonese with the students. This certainly has fulfilled her major objective of learning Cantonese to establish a stronger sense of solidarity with the students and to narrow their social distance (see interview data in chap. 6).

It is important to note that there are instances in the rest of the lesson between the same teacher and the students in which the NET stopped the students' use of L1 in an authoritative manner even though the students were in fact discussing the teacher-set task, a situation quite similar to what has been reported in Guthrie (1984).[79] So what has made the teacher temporarily drop the institutional role of the "language police" in Excerpts 7.3, 7.9 and 8.5? The unconventional setting of the classroom (where students were sitting in groups rather than in rows) and the informal nature of the task (filling in a questionnaire that was not part of the lesson content) contribute to the emergence of this piece of noninstitutional social talk. These echo the results of a study by Poole and Patthey-Chavez (1994) that a different interaction setting, and student–teacher participation structure have resulted in more negotiation of meaning. The frequent laughter from the teacher and students, and the active contributions (although often in Cantonese) from the students show that they enjoy the conversation. To give a balanced picture of the classroom realities of NETs and LETs, we show in the next excerpt how a piece of student-initiated small talk occurred in Mr. Sze's 1D class.

Excerpt 8.6. #Sze (1D, 31/03/00)

In this context, the students are working on some worksheets on comparatives by themselves. The teacher walks around to monitor. It is clear from the interaction below that before B1 initiates, he was discussing the issue with his neighbor. However, it seems that the students are referring to something that is not related to the worksheets, but something brought back by themselves.

1. B1: Ah sir,[80] **keoi waa li-di haai haau-mong** <*Sir? He said that this is an indecent web site*>.
2. LET: Uhmm
3. B2: **M zi hai-mai lei gaa** <*I don't know if it is*>.
4. B1: **Wong-sik mong-jip woo keoi waa li-di haai** <*A porn website he said it is*>.
5. LET: International travel book **zi maa** <*It's only*>. [The two boys laugh at the term "**haau-mong**" <*indecent website*> while the teacher is talking.] **Mou aa** <*No, it's not*>, **li go gwaan-ju me gaa** <*What is this about*>?
6. B2: **Ngo dim-zi zek** <*How do I know*>? **Ngo gin-dou-=** <*I see that-*>
7. LET: =Travel, what does it mean by "travel," what does it mean by "travel"?
8. B2: **Leoi-jau lo** <*It's traveling*>.
9. LET: **Leoi-jau lo** <*It's traveling*>, **mou cuo** <*Yes, that's right*>. **Leoi-jau-sju lo** <*A book on traveling*>, **gwaan me si** <*Nothing of that kind*>. [T walks away]
10. B1: [to B2] **Lei seong dak do aa** <*You've been thinking too much of it*>. [B2 laughs]
11. B1: [sounds like an adult nagging] **Seong siu-di laa** <*Think less of it*>!

Although the two boys seemed to be making a serious enquiry, the subject matter that they were interested in and their private conversation after the teacher has walked away reveal their basic intention of having fun. It is easy to understand why students are interested in the Internet, in particular, online pornography. Young children of their age (12–13) are usually curious about sex, particularly when sex is a taboo and forbidden topic in the classroom and in mainstream Chinese culture in general. B1's adultlike comment on B2 in turns 10 and 11 is significant. It probably implies that B1 was equally obsessed with such topics as B2.

From the two boys' manner and tone of voice, they did not seem to have any intention of challenging, embarrassing, or testing the teacher. The fact that they took the initiative to raise the issue with their teacher reflects their intimate relationship with the teacher. We believe that the students may not easily have done this if the teacher were female, or someone who appeared more solemn than Mr. Sze. From the first author's observation, Mr. Sze is a very friendly teacher, although by no means doting. In the postobservation discussion, he told the first author that these Year 1 students were very childlike. He did not think that the students meant anything mischievous in talking about pornographic Web sites. Even if they did, he thought that he had skillfully normalized the impact of the issue by reaffirming his role as a language teacher (turn 7) when he attempted to teach the meaning of "travel."

Teachers after reading Excerpt 8.6 might think that the Excerpt should have been even more interesting if Mr. Sze were non-Cantonese speaking. If the teacher is sensitive enough, such moments could be turned into valuable opportunities to provide situated language practice for the students. Although it may be more difficult for local teachers to produce the same effects, they could still grasp such opportunities to take students across the linguistic border from L1 to L2, just as Mr. Sze did with teaching the meaning of "travel."

The interaction between Mr. Sze's and his students in Excerpt 8.6 also reminds us of a similar student initiation in Mr. Nelson's 4E class already presented in Excerpt 8.4 when B1 asked the teacher "Do you know what is HSG?" Although both groups of students initiated the conversation, we see the two incidents as being different in nature. While Mr. Sze's students might probably want to know more about the nature of the Web site in focus, Mr. Nelson's already knew what "HSG" meant. Therefore, the latter's initiation was more for making fun and testing the teacher than for gaining knowledge. In this connection, the fun-making intention of Mr. Nelson's 4E probably came from their curiosity to know and to test how much knowledge of local colloquial culture the NET possessed.

As instances of teacher–student interaction, Excerpts 7.3, 8.5, and 8.6 are highly significant in that students were given free spaces to initiate and assert their voices and insert their own meanings and intentions while the teacher also succeeded in building bridges between the students' L1 and L2.

VERBAL CHALLENGES AND FRIENDLY TEASES

According to Straehle (1993), teasing is a language "nip" that can "signal and enhance speaker enjoyment and rapport" (p. 211). Teasing sometimes carries connotations of verbal challenges or "verbal dueling" that is defined as the "exchange of clever and intricate insults and boasts, ... usually happens between males" (Cook, 2000, p. 65). However, teasing mainly originates from the intention to make fun with no ill-will from the teaser and signals a certain degree of familiarity and intimacy. As explicated by Tannen (1986, pp. 15–16), with teasing, the conversational "meaning" is not conveyed merely through the information content or message of individual words, but through "metamessage," or the attitudes of participants toward one another and the talk in which they are engaged. Typical examples of teasing and verbal challenges have been found in Mr. Williams' lessons and isolated instances of a less intense nature also occurred in Mr. Nelson's 4E class.

Excerpt 8.7.   #Williams (2E, 23/04/99)

This occurs in a lesson on oppositional adjectives such as "satisfactory/unsatisfactory." Right at the beginning, the class was very noisy. Most students could not produce any of the adjective pairs that they learned on the previous day. After some reteaching, Mr. Williams asked the students to choose a pair of antonyms and draw pictures to show their contrastive meanings. In the following excerpt, after explaining the task, Mr. Williams suddenly holds off the activity and forewarns the students not to choose adjective pairs that are too easy for their level.

1. NET: I don't want anybody to do, happy //cause happy is too simple=
2. B: //(???)
3. NET: =yeah, listen, listen, listen, shu, shu, (..) Zero, listen, <LISTEN>! (..) Right, nobody does happy cause that is too easy. What about satisfactory? Is that- shuuuuu (…) shuuuu [softer in voice] Listen, listen. Satisfactory, is that too easy?
4. B1: [softly] //yes.
5. B2: [barely audible] //No.
6. NET: (..) No, that is quite difficult one. I would have satisfactory. What about-what about lucky? I think that's too easy.
7. Ss: NO!
8. NET: Too EA:s:y
9. Ss: DIFFICU:LT
10. NET: Rubbish!
11. Ss: Diffi//cult
12. B3: //Davidcult [/deɪˈfrˈkəʊ/, devoicing the /v/, dropping the final /lt/, and stressing the first and the third syllables, common features of Cantonese accented English] [some Ss laugh]
13. B4: [chuckling and reproducing B3's utterance] Davidcult
14. [T stops arguing and goes on to teach some other adjectives.]

Some kind of verbal duel happens from turns 8 to 13 when the teacher and the students exchange bantering in polarized lexical terms ("easy" and "difficult"). This is interesting taking into consideration the topic of the lesson on antonyms and this might explain why Mr. Williams let the bantering go on for three turns. B3's nonsense word "davidcult" in turn 13 is a creative word play in this context. He skillfully blends the name of the teacher, David, and the last syllable of "difficult" to become a hybrid term "davidcult." We believe that B3's creation is prompted by a close resemblance in pronunciations of "diffi-" and "David," and it causes a lot of laughter from the class and B4's repetition of B3's witty creation shows how he relishes the joke. The students' laughter however might have revealed a feeling more complex than simple fun. As argued by Fry (as cited in Cook, 2000, p. 71), laughter can be variously explained as resulting from "feelings of superiority in attack and as compensatory reaction to feelings of inferiority in battle." B3's creation seems an excellent way to tease the teacher's insistence on the students' choosing "difficult" words for the task, and the appearance of this hybrid word has stopped the teacher from further insistence.

Students making fun with the teacher's first name in front of the teacher concerned is probably very unconventional from many local teachers' point of view. Although the students have done nothing to insult the teacher explicitly, playing with the teacher's first name no doubt signifies the students' attempt to cross over the line demarcating the hierarchical status between teachers and students. There seems to be a strong overtone to embarrass the teacher and this may be a form of resistance to the teacher's criticism that their choice of words is too easy. The teacher's dissatisfaction with their performance might have reminded them of their inability to cope with the alienating discourse of English, and their low self-esteem as an ineffective English learner. On the other hand, the students' actions in Excerpt 8.7 also reflect their perception of the teacher as somebody who would not bear any grudge against such playful challenge.[81] It is many students' belief that NETs are stereotypically more friendly and tolerant of students' errors than LETs. Compared with Excerpt 8.7, the verbal duel in Excerpt 8.8 in which students are making explicit negative comments on the teacher seems more tension filled. It also happened to Mr. Williams.

Excerpt 8.8.   #Williams (4E, 22/04/99)

This is a discussion lesson. The teacher asked the students to show their stance toward a list of statements provided by the teacher by standing in different parts of the classroom assigned as either "agree," "disagree," or "uncertain" zones. The students were then asked to justify their choice of stance verbally in front of the class.

1. NET: Mr. Williams is the best teacher in YKT,[82] you disagree, why?
2. B: Ehhh, (.) only play silly games, [Other Ss laugh] but, but eh he is a only one can say English, eh, only one eh English teacher can (??)
3. NET: Fantastic! (???) Right okay now, can't decide, why?
4. G: [asking others] **Dim gaai aa** <*Why*>? **Dim gaai aa** <*Why*>? (0.9)
5. NET: Shuuuuu, everybody must have a reason why. Carol, Carol, (????) (…) Right, okay, Carol, okay, you stand there, tell me. Annie, why, why you disagree? Why do you disagree?
6. A: Because (.) in our class, there are many people sleeping.
7. NET: Okay, great, that's fine. Carol, your your (??) (…) Carol, you have to stand there and (???) (…) Carol?

8. C: (???)
9. NET: Right okay. Okay that's fine. Sometimes very funny and interesting, sometimes very boring. Okay that's fine. Mr. Williams, (...) Mr. Williams-
10. Ss: Shuuuu
11. NET: Mr. Williams is fat.

    [Ss move again, some laughing, making lots of noise.]
12. NET: Okay, okay, shushushu. (...)

    Eric, you strongly agree, you strongly agree, why?
13. E: Because you are fat.
14. NET: Because I am fat= [Many Ss laugh.]
15. E: =Like a pig.
16. NET: Like a PIG! Thank you very much. I'll remember that when I mark your homework.

    [Many Ss laugh loudly.]

The jeering and playfully insulting nature of the students' remarks on the teacher's teaching (turns 2, 6, 8–9) and appearance (turns 13 & 15), and the teacher's attempt to fight back (turn 16) echo a certain tone of "symbolic violence" between the teacher and the students. Judging from the laughter of the students, their insulting comments on the teacher are intentional and meant to be exaggerating. They are apparently deliberate moves by the students to embarrass the teacher. They could also be interpreted as attempts at "biting" (Boxer & Cortes-Conde, as cited in Candlin et al., 2000) most usually found in teasing. Traditionally, Chinese students are taught to respect their teachers. Commenting on their teachers verbally in public, no matter whether the comments are positive or negative, is a very rare practice (Biggs & Watkins, 1996). However, the teacher's deliberate offering of himself to be the subject, or object for discussion, and his lighthearted reactions to the students' comments throughout seem to have encouraged the students to voice their opinions further. Mr. William's implied threat in turn 16 to mark down Eric's homework has not been taken seriously by the class, as is evident from their laughter. A possible reason why Mr. Williams only fought back against Eric and not those previous students who also gave negative comments is because Eric was considered a very intelligent, but rebellious student by Mr. Williams. From what the first author has observed, during lessons, Eric and his friend, Eddie, always "collaborated" to disturb the lessons by joking and chatting loudly in Cantonese. In the postobservation interview, Mr. Williams said that his way of tackling these nonconforming students was to try to "outwit" them through verbal interactions.

A similar instance of student–teacher verbal challenge also appeared in Mr. Nelson's 4E. According to Mr. Nelson, the students were very used to having fun in the lesson by using bad language or ordinary language with sexual connotations in public. During the period of the first author's visit, the students restrained themselves from displaying such verbal practice involving "bad" language (from the authors' judgment). However, according to Mr. Nelson, they seemed to have made some attempts to embarrass him in front of a female visitor, probably in order to attract her attention.[83] Slightly different from the data presented in Excerpts 8.7 and 8.8, the verbal exchanges between Mr. Nelson and his students show characteristics of teasing more than "dueling."

Excerpt 8.9.   #Nelson (4E, 16/03/99)

The following exchange takes place when the teacher has discovered one more careless error on a worksheet he designed. Before this, the teacher already mentioned two and I discovered one. Not long later, a student found another one.

1. NET: [to the whole class, with microphone] Sorry there's one more mistake.
2. Ss: [sounding disappointed and annoyed] Errrrrhhuu!
3. NET: It's because I have used the school computer and there is no spell check on the Chinese program.
4. B: You should check on yourself.
5. NET: I thought I did. Okay should be number eight. It should be <u>empty of people and lacking in, COM</u>fort, C-O-M-F-O-R-T, comfort, line eight, <u>empty of people and lacking in comfort</u>, C-O-M, not N, very so::ry.
   [A student raises his hand.]
6. NET: Is there more? Ahh, I'm so aSHAMED!
   [T walks close to him and talks to him. Five seconds later, two Ss raise a question about the task sheet. The T attempts to answer their questions but soon he discovers that he has made another mistake with spelling.]
7. NET: [to the whole class] I'm very sorry, there is one more.
8. Ss: [sounding surprised] Ahhh?
9. B: How come![84]
10. NET: I've given a test to see how many of my mistakes you can find.
    [Some Ss laugh.] Number nine, should be strange, S-T-R-A-N-G-E (.), strange, so add the R
11. B: You will be fired.
12. NET: [chuckling] Really?

In turn 4, the pupil assumes the teacher's voice by saying "you should check on yourself." Normally, we expect such a comment or advice to be given to students by the teacher. Having it done the other way around not only shows a reversal of roles between Mr. Nelson and his students (which will be perceived as unconventional by most local teachers including the authors), but perhaps also reveals the male student's unconscious intention to embarrass the teacher in the presence of a visitor (see footnote 83). As pointed out by Cook (2000, p. 68), this human psychology has its long tradition in hunter-gatherer societies where the male victors of verbal duels are more likely to attract females because their language skills demonstrate "mental agility and social panache."

Another pupil's comment on the second to last line ("you will be fired"), if interpreted out of context, would sound very abrasive. The fact that it is only produced by a student and the teacher only responded with laughter, however, to a large extent, reveals a "sense of solidarity" and an acceptance of "shared conventions" of such playful bantering (Cook, 2000) between the teacher and the students. It seems that both parties feel very much at ease with this exchange pattern.

There are more cases of teasing of a softer nature across all classrooms than the more tension-creating verbal challenges. The next one from Mr. Williams' 2E gives an interesting contrast with Excerpt 8.9. Whereas verbal challenges always occurred between Mr. Williams and his male students, most of the teasing in Mr. Williams' lessons took place mainly between himself and the female students. We show how one of such instances happened in Excerpt 8.10.

Excerpt 8.10. #Williams (2E, 20/04/99)

The following takes place in an ERS lesson (footnote 62). When the students were supposed to be reading, the teacher walked around to monitor. Some students were obviously not on task. Before G1 initiated the conversation with the teacher, the latter was reminding a male student to behave himself.

1. G1: [with playful tone] //MisTER Wi:lliam [dropping the final /s/]=
2. NET: [to other Ss] //Shuu
3. G1: =What is this?
4. NET: This? Microphone, //do you want to say =
5. G2: [very softly] //microphone.
6. NET: =some//thing for the microphone? Yes?
7. G1: //No.
8. NET: You just said something.
9. G2: MisTER Wi:lliam [dropping the final /s/] is [dropping the /s/] a: handsome boy
10. G1: Handsome bo::y
11. G2: Handsome //BAD boy [laughing]
12. NET: //Don't you, I don't think I am a boy
13. G1: //Handsome bad boy [laughing]
14. NET: //Thank you. Okay.
    [T leaves the girls and gets back to a student he talked to earlier.]

In every sense, G1 is making an attempt (joined by G2 later) to initiate social talk with the teacher. However, as the talk develops, it shows characteristics that are not shared by previous excerpts on social talk. Judging from the tone of voice of the girls, their actions toward the teacher carried heavy connotation of flirting. Literally speaking, the girls have made a direct compliment, in a teasing and probably satirical way, on the teacher's appearance in front of him. This is not what most Chinese students and teachers would expect.[85] Although these girls were only around 14 to 15 years old, they appeared to the first author to be very precocious. Their interest and curiosity about the opposite sex is not difficult to understand. However, their overt display of such an interest through speech should not be viewed as an indiscriminate way of acting. It may be closely bound to their perception of the teacher's tolerance level of such practice and their friendly relationship with him.

During one of the 2E lessons observed, a girl (not in Excerpt 8.10) sitting next to the first author[86] told her that the teacher liked talking about **"haam-sup je"** <*salacious matters*> in the disguise of a seemingly upright manner. The first author has no proof of what she said and has no evidence of hearing any **"haam-sup je"** from the teacher during her visits, but the use of the word "handsome" for Excerpt 8.4 has added to the likelihood of the same underlying meaning of the word being used in Excerpt 8.10, particularly when used with the qualifier "bad." G1 and G2's description of the teacher as a "handsome bad boy" may just be a camouflage expression of their underlying perception of the teacher as someone who is more open to sex. Such a perception might only be the one-sided imagination of the girls, or perhaps the outcome of an overreaction to, or overinterpretation of, some of the teacher's more informal and friendly ways toward female students. Mr. Williams admitted in the postobservation interview that he was more lenient toward the girls than the boys because the girls were more responsive to his instructions. A male teacher's special leniency and friendliness toward female students might have been unduly interpreted as being casual and sexually infatuated by the girls concerned based on their concepts of conventional Chinese moral virtues that males should keep a distance from females or else they would be considered to have sexual interest in the latter.

Even though Mr. Williams might not understand the hidden meaning of "handsome," being described as such by two female students during a lesson was surely embarrassing and awkward. What has been presented to Mr. Williams seems to be a dilemma. While he has succeeded in arousing the interest of the students, at least these girls, to initiate English conversations with him (which he saw as an effective way of improving the students' English), he has at the same time unconsciously instigated other unnecessary associations in these girls, probably through behaving rather differently from other local teachers.

It should be mentioned that G1 and G2 were actually talking into the microphone, which means their speech was recorded. Candlin et al. (2000) mentioned how adolescents sometimes behave differently at the microphone (e.g., switching to English). Perhaps the perception that what is recorded through the microphone would be listened to by an "insignificant other" such as a social worker, or in our case a researcher who is just a temporary visitor, has prompted a more willful display of unconventional actions of the students.

As shown in the previous excerpt, teasing is done during more private interaction between the teacher and the students. This seems to be particularly the case if it was the students who initiated the teasing. In our data, students teasing the teacher in public (apart from perhaps Mr. Nelson and his 4E class in Excerpt 8.9) is only captured once in Ms. Berner's 3E class.

Excerpt 8.11.   #Berner (3E, 05/03/99)

The teacher is guiding the students to prepare a list of questions for an interview with Elsa, the ELTA. A boy proposed a question in broken English to ask about the size and figure of Elsa. After the teacher has taught them the proper term "vital statistics," a male student attempts to prompt the following:

1. B: Ms Berner? What is-
2. NET: I'm not telling you mine [T and Ss both laugh.]
3. B: [shouting out] I know, I know. [Other Ss laugh.]
4. NET: Don't say it, huh huh huh, right.
   [T clears her throat] Is there a nice question you can ask her?

Even though B has not quite finished his question, the circumstance has made it very obvious what he wants to know. It should be noted that the teacher was in fact rather chubby herself, and therefore, her vital statistics would not be "ideal" from most people's point of view. But the teacher's easy attitude toward this issue and the jesting but not ill-willed manner of the students reflect a very relaxed and intimate rapport between her and the students. It is no wonder that Ms. Berner described 3E to be her "fun" class in the postobservation interview.

Comparatively speaking, it is more common for the teacher to tease students in public, as in the following excerpt:

Excerpt 8.12.   #Berner (3E, 05/03/99)

This happened in the subsequent lesson of the one in Excerpt 8.11 when students are conducting the actual interview with Elsa by taking turns to read aloud the questions they prepared in the previous lesson. After one boy asked about the clothes size of the ELTA, the teacher said this to prompt the next question.

1. NET: So lucky Johnny has got the next question. (…)
2. B1: John::ny? [in Cantonese accent, putting undue length on the second syllable]

3. B2: **Faai-di laa** <*Be quick*>! **Ngo-dei m wui siu nei gaa** <*We won't laugh at you*>.
4. NET: Okay, shhhh
5. J: What are-
6. NET: What are your?
7. J: What are your vital^
8. NET: Vital?
9. J: Vital^
10. NET: Statistics. [Many Ss laugh.]

Asking about the ELTA's vital statistics was a question raised by a male student (not Johnny) during the preinterview preparation lesson. Here, during the actual interview, the teacher took the initiative to tease Johnny who got the turn to ask this supposedly interesting, but embarrassing and usually forbidden question in an open interaction in a classroom. Ms. Berner's attempt to tease came from the word "lucky." Without Johnny's consent, Ms. Berner creates an image of Johnny as a male teenager who, like other teenage males, has a special interest in the body figures of the female, and he is "lucky" because he is now given the "privilege" to have this desire satisfied. Other students then joined in the teasing to make fun. "Lucky" Johnny, however, seems to have great difficulty in reading out the question that contains some difficult words, which seems to have produced an anticlimax.

Later, when the ELTA told the class her statistics, several students shouted out some analogies[87] in Cantonese to express their surprise about the "bigness" of the numbers. However, because they said those in Cantonese, Elsa and Ms. Berner were not able to understand, but they were clearly amused by the students' reactions because of the liveliness of the interaction. The students' private discussion of the ELTA's figures seems like a case of gossiping of which the subject being teased may not be aware. This excerpt illustrates mutual teasing happening between the teachers and the students.

A teacher teasing students was also observed in Mr. Sze's lessons with 1B. Apart from reflecting the good rapport between the students and the teacher, the teasing that the teacher did to the students did not carry much intriguing meaning. As discussed in the previous excerpt, the teasing was often carried out in a reciprocal nature; that is, the teacher teases a pupil for the nonsensical or childlike idea just raised by the student himself. Excerpt 8.13 gives one such example.

Excerpt 8.13.   #Sze (1B, 25/03/99)

The class is doing some comprehension tasks based on a reading text on environmental hygiene. It was the teacher's usual practice to talk about some side issues that sprang up from the teaching point in focus. For example, in this excerpt, the teacher commented on the problem with the advice given by the reading text that handkerchiefs should be used when people have caught a cold and want to sneeze.

1. LET: Yes, that's right, you are carrying your bacteria of flu around the classroom. Do you want to do it? Obviously you don't, obviously. You don't want to infect the others when you have a flu. So it's better, okay, to use paper tissue when you got a flu. AFter [heavy stress on "af"] using the paper tissue what do you need to do, if you got a flu? **Doi zu keoi aa** <*Put it in the pocket*>?

2. B1: **Diu zo keoi** <*Throw it away*>.

3. LET: **Diu zo keoi** <*Throw it away*>, **diu bei bin-go** <*Throw it to whom*>?

4. B2: **Laap-saap-tung** <*The rubbish bin*>.

5. LET: **Laap-saap-tung aa** <*The rubbish bin*>. **Gam laap-saap-tung mai cung-mun zu li-go**= <*Then the rubbish bin will be all full of*>=

6. B3: =**Diu-lok gaai** <*Throw it to the street*>.

7. LET: **Diu-lok GAAI tim aa** <*Throw it to the street*>?! [Some Ss laugh.] **Ngo diu nei lok-gaai dak-m-dak aa** <*Can I throw you to the street*>? [Ss laugh.]

The teasing happens in turn 7 (throwing the student out to the street) when the teacher picks up B3's suggestion to throw the used tissue paper out to the street. As a local teacher, Mr. Sze projected a very friendly and informal image in class with his often humorous use of Cantonese to joke with the students. Similar kinds of teasing were observed in other lessons. For example, Mr. Sze sometimes addressed his students (male only) as **"so-tzai"** <*stupid kids*> in an amusing and cheerful way when they had said or done something childlike. This can be regarded as a kind of "soft bite" on the students by the teacher. The first author observed that Mr. Sze tended to have more playful interactions of this type with his male students than with his female students. This could be an interesting contrast with Mr. Williams. Mr. Sze, although behaving in an informal and friendly manner in general, perhaps was more sensitive to the Chinese cultural norms governing interaction between male teachers and female students.

From our data, Ms. Hung is the only teacher who had not been observed to have any teasing with the students. It does not mean that Ms. Hung was not a friendly teacher. She smiled a lot and was encouraging, but students in her lessons seldom displayed verbal play in the public, and never joked with the teacher. However, during interviews, a couple of the sampled groups of students behaved very differently from the lessons. They were more frisky and talkative. One boy (high English proficiency) kept fiddling with his body and spoke with funny voices. Another one told the first author with a smile that he liked Ms. Hung's lessons because the teacher was beautiful. We cannot say the last comment is a kind of teasing, but the amused tone of the student might have reflected his desire for a more informal rapport with the teacher. Perhaps the fact that Ms. Hung is a local female teacher made these boys adopt a set of behaviors that was governed by more sociohistorically conventionalized behavioral norms in class. Because the teacher seldom joked with them, the students tended to be reciprocal in their behavior and showed their respect to the teacher's interaction style by behaving more seriously in class. However, in an interview with a "nonsignificant other" (a temporary visitor), they could behave more as themselves.

TABOO

In their study on nonclassroom-based adolescent discourse in Hong Kong, Candlin et al. (2000) found that adolescents preferred to joke about feces and sex as an act of nonconformity. Because joking and teasing about drugs, sex, and feces are prohibited in schools, adolescents performing these acts in Candlin et al.'s (2000) study may be harboring the intention of releasing their "repressed selves" (p. 78). Interestingly, there are several instances captured in our data in which students talked about, or at least, hinted at issues that are taboos in school contexts.

The first instance of language play on taboo came from Miss Logan's 1B lesson. We should note here that the regular English teacher for 1B was Mr. Sze. To maximize the exposure of students to the teaching of the NET, the school requested Miss Logan to teach one to two lessons every 7-day cycle[88] with almost every class in the school to do oral activities and extensive reading. That is why Miss Logan had this lesson with 1B. In Excerpt 8.14, some students are captured by the recorder joking about feces.

Excerpt 8.14.   #Logan (1B, 30/03/99)
The teacher is teaching adverbs of frequency and she is building up students' concept of varying degrees of frequency these adverbs represented by putting them on a line beginning with "never." The following interaction happened when the teacher asked about what should be placed at the other end.

1. NET: Okay, let's just, first of all, let's put the words on the line (.) Which word should go here?
2. B1: Never.
3. NET: Okay, come out and write it.
   [Some Ss are making playful sounds and laughing.]
4. NET: Which word shhhh, which word should go the other end?
5. B2: Always.
6. NET: Come and write it.
7. B3: **Ngo-si** <*Bowel excretion*>. [a very low-end colloquial Cantonese term with the first and the last sound of "always"]

[Many Ss laugh heartily upon hearing that.]

8. NET: [to B2 who wrote "always" on the board] Thank you.

By taking the first and last sounds of "always" to form the Cantonese term **"ngo-si,"** which is a very low-end colloquial Cantonese expression meaning bowel excretion, B3 is actually conducting phonological play. However, the more striking fact is that these students are joking openly in class on a taboo issue. It has been mentioned that Mr. Sze was the regular English teacher of 1B. From the first author's observation, the students in 1B were extremely cooperative with Mr. Sze. They participated in the lesson actively and responded to the teacher's instructions promptly. They of course said funny and childish things (as in Excerpt 8.13), but never, as far as the first author observed, displayed verbal practices that were incongruous to their institutional student identity. Therefore, the first author was surprised by their verbal play in Miss Logan's lesson. Although they were as responsive (almost always in English) as ever to Miss Logan's elicitation, they were conducting more illegitimate fun talk among their peers in Cantonese, often without the teacher's knowledge and understanding, and sometimes done in an open manner to be heard by most of the class. Such a display of different behaviors in the two teachers' classes may be because of the students' awareness that Mr. Sze was the more long-term authority figure who had significant impact on their school performance, whereas Miss Logan seemed like a decorative bonus. It must be mentioned that Mr. Sze had actually just done the topic Miss Logan taught in the lesson from which Excerpt 8.14 was taken on the day before.[89] However, the students seemed to enjoy the lesson. Nobody had attempted to tell Miss Logan what they had learned in more or less the same approach already. This might be because the students believed that they could enjoy different types of fun during Miss Logan's lessons. This might also show that the students did not really care about what would be taught in the lesson. What is more important is whether they could have fun.

It is difficult to judge from the recording whether Miss Logan heard B3's utterance, but even if she did, it is highly unlikely that she would understand it. Although B3 seems to have displayed the same adeptness in creating phonological associations between the L1 and L2 as discussed before, not many teachers (including the authors) would appreciate the students doing that because of the indecency of the expression. Topics such as sex, feces, and gang culture are traditionally taboos in the Hong Kong classroom. The fact that B3 does it so willfully and the whole class shares the fun so unreservedly in this lesson with Miss Logan but never (from the first author's observation) in Mr. Sze's lessons perhaps reflects the kind of temporary "freedom" that many students said they enjoyed during the NETs' lessons. One type of such freedom is being able to make fun through peer talk and escape possible punishment from the NETs simply because of the latter's inability to accurately identify students' practices that have breached the local sociohistorical conventions governing the linguistic and physical performance of members of the community.

Several typical instances of taboo talk appear in an English room activity lesson of Ms. Berner and her 3E boys. We present one such instance in Excerpt 7.14 showing how students willfully talked about taboo issues including L1-based sex and gang culture in front of the NET by skillfully packaging them in L2. In the next excerpt, which occurs after Excerpt 7.14, we show how the teacher and the students sometimes share the fun of taboo talk.

Excerpt 8.15.   #Berner (3E, 02/03/99)

This is the second activity in the English room activities lesson. The context is the same as the one described in Excerpt 7.14. Under the guidance of the teacher, the students should fill in some speech bubbles on pictures with some cues given. In this excerpt, they come to picture six and the teacher is teaching the phrase "babe magnet" to the students.

1. NET: Yeah, so a babe magnet is someone who locks woman, (??)=
2. B: **Kau-lui aa** <*colloquial Cantonese for 'courting girls'*>.
3. NET: =so cool, very cool, yes? English cool, not Chinese cool, very cool. What's he saying then? What's the babe magnet saying?
4. B: [in sexy tone, with his voice suppressed]Hello? Hi baby? [laughing]
5. NET: Hi baby? [laughing] yeah=
6. B: //Hi, baby?
7. NET: = //okay, write it down, the ballon. Hi, baby?
8. B: **WAA** [exclamation] (**jay jay**) [unintelligible to the researcher]
9. B: **Kau-lui tin-wong dou m-zi haai bin-go** <*You don't even know who's the king of courting girls*>?
10. NET: [laughing] You want to see me later?
11. B: Can I love you? [laughs]
12. NET: See you in Kowloon Tong? [Ss laugh]
13. B: See you in my home?

   [Ss laugh, some are making sounds of inhaling saliva, something always shown on local films to describe the behavior of males when they see sexy girls.]

After the students have figured out what a "babe magnet" is, they are quick to associate it with the popular local culture that they are familiar with; **"kau-nui"**[90] is a slangish Cantonese expression for "courting girls." Such kind of coarse utterance is characteristic of uncultivated people and strictly prohibited in schools. Normally, we would expect teachers to reprimand students for using such expressions during lessons. Ms. Berner's students, however, were again taking advantage of the teacher's lack of knowledge of colloquial Cantonese. On the other hand, the teacher's discursive practice in a sense has reinforced the students' unbridled language play with sex. For example, the teacher joins in the laughter at the students' open reference to sex (turn 4) and she also initiates an utterance with sex connotations (turn 12). The teacher's reference to "Kowloon Tong" reflects a certain degree of her knowledge of local culture. Kowloon Tong is a place in Hong Kong famous for the availability of love motels. "See you in Kowloon Tong" carries the meaning of having an affair (which often includes sex) with someone. As evident from the laughter of the students (turn 12), they all take it in fun.

The fact that only Ms. Berner's 3E boys show such behavior does not mean that they were particularly lousy and bad. The informal context of the lesson and the nature of the tasks all contributed to the students' interactive practice. In normal classroom settings, they only sit with one neighbor. Now they are sitting close with nine others around a table. This physical setting creates a lot of legitimate (encouraged by the teacher) and illegitimate (not permitted by the teacher) interaction spaces for the students. Besides, the absence of the textbooks dilutes the formalness and perhaps, pressure, of a "lesson." All these contextual factors certainly have contributed to the students' discursive practice.

SUMMARY

We show in chapter 8 how students made fun during lesson time, with or without the collaboration or knowledge of the teachers, through four major categories of fun-creating practice, namely phonological play, social talk, teasing, and talking about taboo topics. The manifestations of these categories of fun-making practice serve different functions and reveal different aspects of the dynamics of classroom interaction. It seems that some form of mutual bantering and fun making will be conducive to livening up the classroom atmosphere and in building a friendly teacher–student rapport. In addition, the students sometimes enjoyed the pleasure of defiance and transgression by deliberately using L1-L2 word puns to create jokes about sex or taboo topics in mainstream Chinese adult cultures. It seems that instead of adopting a high-handed approach in stamping out these creative playful practices of students, teachers might try to capitalize on them to turn them into useful English-speaking and English-learning moments.

Students' linguistic play based on phonological and semantic properties of L1 and L2, although highly nonsensical sometimes, reveals their creativity and metalinguistic awareness of the two language systems at work. By manipulating the infinite possibility of the rhyme, rhythm, parallelism, or pun between the L1 and L2, students create individual expressions with new "iconoclastic ideas" (Cook, 2000, p. 201) that may have signified a desire on the part of the students to assert agency (i.e., an individual's capacities to act independently of structural constraints) as language users, and to gain a sense of ownership of the speech.

Social talk and teasing, on the other hand, function to moderate or palliate the institutionalized asymmetrical power relationship between the teachers and the students. By engaging in casual and informal conversations, students and teachers act like friends and teachers sometimes learn from the students' L1 linguistic and cultural knowledge (as in Ms. Berner's case). The exchange of witty challenges, and playful language "bites" in teasing also reflect a friendly, and to a certain extent, egalitarian relationship between the teachers and the students concerned. It sometimes signifies a reversal of roles between the teachers and the students with the latter assuming the authoritative speech register traditionally accorded to the teachers (as in Mr. Nelson's and Mr. Williams' cases).

The taboo talk in the classroom, although being highly sensitive in nature and easy to get out of control, has made available an interaction space for students to emancipate their repressed selves. These might also provide valuable opportunities for teachers to obtain a deeper understanding of the everyday class-specific cultures of the students. From what the students put forward spontaneously for fun-making purposes, teachers could get a glimpse of the inner world of their students. The in-group cultures of the youth, what interests them and what concerns them most are very often revealed through what they utter. If properly utilized, these cultures could be turned into topics that motivate students to participate actively in the talk for interaction.

From what we have presented through the data, there seems to be a whole nexus of socioculturally, ethnically, and gender-related norms behind these playful discursive practices. Direct verbal challenges and criticisms tend to occur only between male teachers and male students, whereas social talk and language "nips" of a softer nature could occur in interactions between different sexes. There seems to be more playful discourses of teasing and talking on taboos in NETs' lessons. One reason might be many students' common perceptions of the NETs (sometimes reinforced by the actions of the NETs concerned) as being more democratic, casual, or informal than LETs. Another reason might be because the students took advantage of the NETs' lack of Cantonese linguistic and cultural knowledge to fully engage in and enjoy their talk, which was traditionally "forbidden" in classroom settings.

An increasing number of scholars (Cook, 2000; Crystal, 1998) advocate that language play has a central role in language learning. However, in second language classrooms such as those in Hong Kong, the verbal play of students often reflects the students' resistance to English and their assertion of a "local Cantonese-based Chinese cultural identity" (Lin, 2000, p. 76), which seems to be working against the purpose of learning English for gaining access to those socioeconomically valued linguistic resources and cultural capital. We have seen in several excerpts in chapters 7 and 8 that the students were highly creative, and seemed to be displaying agency in manipulating the two languages and some were expressing themselves in English. However, in some cases (e.g., Excerpts 7.14), the communication value of their speech is highly restrictive. As pointed out by Candlin et al. (2000), such dynamic and rich communicative features of young people's discourses, if transposed into English, might be conducive to language learning. What could be done to enable students to transpose their dynamic communication practices from L1 to L2? It seems that how these language practices can be capitalized on to empower the students as second language learners and users is an issue that needs to be further explored.

QUESTIONS FOR REFLECTION AND DISCUSSION

1. In your opinion, had Ms. Berner and Mr. Nelson understood Cantonese, would students' playful but sometimes indecent phonological play still occur?

2. How would you react upon hearing playful but impish and nonsensical verbal play from students such as that presented in Excerpts 8.1 and 8.3?

3. How frequent do you have social talk with your students? As a NET/LET, do you see any difficulties or dilemmas in doing social talk with students? For example, would some students take advantage of the friendly relationship and sidetrack the lesson? How can you strike a balance?

4. Do you think it is appropriate for teachers to tease students, or for students to tease the teacher? From your experience, or in your opinion, what would be the advantages or disadvantages for students and teachers to have mutual teasing openly in a classroom?

5. Will you display similar discourse as Ms. Berner in Excerpt 8.15? Will you allow students to draw on slang words such as **kau-nui** (if you understand what it means) during the lesson even though they might show that some learning is taking place? Please explain.

6. If you were Mr. Sze, upon knowing how your class had behaved indecently in the NET's lessons (such as Excerpt 8.14), would you do something to reprimand the students? Why? Why not?

9

Performing "Teachers" and "Students"

TUNING-IN DISCUSSION

1. If you hear expressions such as "Order!" "Objection!," you will immediately think of law courts and barristers. What language or utterances can you think of that signify somebody's identity as "teachers" or "students"?

2. As teachers, do you speak the teacher's "language"? By what means do you think you have acquired that "language"?

To many sociolinguists and pragmatists, it is an interesting topic to debate whether people talk the way they do because of who they (already) are, or people are who they are because of (among other things) the way they talk (Cameron, 1997, p. 49). We mentioned in chapter 5 Pennycook's (2003, p. 528) argument that "[i]t is not that people use language varieties because of who they are, but rather that we perform who we are by (amongst other things) using varieties of language." To the authors of this book, this may simply be a chicken-and-egg debate. We speak the way we speak because of who we are, and we construct who we are by the way we speak. For example, a person utters "objection" in court because he or she is a barrister. On the other hand, the way the person talks and the words they use also identify them as a barrister making a case in court. The important point here is not to essentialize our own identities (i.e., who we are) but to always recognize that our identities can be multiple, conflicting, and fluid, constantly being negotiated and renegotiated. In sociolinguistic terms, somebody's identity is performed through words, in the same vein as Austin's (1962) doing things with words (see footnote 26). According to this strand of sociolinguists, those utterances characteristic of the speech of a barrister do not "preexist" as part of the speech register of that barrister, nor is the identity of a barrister pregiven. The discourse and the identity are both constructed and performed situationally. However, although we totally agree that a person's identity is socially and discursively constructed rather than pregiven, we believe that a performance of that identity through words is not a totally original, creative act. Somebody somewhere sometime must have used similar utterances to perform or discharge a similar identity. This is how Bakhtin's concept of voice comes in useful. Bakhtin (1986) pointed out that every word comes to us already filled with meanings and overtones constructed by someone else who used the same word before. Therefore "the word in a language is half someone else's" (p. 293). For example, when we use the word "handsome" to describe a person, usually a male, we have the awareness and knowledge of how the word has conventionally been used (e.g., smart, good-looking) and we would use it with that awareness in mind. Of course, as further explained by Bakhtin, conventional meanings of an utterance can be "reaccentuated" ironically, indignantly, reverently, and so forth. As shown in chapter 8, some students of Mr. Nelson and Mr. Williams showed signs of using the word "handsome" with an implied meaning different from its conventional meaning known to most people. The students probably did it to assert a form of self-representation that redefines literacy and situated language use, and to construct, affirm, or accentuate a power relation that is casual and nonhierarchical with the teachers. It also shows how people fashion and refashion an identity and relationship with words they use.

The focus of the present chapter is on how the teachers and students performed their "teachership" (or teacher identity) and "studentship" (or student identity) in an institutional setting through words, and how they further asserted and/or refashioned their institutional identities by what they said. We are working on the assumption that both the teachers and the students have brought to the school and classroom settings an awareness and knowledge of how to act and speak like teachers and students of an institutional configuration. In chapters 7 and 8, some such data showing how the teachers and students participated in the lessons has already been presented, sometimes as institutionally expected but sometimes not. In this chapter, we further explore how the teachers and students perform their typical institutional identity through discourse practices, and also in the process, assert, invent, or construct other identities.

There are two broad sections—Performing "Teachers," and Performing "Students." Of course, we understand that in classroom encounters, teachers and students cannot be teased apart, but the two sections only reflect our focuses of the discussion. In the teachers' section, we present data and discuss the discursive practices displayed by the NETs and LETs in motivating, or coercing students into teaching activities, a crucial role of being a teacher. In the students' section, we show how some students performed their student identity in teacher-assigned tasks, often with a self-designed or self-chosen identity. We also show how tension and conflict sometimes arose due to incongruent lesson agendas between teachers and students, and resistance from students toward authoritative discourses.

PERFORMING "TEACHERS"—GETTING STUDENTS ON TASK

With the advent of the communicative approach to language learning, the level of student participation in classroom activities has become a key indicator of effective language learning (e.g., Savignon, 1991). The concept of participation is also gaining importance from a sociocultural perspective. Pavlenko and Lantolf (2000) argued that second language learning is "a struggle of concrete socially constituted and always situated beings to *participate* [italics added] in the symbolically mediated lifeworld ... of another culture" (p. 155). Even though most ESL teachers may not have this sociohistorical and social constructionist view in mind, motivating students to take an active part in classroom activities is almost always their first and foremost concern.

According to classroom discourse analysts such as Sinclair and Coulthard (1975) and Mehan (1979), pedagogical activities in the classrooms are mainly performed with three major types of functional acts; *elicitation* (e.g., What is the name of the story?), *directive* (e.g., Take out your story book), and *informative* (e.g., We are going to read chap. 4). Through these functional acts, students are engaged in classroom tasks. The acts are also found by Mehan (1979, p. 36) to be closely related to different phases of the lesson. For example, the directive and informative sequences contribute to the opening and closing phases, whereas the instructional phase is composed primarily of elicitation sequences. In explicating the different functions of directive and elicitation, Mehan (1979, p. 49) held that "the directive calls for respondents to take procedural action, such as opening books, or moving to see the board in preparation for instruction ... directives and informatives 'frame' the elicitation of academic information that comprises the interior of lessons." Classroom data from the present study, however, reveals that the distribution need not be that clear cut. The three functional acts were often found to appear together in a sequence for a unified purpose in different stages of the lessons observed. In whatever lesson stages these functional acts appeared, the ultimate objective was to ensure that students were cognitively and mentally engaged in the lesson activities, or tasks, administered by the teachers.

In the rest of this section, we show how the teachers employed a combination of discourse practices to get students on task. We first show how directives were used for procedural and pedagogical advisory purposes. We then show how the teachers in this study attempted to employ different discourse strategies[91] [such as code switching, prosodic variations, contextualization cues and signaling resources; see Gumperz, 1982] to engage passive or nonconforming students in the lesson activities. Factors affecting the effectiveness of these strategies are discussed subsequently.

Directives for Procedural Control

Teachers have traditionally used directives as a form of "control talk" (Cazden, 1986), achieving procedural purposes. The use of directives reveals the asymmetrical power relationships between teachers and students in the classroom as they are usually realized as imperatives in linguistic form by the teachers. However, with increased awareness of a more democratic student-centered pedagogical approach, researchers have looked at more indirect directives, often realized as other linguistic forms such as declaratives and interrogatives. These variations reveal what Fairclough (1995) termed as the "democratization of discourse" that refers to the "reduction of overt markers of power asymmetry between people of unequal institutional power—teachers and students" (p. 79). Data from the present study reveal the use of a variety of linguistic acts by the teachers for directing purposes, ranging from least to most direct and authoritative as illustrated in Table 9.1.

The stereotypical Chinese tradition that renders teachers high respect and authority easily makes one think that the LETs may be more prone to employing the strong command and direct types of imperatives in directing students for procedural and pedagogical purposes, whereas NETs would be more prone to employing the other end of the scale. Data from the present study, however, indicate that whereas all teachers used mainly types 3, 4, and 5, types 1 and 2 (most direct and authoritative) appeared extensively in Miss Logan's 2D and Mr. Williams' 4E and 2E, probably

TABLE 9.1
Directives With Varying Degrees of Authoritativeness

Most direct & authoritative	1.	Strong command, e.g., Listen! Shut up!
	2.	Shushing, e.g. shhhhhh…
	3.	Direct imperatives, e.g., Take out your ERS books.
	4.	Polite imperatives, e.g., Take out your books, please.
	5.	Declaratives, e.g., I'd like/want to have three volunteers.
	6.	Teacher-inclusive imperatives as suggestions, e.g., Let's write it on the board.
	7.	Interrogatives as requests, e.g., Can you move forward?
	8.	Interrogatives as suggestions, e.g., Shall we do exercise one now?
Least direct & authoritative	9.	Interrogatives as invitations, e.g., Would you like to try the next one?

because most students in these classes were less well disciplined. Occasional shushings occurred in Ms. Berner's lessons, but were seldom or never observed in classes by Ms. Hung, Mr. Nelson, and Mr. Sze. In the next two subsections, we illustrate how the teachers perfomed directive discourses at both ends.

Illustrating the Least Authoritative Directive Discourse

Mr. Sze provided a striking example of using a lot of items 7 to 9 on the scale to achieve procedural and instructional actions. On several occasions during the first author's visits, Mr. Sze walked into the classroom without immediately starting the lesson. He would spend a few seconds chatting with individual students, sometimes about their homework and sometimes about their behavior. He mainly used Cantonese but sometimes English.[92] After that he would raise the volume of his voice and say to the whole class something such as "Can we start now?" or (after reminding students that they were doing dictation) "Would you like to take it (their dictation book) out now?" On these occasions, students usually replied with a loud, elongated, and exaggerating "YE::S," or said nothing but took the relevant actions.

The first author raised this issue during the postdata collection interview with Mr. Sze and asked him if he thought he was a democratic teacher and if he had ever worried that the students would respond negatively. He replied that, in the first place, he did not notice he had been doing something very different from other teachers. If his students deliberately responded negatively in order to challenge his authority, which had not happened before, he would make them realize who was the "master" of the classroom (but he did not elaborate what he would do). In his interpretation, he presented directives as interrogatives in order to establish a friendly, democratic, and relaxed atmosphere in his lessons. He felt that the students would feel that they were being respected. He added that if students did respond negatively, they might just be playing. With difficult classes such as 1D, Mr. Sze said that he would minimize such linguistic acts and project a more authoritative figure of a teacher. Mr. Sze's justification perhaps reflects Fairclough's (1995) observation that the appearance of democratized discourse may only mean that the previously overt forms of control have been transformed into covert forms; for example, teachers may exercise control through speaking turns allocation, indirect requests, and so forth.

Like Mr. Sze, Mr. Williams was also observed using interrogatives as directives in a seemingly very democratic way by getting students to begin the lesson. However, the effect and consequence were not quite the same. It perhaps shows that the effectiveness of certain strategies for achieving a particular purpose is highly context-specific. Excerpt 9.1 shows how it happens.

Excerpt 9.1.   #Williams (4E, 22/04/99)

This excerpt describes what happened in the first 3 minutes of a lesson early in the morning. When Mr. Williams entered the classroom, many students were shouting and talking to each other in Cantonese. Mr. Williams said nothing and only started talking to the students after entering the classroom for about 2 minutes.

1. NET: Four E, are you all awake this morning?
2. Ss: No.
3. NET: Have you all finished breakfast?
4. Ss: No.
5. NET: Are you all ready to do some English?
6. Ss: No. [A few male students say yes very softly.]
7. NET: Good. [Ss laugh] Nothing, nothing unusual then today. Okay, I don't- you don't need anything at this moment apart from the pen. You don't need anything apart from the pen. [Voice volume increases.] <Are you listening?>
8. Ss: [in a perfunctory manner]Yeah yeah.

Mr. Williams' interrogatives in turns 1 & 3 seem to be made for socialization purposes. The authors have seen local teachers ask similar questions as a kind of ice-breaker, or conversation-opener. Students' chorus responses in turns 2 & 4 are not unusual taking into consideration the time of the lesson and the habit of many Hong Kong students to skip breakfast due to waking up late. Mr. Williams' last interrogative in turn 5, however, merits a critical interpretation. As experienced teachers, the authors would interpret Mr. Williams' "Are you ready to do some English?" as a rhetorical question that signals the beginning of the lesson. On the surface, it serves the same democratic function as Mr. Sze's "Can we …?" and "Would you want to …?" What is interesting about Mr. Williams' interrogative is the negative response from many, if not all, of the students to his questions. Of course the last "no" from the students may only be a result of playful bantering between the teacher and the students, which was a common feature of Mr. Williams' lessons. Still, it sounds a bit embarrassing. Local teachers might just pretend not to have heard it and begin the lesson anyway, or ask the students what they want to do then, or show dissatisfaction by talking about the proper behavior of students and how valuable the limited lesson time is. Mr. Williams, however, accepts students' negative response as normal with a positive evaluation remark "Good." The authors are not sure how much the students have sensed the sarcastic implication of the teacher on their general behavior by saying "nothing unusual," but from the students' laughter, we guess they received the teacher's ironic humor quite well.

Compared to Mr. Sze's experience described earlier in this section, Mr. Williams' attempt to democratize his discourse has met with different student reactions. It seems that Mr. Williams' 4E students tended to take the teacher's democratized discourse more literally than Mr. Sze's 1B class. They might be doing that just for the fun and excitement they would obtain from openly challenging the teacher. They might also be testing the teacher's limits for overt nonconforming behavior of students. A LET like Mr. Sze probably would not have opened up this opportunity for the students to play with their power, or the students would not have said "no" so directly and readily because their sociocultural knowledge of the Chinese traditional virtue of respecting the teachers would have reduced their readiness to challenge the local teachers just to avoid getting into unnecessary trouble because they know that most local teachers tend to take students' overt nonconforming behaviors very seriously.

Illustrating the Most Authoritative Directive Discourse

Among the six teachers, Mr. Williams seems to be the only one who has been observed to employ a range of directives for procedural control in his lessons, including directives from both ends. After illustrating his least authoritative directive discourse in Excerpt 9.1, we illustrate in the next excerpt one of his more authoritative examples.

Excerpt 9.2.   #Williams (2A, 23/04/99)

It happened at the very beginning of the second of a double lesson. In the first lesson, students have learned some prefixes. In this lesson, the teacher asked the class to design a board game to teach those English prefixes, and then explain their design to the whole class. However, most students could not do the explanation (see Excerpt 9.8). The teacher then decided to change the format of the task.

1. NET: I want you to take your drawing, and I want you to explain your game to the other group. And then they can explain their game to you. Okay now ALL the explanation must be in English.
   [A student makes a strange sound at this point. Other Ss remain silent.]
   (.) Okay? This is- it's no point in doing this if you are speaking in Cantonese, NO point, wasting our time, all the explanation must be in English, okay? Okay. So all the groups in this- (.) all the groups in this half of the room stay where you are, right? And all the groups from this part of the room- (.) now that won't work, will it? Too congested. Okay, find another group, find another group. Let's have everybody standing up, everybody standing up.
2. B: I don't want to stand up.
3. NET: I don't CARE what you want to do, I am the BOSS I'm telling you stand UP! Okay come on everybody stand up, stand up. (…) [noises of chairs and desks moving]

Throughout this Excerpt, Mr. Williams uses a lot of direct imperatives in turn 1 that reveals the teacher's expectation for absolute observance of his instructions from the students. When B publicly expresses his refusal to follow the teacher's instruction (turn 2), Mr. Williams exercises his authority (turn 3) with a forceful directive containing three strongly stressed words (CARE, BOSS, and UP). Similar statements from Mr. Williams appeared twice in this lesson. In the other one, after shouting "SHUT UP," he said, "I talk and you have to listen okay?" In the postobservation interview, the first author explored Mr. Williams' rapport with these classes. Surprisingly, Mr. Williams did not express any bad feelings toward the students' behavior (which was unlike Ms. Berner who said explicitly that her 1A was a headache). He thought that teachers should show their emotions and exercise their authority when situations warranted it. Mr. Sze expressed similar views that even though he tried to be democratic and relaxed with the students, when things went wrong, he would make students know who was in charge. Because no data showing Mr. Sze exercising his authority have been captured, we could not make any comparisons here. However, it seems that even though Mr. Williams and Mr. Sze came from different backgrounds, they shared similar perspectives that staying in control of the classroom activities is part of a teacher's performance. As regards possible factors causing students' resistance in Excerpt 9.2, more discussion is given after presenting Excerpt 9.8.

Directives for Advisory Purposes

Directives have traditionally been linked with the achievement of procedural verbal and nonverbal actions. In our data, however, there are occasions where directives were used to give advice. The data came from Ms. Hung's 1E class when she used directives to advise students on desirable reading behavior. Excerpt 9.3 shows how it happens.

Excerpt 9.3.   #Hung (1E, 12/10/98)

This is an ERS lesson. Ms. Hung asked students to come to the front of the class to conduct reading conferences with her. In this excerpt, she is checking one student's reading record.

1   LET: Na[93] this is, yeah, this is something important. (.) So for important

2   things, if you don't understand this this is a very important thing this

3   →   is the title, then (.) you must look up in the dictionary,

4   →   and then, think about the story,

5   →   and write it down there (.) okay? you can write it here,

6   the meaning f-foul play (.) now I'll ask you next time what foul play

7   means, okay?

8 → So remember when you read a story you must, understand it.

9 → If you don't understand it, you MUST find a way to try to understand

10 → it, either look it up in the dictionary? or ask some other classmates?

11 → or ask the teacher(.)

12 huh, otherwise you can't, enjoy this story (..)

13 → Try to set a::, target.

Lines marked with an arrow in Excerpt 9.3 contain directives most of which are direct imperatives, and conditionals with obligatory modals ("must"). They are used by Ms. Hung to advise the student concerned on the kind of desirable reading habits, and the steps and procedures in reading he should develop. In fact, the use of the modals "have to," "should," and "must" appeared very frequently in this ERS lesson. Apart from this excerpt, Ms. Hung was found in this lesson to have used quite a few directives of this nature with other students:

> *"Before you go to bed, uh, spare twenty minutes, it's very very useful, it's very good."*

> *"Try to read a bit more every day, alright? Huh, and then you have to read about 10, this much okay? Thank you."*

> *"If you think the E books are too difficult, ehm, then you'd better read F books."*

This kind of "advisory directive" has also been captured in some of Ms. Hung's other lessons when she commented on students' performance in an oral presentation task at the beginning of every lesson with a view to training students for the public exam. Most of the advisory directives given by Ms. Hung as illustrated in Excerpt 9.3 and other lessons done by her are not for immediate effect. For example, Ms. Hung often said, "Next time, you speak louder."

Interestingly, advisory directives like the one made by Ms. Hung have not been found in other participants' ERS lessons. According to Yu (1997), teachers are expected to hold regular conferences with individual students in ERS lessons to discuss "their reading habits, reading strategies, reading attitudes, share thoughts and ideas about the books they have read" (p. 5). Although several ERS lessons (by Mr. William, Miss Logan, Ms. Berner, and Ms. Hung) were observed, only Ms. Hung and Ms. Berner had conducted formal reading conferences with the students.[94] However, Ms. Berner only shared with the students thoughts and ideas about the books they read and had not done what Ms. Hung had done to develop students' reading habits and attitudes. This may reflect what Ms. Hung expressed in an interview, that apart from teaching the language, she should also be responsible for promoting the "all-round development" of the students (see interview data, chap. 6). Ms. Hung's explicit urging and expectations on the desirable behavior of the students outside school probably reflected her Chinese traditional concepts of being a teacher who, apart from imparting subject knowledge, should guide students to develop proper behavior as a student, which includes a good attitude toward learning.

Engaging Reticent or Nonconforming Students

Tsui (1996) has comprehensively documented Hong Kong students' reticence and passiveness in second language classrooms. Whether this is due to anxiety, lack of motivation, lack of knowledge to respond, or a tendency to avoid public display of knowledge in front of peers, their reluctance, and sometimes resistance, to respond to the teachers' elicitation, or to participate actively in the teacher-designed activities have been a big headache and challenge to many teachers. In our data, cases where the students concerned were not responding or participating as expected by the teachers are by no means uncommon. Different teachers were observed employing different communication and discourse strategies to engage the students and to keep the lessons in progress, ranging from a more authoritative type to a more affective type. We present these strategies in the following sections beginning with the most authoritative type.

Exercising Authority

Getting students on task by exercising teachers' institutional authority appeared in three teachers' lessons, those of Mr. Williams, Miss Logan, and Mr. Nelson. We have already shown how Mr. Williams used this strategy in Excerpt 9.2 to command a nonconforming pupil to follow his instructions by claiming to be the "boss" of the class. Whereas Mr. Williams' attempt to exercise authority produced some impact as shown in Excerpt 9.2, Miss Logan's use of authority in 2D, which will be shown in the following excerpt, was not as effective. According to Miss Logan and some other local teachers, 2D was notorious for poor classroom discipline. The fact that Miss Logan only saw the class for two lessons per week[95] made the situation worse because it was difficult for the teacher and students to establish a good rapport. The lesson from which the following excerpt emerges is a double lesson (80 minutes long) on extensive reading and oral activities. The school placed great expectations on Miss Logan as a native speaker to develop the students' English oral skills, and therefore she had to take at least one oral lesson with almost all classes in the school. The interaction presented in Excerpt 9.4 show how the whole business of oral practice fails to work and how Miss Logan exercises her authority in an attempt to get things in order.

Excerpt 9.4.   #Logan (2D, 31/03/00)

The teacher began some oral work after the students had done the ERS lesson. During the ERS lesson, most students were chatting in Cantonese under the cover of their storybooks. Then in the oral lesson, very few students paid attention to the teacher when the latter attempted to conduct an oral activity. In this excerpt, the teacher exercises her authority by threatening to send students outside the classroom, and take up their lunchtime if they continue to behave poorly. Due to the length of the whole incident that lasted for about 3 minutes, only significant utterances are presented. The counter numbers in (( )) [(5 sec for every 0.1)] marks the approximate interval between utterances.

At the beginning of this excerpt, the teacher was revising some vocabulary items (names of fixtures in an apartment) the students were expected to use in the oral activity "Finding Grandma's False Teeth."

1. NET: ((39.4)) Make sure that you know all these words. What's this?
   [Some Ss answer. T repeats items from Ss if correct. Same pattern repeats 3 times.]
   {....}
2. NET: ((40.1))Write the word on this, sink, or wash basin, I should see all of you with your pens writing the words, here. (...) S-I-N-K, sink.
   (Ss are chatting, noise level begins to rise)
   {....}
3. ((40.6))[Ss sitting near the recorder talk about their English test results. One says that he has got only 16 marks.]
4. NET: [with voice raised] <I think> some of you want to go outside.
   [Some Ss shush and become quiet for 2 seconds.]
5. NET: It's clear that you don't want to listen to me, you don't want to learn and study English.
   [3 to 4 boys are still talking, 1 or 2 more begin to join]
   [T writes on the board.]
   {...}
6. NET: ((41.2)) I think I just have to stay here for lunch time if this continues.
   [One B says 'OH'.]
7. NET: ((41.5))[to two boys near the recorder arguing in Cantonese, very gently] Alright, stand up, I had enough of this, stand up. (.) [a bit louder] <Stand UP!>
8. B: **Zung-hou laa** <*That's better*>. [This utterance is clear on the recording.]
9. NET: When I think you can stop talking, I will let you sit down again.
10. B: Och, okay.

It seems quite clear from Excerpt 9.4 that the teacher does most of the task-related talking. Students' responses to Miss Logan's elicitations are indistinct (they often could hardly be recognized on our recordings) and often overwhelmed by other students' chatting and laughing. Being present in the lesson, the first author felt extremely uneasy about the lesson atmosphere. Before exercising her authority, Miss Logan made an attempt to appeal to students' sense of responsibility with a negative assertion "You don't want to learn and study English" (turn 5), but to no effect. Even her exercising of authority does not seem to have generated too much impact. Most students in the class either continue to talk and laugh in Cantonese and ignore the teacher, or to look dull and expressionless. Sending one pupil out of the classroom and threatening to take away more time of the students' lunch break have not stopped some students from chatting. When the bell rang, Miss Logan allowed most students to leave, just keeping five to six students behind. However, when they gathered in the front of the classroom standing around the teacher, the teacher said nothing to them. The first author asked the students in Cantonese if they thought they should apologize to Miss Logan, most just had their heads drooped, smiled with embarrassment, but said nothing. Miss Logan sat in front of them for a while and then asked them to leave. The first author did not mention this incident with Miss Logan in the postobservation meeting because she could sense that Miss Logan did not want to talk about it.

Is Miss Logan's experience a unique problem with the NETs? We believe most local teachers would not find these disciplinary problems surprising. They are rather common in classrooms with young or novice teachers. However, Miss Logan was not a particularly young or novice teacher during our study. Her strategies in handling the class were quite popular among local teachers too. Asking students to stand at the back of the classroom, or depriving misbehaving students of their recess and lunchtime were some of the disciplinary strategies the authors, particularly the first author, employed when we were secondary school teachers.[96] In this respect, Miss Logan seemed to have already mastered some locally popular strategies in performing the disciplinary role of a teacher. However, from the authors' personal experience, these strategies usually generate only temporary effects, perhaps because the high-handed or threatening nature of these measures does little to motivate the students to participate in the lesson. The question is, apart from employing these strategies, what else could Miss Logan have done in such a situation?

The authors (Lin & Luk, 2002) documented how a young and inexperienced student teacher, Tracy (a pseudo name), tackled chaotic disciplinary problems in a working-class school, quite like those experienced by Miss Logan, on the first day of her teaching practice, and succeeded in motivating the students to get on with the task. Tracy did so by stopping the cooperative learning pair work with which students were not familiar, and talked to them in Cantonese for 15 minutes about how she struggled with learning English when she was young in an underprivileged environment. She encouraged the students to value the opportunities of learning English and assured them that they all would achieve what she had. This example perhaps shows that resistant students like those with Tracy and Miss Logan might respond better to the teacher's attempt to negotiate than to discipline with high authority. One benefit, therefore, for bilingual ESL teachers such as Tracy is that they could do this negotiation and affective sharing of personal experiences and feelings in the students' L1. Several students from 2E, another difficult class of Miss Logan, expressed during the interview that they were happy to be taught by Miss Logan (because she spoke "better" English), but they were also unhappy because Miss Logan could not handle the discipline of the class. Most of their classmates did not respond to the teacher because they did not understand what she was doing. One pupil said that it would be much better if Miss Logan knew Cantonese. Of course, these comments came from a class considered to be weak in academic performance. As suggested in chapter 7, students should bear some of the responsibility in the process of sense making in the classroom. After all, students from a better class of Miss Logan, 2B, did not feel that they had serious communication problems[97] with the teacher because they would pay attention to the teacher's explanations and paralinguistic aids such as gestures and drawings. However, the situation presented in Excerpt 9.4 might reveal the difficulties and constraints of a NET in handling uncooperative and unmotivated students if they do not understand the students' L1 and do not share students' experience in growing up and studying in Hong Kong.

Mr. Nelson is another teacher who was observed to have resorted to his authority to deal with nonconforming students. As is shown, his case is quite different from those of Mr. Williams and Miss Logan. Whereas the latter two conveyed a connotation of anger when exercising their authority, Mr. Nelson did it in a light-hearted way. Mr. Nelson's students were generally highly motivated for their study. Even though most of them were more interested in science subjects and inevitably putting less effort into learning English, they knew the importance of English for passing exams and their further studies. The students occasionally showed signs of resistance for the teacher's teaching methods, perhaps only to see if they could take advantage of the teacher's leniency for their own benefits. The following excerpt shows one such instance.

Excerpt 9.5.   #Nelson (4E, 17/03/99)

This took place almost at the end of a drama writing lesson. The teacher is talking to a student who fails to produce anything substantial after the activity has been going on for more than 30 minutes.

1. NET: I haven't seen a drama being written yet.
2. B: Is that (???) [inaudible speech]
3. NET: I want to see this, otherwise, I'll make you stay after school to do it.
4. B: Really?
5. NET: Yes!
6. B: I don't think so.
7. NET: I think so.
8. B: I think you can't.
9. NET: I CAN [amused but serious and firm in tone]

Mr. Nelson threatens to detain "B" after school to finish his drama (turn 3), a threat the student doubts (turn 4). A possible reason may be due to the image of Mr. Nelson, who appeared to the first author to be very gentle and friendly. From the first author's observation, most students seemed to be treating him as their friend, and not so much as a "teacher" in the Confucian tradition. During our postobservation interview, Mr. Nelson asked the first author if she found some students' insulting comments on him unacceptable, for example, calling him "stupid." The first author told him the students might have perceived their relationship with him as rather egalitarian. They might have gone too far in front of a NET, thinking that NETs were more open minded and democratic (the students' general cultural stereotypes of NETs). When asked about what he thought, Mr. Nelson said that he basically enjoyed being the students' friend, but he had a baseline that students should not cross; otherwise, he would exercise his authority as their teacher. Over this point, Mr. Nelson's view seems to concur with Mr. Sze's.

In the next two instances, the NET concerned appealed to an external authority, that of a local teacher, to urge students to do something. One such instance happened in Mr. Williams's 2E lesson. Another one happened with Miss Logan.

Excerpt 9.6.   #Williams (2E, 20/04/99)

1. NET: ERS no book?
2. B: //because
3. NET: //Oh DEAR!=
4. B: =Tomorrow I'll buy.
5. NET: Okay, alright so you need to explain to Ms. Wong, and she is going to (.) Ms. Wong, yeah, Joseph, Ms. Wong is going to kill you, isn't she? (.) Okay, well, it's alright with me but you have to explain to Ms. Wong as well. Have you got the reading book? Reading book? Alright, okay.

Ms. Wong was the English panel chairperson. Asking the student to explain his absent-mindedness to Ms. Wong certainly adds to the seriousness of the case. Although forgetting to bring a book is not a big issue and Mr. Williams might just want to tease the student, this instance perhaps also reflects Mr. Williams' perception of the power differentiation between himself and Ms. Wong. He has also established a different image of himself and Ms. Wong—he seems more lenient and would accept the pupil's explanation, whereas Ms. Wong appears more "fearsome" (turn 5, "going to kill you"). During the extensive reading lessons, Ms. Wong and Mr. Williams were present in the classroom. Although Mr. Williams was the class's regular English teacher, the students seemed to behave more appropriately in the presence of Ms. Wong. They became noisier whenever Ms. Wong left the classroom and much quieter once she came back. Mr. Williams' appeal to external authority seemed to be effective. However, the first author had several interactions with Ms. Wong and found that she was a gentle teacher. The authority that Ms. Wong enjoyed probably did not come from the fact that she was a fierce teacher. Rather, her position as the English panel chairperson probably put her on a higher hierarchical status than Mr. Williams in the students' perceptions. In the next excerpt, Miss Logan did not portray a fierce or fearsome image of the local teachers, but similar to Mr. Williams, she appealed to the authority of the local homeroom teacher.

Excerpt 9.7.   #Logan (2D, 31/03/00)

This is also an ERS lesson.

1. NET: Take out your ERS book.
2. B: No no no, no no no, no no no no no [singing in the tune of "Jingle Bells"]
3. NET: (…)But you know that you have ERS today.

   (0.6) Next time, I am going to take the names of students who have forgotten^ [Ss' noise gets higher, talking and laughing in Cantonese. T raises her pitch] Students who have forgotten their ERS book, I'll take your name and give it to your homeroom teacher.

   [Some Ss shush.]

In Miss Logan's case, even though she only saw the students for two lessons every 7 school days, in normal situations, she should take full responsibility for the discipline of the class during her own lessons. From the long pausing in turn 3, it seems that Miss Logan is considering a way to handle this difficult class. The first author remembers when she started teaching after university, she also took advantage of the special status of the homeroom or class teacher to discipline misbehaving students. Some experienced teachers later told the first author that unless the situation was beyond control, this strategy might not be effective because she might have looked incompetent in functioning as an independent teacher in the eyes of the students. The comment from some of Miss Logan's students during the interviews on her inability to handle disciplinary problems (see analysis after Excerpt 9.4) perhaps reflects the undesirable effect of resorting to external authority in handling minor issues such as not bringing their textbooks.

Two more strategies for engaging reticent and/or nonconforming students that are not authoritative in nature are presented in the rest of this section, "Making Concessions," and "Appealing to Students' Face." As can be expected, these strategies vary in their overall effectiveness. We begin with what seems to be less effective. It should be noted that strategies classified under each category reveal specific core focus, but may share overlapping features.

Making Concessions

Making concessions means the teacher changes the original plan of the activities because of few or inappropriate student responses. These concessions could take different forms, but usually result in less desirable pedagogical outcomes compared to what is originally expected. In Excerpt 9.8, we show how Mr. Williams makes concessions by speaking for the students. In Excerpt 9.9, we show how Miss Logan changes from one task to another so that her students could be exempted from the original task altogether. Then in Excerpts 9.10 and 9.11, Ms. Berner and Ms. Hung reduce the level of difficulty of their tasks to obtain more active pupil participation. The following excerpt of Mr. Williams' 2A shares the same context as Excerpt 9.2 but took place before that. The students were asked to design a board game to teach antinomy. Toward the end of the lesson, Mr. Williams invited some pairs of students to come out to explain in front of the class the design of their games. Excerpt 9.8 shows what happened to the first pair of students.

Excerpt 9.8.   #Williams (2A, 23/04/99)

1. NET: Yes, you ca-, come on, Rainy, you can explain it.
2. R: (??)
3. NET: I know you haven't finished but you can still explain it.
    [Some girls seem to be arguing and saying somebody else's name.]
4. NET: Oh, dear me! Dear me! Shuuuu!
    [A boy repeats the T's "Oh dear me!" in a playful manner three times.]
5. NET: (0.6) [probably responding to some Ss' speech but indistinct on the tape] You can't criticize because you wouldn't stand up and do yours. Rainy, Vincy, come on, somebody's got to explain that game. (…) Right okay, quiet please, shu shu shu shu shu shu.
6. (0.7) [The girls come out.]
7. NET: Okay quiet ple:ase. Again, can you hold it up Vincy, hold it up, Ellen, come on, face this way please. Again, it's not finished, but you can get, you can get an idea of how the game would work. Can you see these pictures, Tammy, can you see these pictures from the back. (..) Mh, it's difficult. Okay, the idea is, that you have, you have the words written on the board, and then some, and then the prefixes written here on like a, like a, right, like a note pad and you can flick through all of the prefixes to find the one which goes with the word, [turning to Rainy and Vincy] and how do you know when it is right?
8. (…) [The girls begin to talk to each other in Cantonese, laughing.]
9. NET: (…) Okay ehh (.) shuuuuu shu shu shu! JACK! So the right answer (.) the right answer is written, behind the word, you can lift the word and have a look, check the answer underneath, thank you very much, but why didn't you say that? Okay, thank you, sit down.

When Rainy and Vincy still fail to produce the explanation after much pleading and encouragement from the teacher, the teacher attempts to do the explanation himself (turn 7, lines 5–8). When he feels that he has done enough demonstration and attempts to involve the girls in the explanation by raising a display question in turn 7 ("how do you know when it is right"), he finds that even after a long pause, the girls cannot produce an appropriate response (turn 8). His last resort is to continue the explanation himself and send the girls back to their seats after thanking them (turn 9).

From our experience, this kind of scenario is not unusual and probably may happen frequently in local teachers' classroom. The first author remembers when she tried to conduct a similar activity in the first year of her teaching career, similar student performance scared her off from conducting a comparable activity again, putting all the blame on the students' passivity. Mr. Williams' unsuccessful attempts to get other students to explain their games in the rest of the lesson seem to suggest that his strategy to speak for the students and demonstrate how the task could be done has not been very effective. The students' attempts to avoid doing the explanation could be understood from the following perspective. Given the sociocultural background of the students (most came from working classes), their conventional learning styles, which are being produced and reproduced by the ways they are taught in many working class schools, (e.g., being more accustomed to reproducing text in chorus), and rather limited English proficiency, doing a spontaneous presentation in English in public was an extremely difficult task for them. From what has been observed, the students dared not reject the teacher's request directly, nor did they totally ignore the teacher. It may be because the students picked by the teacher were the better ones and they perceived this to be the students' obligation to perform in class. However, they were reluctant to do it partly because they probably had not experienced this kind of task before and partly because they did not know how to begin. When they were called on, they looked at each other, laughed uneasily, and stood up very slowly. Almost 10 min (out of a 40-min lesson) were spent on this stage of the lesson with either dead air, or Cantonese chats and giggles among the students. It seems that the students may need more explicit instruction by the teacher on how to formulate an explanation relevant to the task (see Lin & Luk, 2002 for the importance of giving clear instructions and explanations of task goals especially among working-class students who are not used to task requirements in middle class progressive pedagogies). Just watching the teacher do it once seems insufficient. However, Mr. Williams does not seem to realize the crux of the problem.[98] He later changed the format of the presentations (see Excerpt 9.2) so that students explained their design to one another. This change might promote interaction (could be in L1 or L2) among the students, but might not necessarily enable the students to master the institutionally expected skills of presentation.

In contrast, Miss Logan in the next excerpt makes concessions so that students could avoid doing the original task altogether. Excerpt 9.9 comes from the same lesson as Excerpt 9.4.

Excerpt 9.9.   #Logan (2D, 31/03/00)

After preparing students for the relevant vocabulary items and structures, Miss Logan attempted to conduct an oral activity "Finding Grandma's False Teeth" with the whole class. She tries to elicit questions from the students about the whereabouts of grandma's false teeth. Due to the length of the transcripts, only the significant parts are presented. The counter number in (( )) shows the approximate length of the incident, with 0.1 representing 5 seconds.

1. NET: ((47.8))You can ask me some questions now. Are they in the bla bla bla? Are they under the bla bla bla? (.) Can you guess? (..) Yes, are they-? (.) Oh, they are not in the toi-, they are not in the bathroom cabinet, they are NOT under the towel, they are NOT under the bed, they are NOT in the sink.

   [NET's voice raises a bit] <Any> questions? [Ss shush.]

2. {....}((48.6—49.1: T continues to prompt Ss for the target language.))

3. NET: Okay, 10 minutes for you two, 10 minutes of your lunch time, you are staying here.

   [some sounds of surprise and laughter from the students]

4. NET: Question, are they in the bath? No they're not. [tapping on the board]

   [T continues to ask and answer with similar utterances]

   {....}((49.8))

5. NET: I'm not going to give you any sentences. (.) You just have to ask me. Right we're just practicing easy sentences. I know you can do it. Ask these questions to find out where the teeth are in the bed? I think you know all these words. Bed, What's this word—what's this thing? A place for you to keep your clothes. What's this called? (..) Wardrobe, okay, say the word, wardrobe.

6. Ss: [from very few] Wardrobe

7. NET: Write the word, W-A-R-D-R-O-B-E, wardrobe. [T goes on to revise "mat, table, chair, bed, etc."; most were revised before.]

   [after another initiation with no response from the Ss after 8 seconds]

8. [T goes on to revise "mat, table, chair, bed, etc."; most were revised before.]

   {....} ((51.7))

9. NET: [after another initiation with no response from the pps after 8 sec] Well okay we'll put these, papers away, I think we can throw them into the bins, most of us cos' you haven't listened, or learned or tried to practice any English, so we'll forget trying to speak any English,

10. (0.12) [Ss are chatting quietly.]

    {....}((52.3))

11. NET: I'll talk to you some listening (..) Right listen to what I tell you and then I'll ask you a question. (.) Right, this is-? I'm not even going to ask you, (.) because you will not talk to me.

12. [T explains the listening activity during which she tells Ss that 5 minutes will be taken away from their lunch time. Some Ss chuckle.]
   ((55.2))

13. NET: So if anybody was listening, you can tell me where is the fly, now. Where is the fly now? Near which number, you can see numbers, (..) Which number?
   [some tapping sounds made by the Ss, some laughter] Number^ (...) which number?

14. B: Seventeen.

15. NET: Seventeen, that's the one, (.) number?

16. B: Seven.

17. NET: Seven. Which lady had the fly in her mouth, the blonde lady or the dark lady?

18. B: Blonde.

19. NET: The blonde lady, okay (..) Okay, for the rest-, (.) for the rest of the lesson, you are going to write a description= (..) [T shows a picture on OHP] =of this picture. (..) You are going to describe this room. (..) I'll give you about 6 minutes to write the description.
   {....}((56.8))

20. NET: As you don't want to listen, you don't want to speak, so you can write. First of all, put your name on the top, everybody, write your name and number at the top of the paper. (...) <WRITE YOUR NAME AND NUMBER AT THE TOP OF THE PAPER>
   {....}((57.6))

21. NET: I will collect your writing at the end. No talking. You do not want to speak English, you may not speak Chinese. (..) you will write without speaking for the rest of the lesson.

The tension between the teacher and the students was strong in those two lessons. It can be seen in Excerpt 9.9 that in her attempt to elicit the target utterances from the students, Miss Logan has employed some other strategies before making the concessions. Like Mr. Williams, she demonstrates exemplar utterances (turn 1). She tries to scaffold some utterances with the students, and revise the vocabulary items again (turn 7). She also reassures the students of their competence to do this easy task (turn 5, "I know you can do it"). When all these strategies fail to produce much effect, in the face of the students' indifferent and unenthusiastic attitude, Miss Logan modifies the nature of her pedagogic activities two times. First she changes the oral activity into a listening one (turn 11), and then to a writing task (turn 19). The changes, ironically, are made so that the students do not need to have any direct interaction with the teacher, as is reiterated by the teacher in turns 20 and 21. This final concession seems to have defeated the major objective of having a NET to develop the students' oral abilities.

As discussed earlier in this chapter, a difficult class such as 2D is by no means unusual in Hong Kong and Miss Logan's experience is by no means unique. In fact, the lack of student responses is a common problem with even some good classes as evident in the next two excerpts with Ms. Berner and Miss Hung. It is interesting to compare how the two teachers employed other strategies, in addition to making concessions, in pursuit of student responses.

Excerpt 9.10.   #Berner (3B, 11/09/97)

In this excerpt, Ms. Berner prepared a year 3 class for a textbook-based listening task that is about two pop song groups. She tries to motivate the students by playing a song sung by one of the pop song groups. After playing the song, she tries to elicit the students' feedback on the song.

1. NET: Alright . Ehmm "Let it be" by the Beatles (.) Can you say anything about that song. Do you like it? (..) Yes? No? Do you like it? (..)
   //Put up your hand if you like the song (.) okay?
2. B: [very softly] //yes
3. NET: Uhm (..) if you look at the words of the song (.) do you think (..) it's a song which tells you (.) to be (.) um, happy? Peaceful? Optimistic? Hopeful? Or? Do you think it's a very, sad song? Does it say ehh, nothing works, everything's wrong? What do you think? Do you think it's a happy song or, that tells you to accept things, or do you think it's a sad song, which says there's no hope? Put up your hand if you think it's happy, (..) Put your hand up if you think it's sad. (..) Alright, if you think it's sad, let's have a look at the, the words.

In turn 1, Ms. Berner modifies her elicitation strategies from a request for free response (Can you say something about that song?), to a yes–no question (Do you like it?), and to a directive for physical response (Put up your hand if you like the song.). In turn 3, a similar cycle of elicitation is used. It seems to the authors that this cycle of strategies of Ms. Berner is a kind of involuntary concession made interactively in order for the lesson to proceed. Throughout Excerpt 9.10, most students have not said a word. Even though Ms. Berner is able to obtain some physical responses from the students by modifying her elicitation strategies, it is apparently not what the teacher desired. Actually, a similar concessional strategy (asking students to put up their hands as a means of expression) was employed two more times during the same lesson. Ms. Berner did most of the talking in that lesson. After the lesson, she talked about her disappointment over the students' behavior. By spending so much time identifying two songs to motivate the students, she expected a much more lively expression of opinions from the students. This might be similar to Tracy, the teacher-trainee's experience as described in Lin and Luk (2002). Tracy had thought that the song-listening cloze task (fill in blanks in the lyrics) would be attractive to her students, but to her disappointment, they did not seem enthusiastic. Tracy had to switch to Cantonese (the students' L1) to explain to them why she was doing this task with them and why this task was useful to them to motivate them to do the task.

Ms. Hung also experienced a frequent lack of response from her third-year class during a lesson in the first author's pilot study. In Excerpt 9.11 below, we show how Ms. Hung varies her elicitation strategies.

Except 9.11.   #Hung (3E, 12/10/98)

Ms. Hung is doing a class reader with 3E. The story is about a girl quitting school in order to get married.

1. LET: Green house, (.) green house[99] (.) Better life, whose better life? (…) Whose better life is it? (…) Do you know how to read the word? (..) Yes or no? Yes, whose better life is it? (…) If you know the answer, it's your duty to put up your hand. (.) Do you know a student's duty? (.) Yes or no? Okay, so it's your duty if you know the answer, you MUST, le:arn to put up your hand, yes?
2. B1: Peggy.
3. LET: Peggy very good. Ah, so it's Peggy. (.) Ah, Peggy's (..) better life (.) Yellow house, am I right?
4. B1: Yes.
5. LET: Thank you. (…) Right, (.) okay now, (…) ehm (…) what does, Peggy want to do? Na you've read the story, you know that Peggy wants a better life. (.) What is a better life for her? (..) What does she want to do in this story? What does she want to do? Okay, tell your neighbor now, what do YOU think Peggy wants to do.
6. [Ss begin to talk to one another]
7. LET: Okay? tell your neighbor, what does Peggy want to do? (.) Now pair work, you tell your neighbor what you think Peggy wants to do.
    (0.18) Does she want to get a job?

It can be seen in Excerpt 9.11 that when no responses from the students came forward, Ms. Hung used the following strategies:

1. pauses to wait;
2. repeats the questions in exact or similar wordings (turn 1, "Whose better life is it?"; turn 5, "What does Peggy want to do?");
3. appeals to student's sense of institutional roles and obligations in class (turn 1, lines 4–6, "Do you know a student's duty?");

4. transforms an information question (turn 5, "What does Peggy want to do?") into a yes–no question (turn 7, "Does she want to get a job?"); and

5. directs students for peer interaction (end of turn 5 and turn 7).

Of these five strategies, (1), (2), and (4) have also been adopted by Ms. Berner in Excerpt 9.10. It seems that Ms. Hung has more elicitation strategies at hand during silent responses from students. The use of (3) was in line with Ms. Hung's strong sense of obligation as a teacher who is also responsible for shaping the proper behavior of students, apart from transmitting knowledge. Strategy (5) seems to be the most effective as students actually begin to talk to one another. A bit different from that of Ms. Berner, Ms. Hung is able to elicit not just physical behavior, but verbal communication from the students. By standing very near some students in the classroom, the first author could hear that they were really talking about the story, very often in mixed code of Cantonese and English. This incident seems to have revealed that students' reluctance to respond may not be due to a lack of knowledge, but rather a lack of confidence in speaking English, or a reluctance to display knowledge in public for fear of getting it wrong and feeling embarrassed. Perhaps instead of requiring students to display their knowledge in public (i.e., in front of the whole class), which is face-threatening, the task could be designed to allow for alternative ways of displaying their knowledge, for example, students discuss answers to questions in small groups with the teacher circulating from group to group to listen to their answers.

Even though the four excerpts under this section show different natures of student reticence or silent response, they seem to share one thing in common, that is, they all reveal a certain degree of social incongruity between the home backgrounds (or habitus) of the students and the school performance expected by the teachers. In Mr. Williams's case, the discourse gaps produced by the class differences between the teacher and the students resulted in the students' passivity. In Miss Logan's case, "Finding Grandma's False Teeth" seems to be an activity totally detached from the students' everyday living experience (see Luk, 2005a, for related discussions). As for Ms. Berner's 3B and Ms. Hung's 3E, they were good classes with generally obedient and diligent students. Class 3B was sometimes rather dull but 3E had shown extremely active responses in some activities. One reason for their silences may again be due to the choice of pedagogical materials. In Ms. Berner's case, using pop (or ex-pop) singers as teaching content sounds fascinating, but the choice of Beatles and the Rolling Stones did not seem to be culturally appropriate to these young Hong Kong students who seem to be more keen on Canton pop media and music rather than on Western ones. Even the authors who were much older than these students had difficulties in identifying emotionally with these two pop groups that gained fame in the 1960s, not to say the students who were only 15 years old. Besides, the lyrics of the songs Ms. Berner had made great effort to locate seemed too difficult to the students because of the highly Western culture-specific and generation-specific ideologies (e.g., talking about Catholicism and drugs—the hippie culture of that generation in the 1960s in the West). Of course, the teacher should not take all the blame because the reading text that students were supposed to read was on these two pop groups. Most teachers in Hong Kong exercise the common practice of teaching according to the textbook topics. Even though junior forms do not have to do any public examinations, most teachers are under the pressure of covering a number of textbook chapters for the standardized internal examinations. From what the first author observed, most of the students in Excerpt 9.10 listened to the teacher patiently and attentively during the lesson, making every effort to respond whenever they could. As students from the good class (i.e., they are the motivated and academically able students in the school), they certainly understood the need to study the textbook chapter well for their tests and examinations, but this did not reduce the remoteness of the lesson topic from their everyday lives.

As for Ms. Hung, although the story is about a school-age girl, the students might find it difficult to derive personal relevance from the story. The story is about Peggy who wanted to quit school in order to find a job and marry her lover. To Ms. Hung's students, this may be totally unintelligible because they were among the top 30% of students in terms of academic achievements in Hong Kong. Their prime concern at school was how to get good results in public examinations so that they could enter their first choice of discipline in the universities. We believe some work needs to be done by the teacher to establish the right schemata (both linguistic and ideological) in the students for them to understand the story. The students' unwillingness, if not resistance, to voice out the answers in public might have reflected their lack of confidence in talking about something so culturally remote and alien to them. To the authors, these silences from the students were thus largely a result of incompatibility of cultural resources and identities expected by the teachers and those actually possessed by the class. It is not possible for the students to develop any resonance with the behavior of the main character of the story. In Bourdieu's terms, the students' habitus is incompatible with the habitus required by the school curriculum, and sometimes, that of the teacher's (see Lin, 1999). Similar to Ms. Berner's case, Ms. Hung was also under the pressure of covering the storybook as chosen by the English panel of the school because it constituted one of the test topics in the final examination.

Sometimes students do not proffer any responses to teachers' initiation not because of anxiety, lack of knowledge, or lack of confidence, but out of concern for losing face. In the next section, we discuss how teachers reacted during such incidents.

Appealing to the Students' Sense of Face

Goffman (1955, as cited in Bond & Hwang, 1986, p. 244) defined the term "face" as "the positive social value a person effectively claims for himself by the line others assume he has taken during a particular contact. Face is an image of self delineated in terms of approved social attributes." To most secondary school students, their sense of face or image of self mainly hinges on how they are viewed by peers. In this subsection, we show how Mr. Sze, Mr. Nelson, and Mr. Williams adopted face-related strategies in motivating students to participate in the lesson activities. We first illustrate in Excerpt 9.12 how Mr. Sze alleviates students' fear of losing face by modifying his activity format. During the first author's study, Mr. Sze was seldom observed to have experienced difficulties in motivating students to take part in the classroom activities. In the following excerpt, Mr. Sze experiences some problems with motivating certain students in his 1D class (a comparatively weak class) to produce an utterance in English.

Excerpt 9.12.   #Mr. Sze (1D, 31/03/00)

The teacher is teaching comparatives using a competition. The students are divided into two sides and each side takes turns to make sentences, comparing two of their classmates standing in front of the class. Some students do not find the activity appealing.

1. LET: [speaking to one of the groups] **Wai, jat-tiu dou mou aa** <*Come on, not even one sentence*>? [urging the other group] **Jiu bei-faan A gaa-laa-wo** <*I have to give the turn back to A*>. (??) **M-dak aa** <*No*>, **haa-jat-lun laa** <*Next round.*> Jane, **si-m-si haa** <*Want to try*>?

2. J: **M-hou laa** <*No*>, **haa-jat-lun ngo gai-fan aa** <*Next round I'll be the marker*>. **Hou mun aa** <*Very boring*>.

3. LET: [talking to another pp] **Mou laa** <*It's over*>. Three-**wong zi wai** [name of a student]

4. W: Jacky is eh (harder)?

5. LET: Jacky is **me aa** <*what*>?

6. W: (??)

7. LET: Harder than, **ji-gaa gong gan** number one **aa** <*We're talking about number one now*>.

8. B1: Sze sir, **nei m-hai waa bei ngo teng gam mou-liu aa** <*You're not telling me that you're so senseless*>. [T may or may not have heard it.]

9. LET: Three two one, di:::: [imitating the sound of a bell]. Tall again. **Faai-di laa** <*Be quick*>! **M sai paa-cau aa** <*Don't feel shy*>, Angel? Connie is taller than Jacky.

10. A: Jacky, Och, Connie is taller than Jacky.

11. LET: Very good, one more mark. **Gam keoi-dei hai bou-daap gaa** <*They are taking the second chance to answer*>, **gam dai-ji-tiu jau hai keoi-dei laak** <*Then this one is their turn again*>. Noisy, noisy?

12. B1: [speaking in his seat, very near the recorder] **Nei m-hai waan gam mou-liu ge jau-hei** <*You're not playing such senseless game*>.

13. LET: Three, //two=

14. Ss: //two, //one
15. LET: =//one, Heidi? **Si-daan laa** <*Anything will do*>, **li-di gam zu-gun ge je** <*Such a subjective thing*>, **ngap-dak-ceot zau dak ga-laa** <*Just say anything that comes to you*>.
16. H: They are very noisy. [laughter]

It is in fact difficult to say for sure from reading the transcripts whether students did not take part in an activity because of their lack of knowledge and confidence or due to resistance, unless one was present in the scene. The situation got trickier, particularly when only a certain number of students showed the same kind of enthusiasm as the others. When this happened to Mr. Sze (as evident from Jane's response in turn 2, and B1's comment in turns 8 & 12), the following strategies were used, as illustrated by Excerpt 9.12.

1. using L1 to show solidarity and to facilitate communication with the weaker ones;
2. minimizing the challenges of the activity (turn 1, "just one utterance is expected")
3. arousing their collective group spirit by referring to the rules that if they did not respond, the chance would be given to the other group (turn 1, "I have to give the turn back to A.")
4. reassuring students that any utterance from them would stand a high chance of being accepted (turn 15, "Just say anything that comes to you.")
5. showing understanding of students' consciousness of face threats, hoping that such display of understanding would alleviate their worries (turn 9, "Don't feel shy.")

It is clear from the sequential development of the teacher–pupil exchanges that Mr. Sze's initial attempts (turn 1) to motivate Jane and her group to make an utterance were not very successful. However, Mr. Sze was able to employ multifaceted psychological strategies, combining cognitive and affective aspects to motivate the students. Unlike Ms. Hung, Mr. Sze seldom paused for a long time for students to respond. All his urges in Excerpt 9.12 are informatives in L1. He does not repeat the elicitation question, nor does he appeal to his authority as the teacher. Basically, he attempts to appeal to students' concern for face (by being able to do a simple task), and adolescents' desire for peer recognition and group solidarity (being able to contribute to the group they belong to). After repeated efforts and with different strategies, later in the lesson, both groups became more involved in the activity. Student B1, who previously commented on the nonsensical and childish nature of the activity, took the initiative to write sentences on the board. B1's change of behavior may partly be due to the teacher's discourse strategies, but also partly due to the teacher's modification of the format of the activity later.

From the first author's observation, the whole class seemed to have taken a more active part in the sentence-making activity after the teacher stopped using real persons for comparisons. If the first author's observation is valid, this scenario calls for further investigation. Inviting students to serve as "models" for some language work is a favorite strategy of many teachers (Ms. Berner had done the same on a similar topic, see Excerpt 7.8). Sometimes students respond well but sometimes they do not, and in most cases they looked embarrassed. Our interpretation has to go back to the choice of topic. When Mr. Sze asked other students to compare two of their classmates, it involved face threats because any comparisons would make one of the students a lesser person. Some students might resist doing an activity like this because the students under comparison may be their friends, or they may fear that they would be the next choice of real-person model. Therefore, whether consciously or unconsciously, Mr. Sze's decision to stop using real persons in the comparison seems a wise move.

In Excerpts 9.13 and 9.14, Mr. Nelson and Mr. Williams respectively appeal to students' general desire to maintain a positive image appropriate to the social situation and to secure a favorable evaluation from others (Bond & Kwang, 1986) in their attempts to engage students on task.

Excerpt 9.13.   #Nelson (4E, 16/03/99)

This happened toward the end of the lesson in which the students were asked to formulate questions based on some given answers. B1 in the following excerpt does not write down anything after some time.

1. NET: [talking to B1] Are you resting again?
2. B1: I am confused.
3. NET: What you should do?
4. B1: We should write down some question //about these answers
5. NET: //Yes yes, so what questions will you write down to get these answers?
6. B1: (???)
7. NET: Write down the questions.
8. B1: But it's in my mind, it should not be write down.
9. NET: But I want to check it.
10. B1: You want to check it?
11. NET: Yes, and //Gary wants to see it=
12. G: //check his brain.
13. NET: =cos he told me you are a very lazy boy.
14. G: Yes.
15. NET: See?
16. G: Very lazy.

17. B1: I am very clever.

18. NET: Then show us how clever you are.

In Excerpt 9.13, Mr. Nelson uses two face-related strategies:

1. using peer pressure by saying to B1 that his classmate (Gary) would like to see his work (turn 11) and by getting the support of Gary (turn 14);
2. appealing to B1's desire not to lose face by deliberately challenging B1 that he was considered a lazy boy by his classmate (line 13), and when B1 protests that he is in fact very clever, taking the opportunity to urge him to show his cleverness by writing down the questions.

Note in turn 9, Mr. Nelson first says that he wants to check B1's questions, but perhaps immediately realizing that this might not present a strong case, he adopts the previous strategies. The teacher's comment in turn 13 is a clear attempt to goad B1 into action by ridiculing him for his laziness. An informal chat with Mr. Nelson later confirms that as a teacher he would not tolerate students' laziness, especially if they had the ability to do the activity competently. It seems that diligence is a cross-cultural virtue. However, it is also Chinese traditional wisdom that laziness will only lead to failure. Students in Mr. Nelson's school were among the top batch of students in Hong Kong in terms of academic performance. The examination culture in Hong Kong has made them aware of the need to work very hard to survive in the highly competitive public examination system to further their studies. Being considered a lazy pupil by the teacher and his classmates might have reminded B1 that if he does not work hard, he will lose his competitive edge and lag behind the others.

Mr. Williams' appealing to students' face consciousness presented in the next excerpt also shows how students' face consciousness is often tied with their awareness of their institutional role as a student. It is quite similar to Ms. Hung's strategy (3) in Excerpt 9.11, which appeals to students' sense of institutional roles and obligations in class.

Excerpt 9.14. #Williams (2E, 20/04/99)

This interaction began after Mr. Williams found out that the pupil, Brian (Br), had not done his homework.

1. NET: Have you got your composition book now, here? (…) Where is it? (.)

2. [Br murmurs something, not clear on the tape.]

3. NET: Give it to me? (.) I don't think so. When did you give me the book?

4 Br: [in very low voice] I don't know.

5	NET:	Bria:n. (0.6)
6	Br:	I use the new book to do the composition. Tomorrow (..) to give you.
7(1)	NET:	Okay, 8:30 tomorrow in the staff room, okay (.) don't forget,
(2)		and I'm very-, Brian, I'm very disappointed because YOU used to be
(3)		a very good student, but now, you're not a very good student. You
(4)		are not, you're not trying, you're not trying hard in English lessons
(5)		any more, very lazy. (..) Now you can't, you can't do better than this.
(6)		I remember in September, you were a very good student. (.) and now
(7)		you're not so good. I think if you change your seat and don't sit here
(8)		with these naughty boys and you sit in the front with Stephen, and
(9)		some of the other good students, I think your attitude will improve,
(10)		your performance will improve, Also you sit such a long way from
(11)		the teacher, and it's very easy to sleep and read comic books, and er
(12)		things like that. So I'm going to speak to Mr. Ng [the class teacher] and ask him if you can change seat and sit near the front.
(13)		Do you think it's a good idea?
8	Br:	Yes.

A sequential analysis of Mr. Williams' long monologue in turn 7 reveals three distinct strategies in his attempt to bring Brian back to the right track.

1. He compliments on the past good behavior of Brian (lines 2 to 3) to appeal to his conscience of what a good student should be like (line 4) and contrasts his present behavior with that in the past;
2. He offers Brian a solution to his problem (lines 12–13) and assures him of the positive consequence (lines 9–10);
3. He seeks Brian's opinion about his suggestion (line 13, "Do you think it's a good idea?"), thus respecting the student as an autonomous being.

Brian's positive response at the end of the interaction shows that he is still concerned about maintaining a good student image in the teacher's mind. Mr. Williams' effort to give such personal attention to students at-risk is a good example showing how a NET could also effectively play a counselor's role. A similar instance showing effective appeal to students' face as a motivating factor happened in Mr. Nelson's 4E lesson. A student who refused to work with his classmates agreed to do so after the teacher pleaded for him to cooperate. To a certain extent, he conceded because he did not want the teacher to think he was a troublemaker.

However, not all instances of psychological strategy worked well in our data. A typical instance occurred in Mr. Williams' 2E. In that lesson, a few male students (including Zero mentioned in Excerpt 7.12) openly defied the teacher's authority by chatting loudly in Cantonese despite several warnings from the teacher. The majority of the students were in fact unmotivated. To keep the class under control, Mr. Williams first exercised absolute teacher authority by shushing frequently, banging on the desk, and shouting "shut up" several times. Later, he started to employ softer strategies by praising students (including those who had just misbehaved) who fulfilled the very simple task of telling the class what antonyms were represented on a picture they drew during the lesson (related information is available in Excerpt 8.8). For example, he praised the drawing of Zero whom he had just warned. He clapped hands to show appreciation whenever a pupil presented an English utterance. However, the students did not respond well to Mr. Williams' face related gestures. Almost nobody else followed suit and clapped as well. On a few occasions, individual students did just the opposite. They clapped hands at a strong and regular beat when nobody else (not even the teacher) was clapping. It made the clapping sounds stand out very distinctly while the teacher was talking. Besides, whenever the teacher praised a pupil on their performance, somebody would be heard laughing. From the teacher's occasional reprimanding, Jerry (Zero's good friend) seems to be the major "culprit" for all these nonverbal defiant acts.

Having observed the lessons given by Mr. Williams and other teachers, the first author considers that the ineffectiveness of Mr. Williams' appeal to students' face consciousness described earlier should have nothing to do with the strategy itself. Clapping hands is a common practice to compliment performance at primary level and Ms. Hung and Mr. Sze used this strategy with their F1 classes. Usually, the whole class would join in clapping to demonstrate encouragement, appreciation, and praise for their classmates' performance. The cause for the tension that emerged in that 3E lesson of Mr. Williams might need to be traced back to other occasions. We hinted in Excerpt 7.12 that the miscommunication between Mr. Williams and Zero resulting in Zero being considered a dishonest pupil might have planted some seeds of resentment in the latter's mind. Mr. Williams' more high-handed attitude toward boys in his classes might have undermined his relationships with them in general. Using Bond and Hwang's (1986) terms, Zero and Jerry might be staging their "retaliation" (to hurt the teacher's face deliberately) because Mr. Williams as the allocator of *mianzi* (standard Chinese term for "face") had, at an earlier time, failed to give them the expected "face." This incident again shows that the effectiveness of a certain strategy is highly situational or context dependent, and the causes and effects of certain phenomena cannot be viewed in isolation but situated in the history of teacher–student relationships. How people perform through discourse carries connotations and memories of preceding incidents, or preceding utterances from other people. These are also insights that can be better captured by qualitative ethnographic and discourse analysis research approaches rather than positivist experimental or questionnaire survey approaches.

PERFORMING "STUDENTS"—PARTICIPATING IN TASKS

In the previous sections, we look at how teachers performed their "teachership" in getting students on task. From the various excerpts and discussions, readers have also seen how students responded in various ways to the teachers' performance. In the following sections, we shift our focus to the students. We show how students performed their "studentship" in teacher-designed tasks. We also show how some students may contest the teachers' construction of their own identities, and transform the originally authoritative discourse into self-relevance discourse agentically.

Enacting a Teacher-Designed Agency Role

The teacher designs almost all classroom activities in Hong Kong. In extreme cases of these activities, students may be speaking in a way that is totally of the teacher's desire and design, for example, reproducing verbally the written words from the textbooks in the answers-checking activity or the "operations-oriented activities" in Lin's (1996b) doctoral study. Students' roles in these cases are similar to that of the "animator" but not the "author and/or principal" of an utterance in Goffman's (1981) configuration of speaking roles. In more communicative-oriented activities, the students are usually assigned roles that allow them to express in their own words their intentions, feelings, and ideas within a given target language structure, but the roles are still usually designed by the teacher.

In the excerpts presented in this section, we show how students enacted teacher-designed/assigned agency roles in the presence of the teacher. The teachers handed over these agency roles to the students through variations on the conventional IRF pattern. By nature, the setting and rationale for the activities presented in the next few excerpts are quite similar to the "student initiative-oriented activities" described in Lin (1996b) during which the teacher "designates the role of the questioner to a student or a group of students" (p. 189). Similar to Lin's (1996b) case, it is also shown that students' agency roles in these activities are conditional in nature because they are subject to the teachers' design, designation, sanction, and confirmation. The teachers often monitored the students' utterances.

Excerpt 9.15.   #Hung (1E, 15/10/98)

Ms. Hung conducted an activity in which one pupil first individually identified a picture or an article from the newspaper the class is reading, and described it orally to the class. Other students, hearing the descriptions, tried to locate the article or picture from the newspaper. The first pupil to get it right scored one mark for his respective house.[99]

1. LET: Blue house right very good. Ask questions, yes, ask questions, yes please.
2. B1: There are some cartoons here, on the page, there is some cartoons.

3. LET: Cartoons on there? In the page^, okay, house?

4. B1: Blue.

5. LET: Blue House. (..) Some cartoons, yes.

6. B2: Page 5.

7. LET: Page 5, is that correct?

8. B1: No, it is not correct.

9. LET: No, not page 5 (..) Second last boy.

10. B3: Ten.

11. LET: Page 10, is //it okay?

12. B1: //No.

13. LET: Now you have to tell page 10 which particular part yes please?

14. B4: Student Standard page 8.

15. LET: Student Standard page 8?

16. B1: Yeah.

17. LET: Ehhuh correct, this one is tricky there are many cartoons, are there many cartoons?

18. Ss: Yes //ye::s.

19. LET: //Cartoons everywhere, next time you need to give a better question, cartoon showi::ng^ okay. So what does that cartoon show, house please?

It can be seen clearly that B1's initiation in the linguistic form of an informative (turn 2) is a result of the teacher's directive on the previous line. The teacher's partial repetition in the next turn (turn 3) serves an echoing purpose of B1's initiation. It is neither a response to nor a feedback on B1's initiation. B2's utterance in turn 6 is the actual response to B1's initiation. B1's evaluative feedback in turns 8, 12, and 16 complete his reversed role as classroom discourse initiator. In this context, he is the sole person with the necessary knowledge to pass evaluative feedback on others' responses. A linear representation of the discourse sequence could be as follows. Acts in the brackets are optional.

T invites bidding for turn → S1 bids and initiates (T repeats initiation) → S responds (T repeats response) → S1 evaluates (T comments)

Key: S1—the first student who takes up the speaking turn

S—an indefinite student

Actually, the teacher could have done the description part as well. Handing over to the students the right to choose what to describe and how to initiate shows Ms. Hung's attempt to provide students with the experience of a more agentive speaking role. Of course, we should not overlook the phenomenon that the teacher is still very anxious to control the flow of the interaction in this activity. She tends to repeat not only the initiations but also the responses from other students. Perhaps she is anxious to make sure everybody hears the utterances clearly. She also provides an advisory directive (see Excerpt 9.3) in turn 19. As highlighted by Heras (1994), even though there are classroom interaction instances in which a student may be handed the role of a teacher, he or she often does not hold the institutional position of teacher (p. 280). The teacher's evaluation of B1's initiation in turn 19 is a clear indication of this role relationship in the classroom.

The following example, which occurs in Ms. Berner's 3E class, shows clearly how the students are playing only the animator role (Goffman, 1981) in a communicative task by reproducing prewritten utterances. The teacher, similar to Ms. Hung in Excerpt 9.15, is also performing the significant controlling and monitoring role even though she is not supposed to have a direct communicative involvement in the communication.

Excerpt 9.16. #Berner (3E, 05/03/99)

This excerpt shares the same context as Excerpts 8.1, 8.2, 8.3, and 8.12. It shows how the students, under close monitoring of the teacher, take turns to ask Elsa a list of preset questions. A similar pattern recurs in the rest of the lesson.

1. NET: Simon? you ask the first question.
2. Si: (??)
3. NET: You've got to be much louder, Simon?
4. Si: [loudly but in a playful tone] Where were you bor::::n.
5. E: [cheerfully] I was born in ENGla:nd.
6. NET: Where is that place?
7. E: In Shropshire.
8. B1: **Me-aa** <*What*>?
9. B2: How to spell?
10. E: S-H= [without yet releasing the ending /tʃ/of "h"]
11. NET: =Come on, come on, question, how do you spell that please?
12. B2: How do you spell that please?
13. E: S^
14. Ss: S^
15. E: H^
16. Ss: H^
17. [Ss repeating after Elsa, imitating her tone in a very neat but playful manner.]
18. NET: [immediately after Elsa has finished spelling] Shropshire.
19. Ss: Shropshire.
20. B: Repeat [probably gone unnoticed]

21. NET: Okay, next question please Chan.

22. B: **Duk do jat-ci** <*Say it once more*>, one more [Probably nobody has heard.]

23. C: When were you burn [sic]?

24. E: When was I bor::n?

25. C: born, born.

26. E: Mm, [looking at Ms. Berner] shall I tell them?

27. NET: Yeah, do tell them.

28. E: 1979.

Whereas students in Excerpt 9.15 bid for turns to initiate with the teacher's nomination, students in Excerpt 9.16 mainly have their initiation turns assigned by the teacher. In both cases the students make the "initiation" as a "response" to the teacher's earlier initiation. In a smooth sequence, the students' initiation would be followed by Elsa's response. Feedback or evaluation moves in the IRF tradition (that is, evaluating the quality of the response) are not expected, although there were occasions when students commented on Elsa's answers in Cantonese (not available in Excerpt 9.16). For example, they showed admiration that Elsa would be going to university soon. However, in that lesson, feedback or evaluation did not necessarily come from the pupil who initiated the question. Sometimes, as shown in turns 8 and 9, students other than the questioner may request clarification in relation to Elsa's response. It is usually a request for Elsa to spell her answers. Probably due to the students' limited English knowledge and the very culture specific nature of Elsa's answers, Elsa had to spell almost every word she gave. It is interesting to note that at times, the teacher interrupted before Elsa responded to correct the students' improper question form (as in turn 11). In turn 26, Elsa even sought opinion from the teacher before answering. The heavy teacher influence in this interview is apparent. Here is an attempt to represent the discourse sequence linearly:

T allocates speaking turn → S1 "initiates" (T comments/edits) → G (guest) responds or conducts side talk with T before responding (as in turn 26) → T allocates next turn or S follow-up initiates or comments

These discourse features once again illustrate Heras's (1994) observation that roles and their corresponding power could be separated. In this activity, although the students were given the role to initiate, they did not enjoy the authority or power of the teacher. The teacher assigned the initiator role. Even though students were supposed to be free to initiate any questions they like, due to their limited English proficiency, most only read out from the list of questions Ms. Berner had prepared with them on the previous day. After a few cycles of question and answer, Ms. Berner could even predict what the next question would be (as evident in Excerpt 8.12). All these features rendered the students' role in this activity more like the "animator" rather than the "author" or "principal" of the utterances. The questions that come from their mouth may not be what they really wanted to ask. However, it does not mean that these activities are not worth doing. At least we see students taking the initiative to request, in English, that Elsa spell her answers. Seeking clarification is a crucial strategy in communication. This opportunity to have a change in their mundane classroom role from an answerer to a questioner probably furnishes the students with some novel experience as an English user.

The next excerpt shows how Mr. Nelson's 4E students manipulate the communicative space given to them in the production of a highly spontaneous and creative enactment of the teacher-designed and assigned agency role. The activity (an oral presentation) was institutionalized by the school as a curriculum activity, mainly in response to the public examination requirements for students to do an oral presentation as part of the speaking test. Everyday during the first author's visit, two to three students in Mr. Nelson's and Ms. Hung's classes had to do a 2-min presentation, either on current news stories or any topic of their own choice. Probably to make the presentations more meaningful, Mr. Nelson and Ms. Hung required students to do follow-up activities after the presentations. What they did varied. Ms. Hung required the presenter to raise questions based on his presentation. Mr. Nelson, on the other hand, asked students in the audience to raise questions or give comments on the presentation they had just heard. The following excerpt shows an interesting occasion.

Excerpt 9.17.   #Nelson (4E, 16/03/99)

After a student called Thomas (Th) has done his presentation about being a teacher, Mr. Nelson invited Frankie (F) and Robert (R) to ask questions.

1. F: (??) students become (??), so if you were a teacher, what will you do to (?)
2. Ss: [making cat-calls] WAAOUH [laughing]
3. Th: If I'm teacher, I will eh I will make mo:re mo:re project work for the students to do (..) and provide more interesting job for them for the student (..) [Some Ss laugh.] so they will not feel boring during the lesson
   // and they will learn more
4. NET: // [amused] okay (??)
5. R: The teacher sometimes will make mistakes. What will the teacher do if the teacher make a mistake, and how to be a teacher with no mistake, the teacher will make mistake, sometimes will make mistakes=
6. Ss: =what kind of mistake?=
7. R: =what //will the, some mistakes
8. Ss: //[laughing] what kind some mistakes

9. NET: For example?
10. R: Some eh spelling mistakes
11. NET: Okay. [Many Ss are talking at the same time.]
12. Th: Ehh vocab meaning. I think it is not the problem because ehm, all—anybody will make mistakes, not just the teachers.
13. NET: Okay, thank you.

Excerpt 9.17 shows an interesting discussion (although the English is often inaccurate) among the students, with occasional peripheral participation and monitoring of the teacher. Even though Frankie's and Robert's initiation turns in the excerpt were assigned by the teacher, their instant reactions reflected that they were quite well prepared to speak out their minds. It is particularly amusing to note the references, which I suspect were deliberate acts, made to the use of project work (turn 3), and teachers' making mistakes (turn 5) by Frankie and Robert. The latter case reminds us of Excerpt 8.9 that shows how some students criticized Mr. Nelson in a jocular manner for making careless mistakes. The students' general attitude toward project work, as revealed in the interview, was that on the one hand, project work was as an interesting task, but on the other hand, doing project work only may not benefit them in their examinations. Therefore, these utterances from the students might be interpreted as deliberate acts to make their voices heard by the teacher in a satirical but harmless way. Or viewed from another perspective, it might have shown how a temporary change of identity of Thomas made him assume the institutional voice of the teacher who therefore felt obliged to defend his pedagogical principles and professional integrity.

As a whole, all excerpts in this section show how students could enjoy a certain degree of agency and assert some form of their identities during teacher-designed activities through variations on an institutionalized interaction pattern. Although the agency status of the students is conditional and temporary, the emergence of these activities opens up potentials in reshaping the power relationships in the classroom and contributing to the objective of developing students into increasingly competent and effective language users.

Transforming a Teacher-Designed Identity

In the previous section, we have seen how students enacted their student identity in the presence of the teachers. In this section, we show how a group of students transformed the teacher-designed English language student identity in the absence of the teacher. The next excerpt shows a communicative-oriented task conducted in the form of group work. Due to the large class size (about 40 students), teacher's monitoring of individual groups may be minimal, thus creating space for students to derail the teacher-expected patterns of talk. In Excerpt 9.18, we show how some students working in a small group display their everyday identities (including being a student and a youngster immersed in Hong Kong Conton pop culture) during a communicative activity in the absence of the teacher and how it ends up transforming the original identity designed by the teacher. It comes from Miss Logan's 2B. Similar instances were also recorded in some other lessons of Miss Logan (see Luk, 2005b), and in Ms. Hung's (see Footnote 76) and Ms. Berner's classes.

Excerpt 9.18.   Logan (2B #25/03/99)

This excerpt shows a group activity in a F.2 class. After the teacher presented the language focus, past progressive, with a make-up schedule, the students are told to work in small groups to practise the structures by asking and answering in turns what the others were doing at a certain time on a certain day. The following conversation takes place among two girls (G1, G2) and two boys (B1, B2).

1. G1: What were you doing at- **m-hai** <*Oh no*>, yesterday evening at 5:00?
2. B1: [laughing] **Ngo hei-kuen** <*I give up*>. (…)
3. G2: I was, I was-
4. B1: Speak loudly.
5. G2: I was watching television.
6. B1: Really? [chuckling]
7. G2: [at a very high pitch] Yes yes.
8. [Off-task talk for 10 seconds.]
9. G1: **M dak** <*It's not okay*>, **ngo jiu zoi man gwo** <*I'll ask again*>. What were you doing yesterday evening at 5:00?
10. B1: **Nei gong ngo aa** <*You mean me*>?
11. G1: **Saam-go dou jiu daap** <*All three of you should answer*>.
12. B2: **Me waa** <*What*>? **Gei-do** o'clock **waa** <*At what o'clock*>?
13. G1: 5:00.
14. B2: 5:00 **aa.**
15. G2: I was watching television
16. G1: Spencer?
17. B1: I was sleeping.
18. B2: I was fighting.
19. G1: **Me-aa** <*What*>?
20. B2: Fighting.
21. B1: Figh//ting [chuckling]
22. G1: //Fighting **aa** [Cantonese particle to show doubtfulness]? **Daa-gaau aa** <*Fighting*>?
23. G2: Sleeping?

24. B2: **M-hai** <*No*>. Fighting Spencer.

25. B1: **Nei dou so ge** <*You're insane*>! **Ngo fan-gaau dim bei nei daa aa** <*I was sleeping. How come I got hit by you*>?

26. B2: **Zau hai fan-gan-gaau sin daa aa-maa** <*It's because you're sleeping that I could hit you*>.

27. [The two girls continue to ask each other the question while the boys are chatting on their own.]

28. G2: What, what were you doing yesterday evening at 7:00? (..) Jerry?

29. B2: **Cat-dim zou mat le** <*Doing what at 7:00*>?

30. G2: **Daa-gei lo** <*Playing electronic games*>.

31. B2: [sounds like thinking hard] **Cat-dim zou mat le** <*Doing what at 7:00*>?

32. G2: **Daa-gei lo** <*Playing electronic games*>.

33. B2: **Ei^** [a Cantonese particle to show that you suddenly remember something]

    yes, **m-wui** <*No, I won't*>, **m-hai** <*No*>, **fan dou baat-dim sin daa-gei aa maa ngo** <*I slept till eight o'clock before playing the electronic games*>.

    I was sleeping **aa dou-hai** <*just the same*>.

34. G1: **Wan jan daap ngo dak-m-dak aa** <*Can somebody answer me*>?

35. G2: I was seeing (???)

36. G1: Spencer **le** [a Cantonese particle meaning "how about"]?

37. B1: **Ngo dou hai** <*I was also*> sleeping [laughing]

38. B2: [with playful tone] to found [sic] **zau-gong aa-waa** <*To look for Duke Chau*[101]>.

39. G2: **Nei le** <*How about you*>? What were you doing yesterday evening at five o'clock?

40. [The two boys begin to talk about football stars in Cantonese.]

41. G1: I was watching television.

42. G2: Also watching television.

The teacher designed the activity the students are doing in Excerpt 9.18 as a communicative activity for oral practice. From the authors' experience as English teachers, activities like this have proved popular with teachers in Hong Kong practicing the communicative language teaching approach, because of the dual focus it is supposed to handle. On the one hand it provides recurrent practice of the linguistic structures and vocabulary items in focus. On the other, by establishing an information gap, the activity also provides meaning-based interaction.

However, from Excerpt 9.18, we see that although the four students are interacting as a group, not every one of them has the same intent to carry out the communicative activity as instructed by the teacher (i.e., using only English). G1 and G2 seem more cooperative and conscious of their institutional role. The two boys, on the other hand, do not seem to take the activity very seriously. They not only fail to initiate any questions with the other two girls, but also answer half-heartedly. The truthfulness of the answers they provided, such as fighting and sleeping, is suspicious. It seems that the students interpreted the task differently. The girls seemed to be focusing on the "structure aspect" of the task (as evident in G1's insistence on forming the questions in the same word order as the teacher's example, line 1). The boys, however, tended to focus on the "meaning aspect" of the task and their underlying objective seems to be more for fun than for practicing English.

The boys in Excerpt 9.18 conducted the task mostly in Cantonese, which is not the expectation of the teacher. It is interesting to note that the girls for a time join the interaction in Cantonese. From turn 29 to 33, the students are seen engaging in an interesting argument about what the boys were doing. To the authors, this is real and natural communication. The only problem for many teachers is the fact that the communication is not done in the target language. Most teachers may immediately attribute the reason for such code switching to a lack of sufficient language of the students to express themselves in English. That is a highly likely reason, but a more valid reason may be the lack of a perceived need by the students concerned to express something, in particular personal feelings in L2 to their L1-speaking peers. This lack of a perceived need to use English may also be related to how they positioned themselves in the business of learning English. To most students in Hong Kong coming from a lower socioeconomic status group like those in Miss Logan's school, using English with their peers for interpersonal communication is a socially and culturally incongruent behavior. It does not match their local Canton pop cultural (or "home") identity. It may be fine to use English for practicing the linguistic structures of the language (thus fulfilling their student identity), but when personal meanings come into play (which links to their home identity), they feel more resistant to using English, particularly when the meanings are expected to be conveyed to their peers who share the same L1. This makes the use of English unnecessary and socially awkward and culturally inappropriate. Therefore, their desire to display their L2 learner and user identity is low. What makes the interaction more interesting and relevant to their everyday culture and experience (or internally persuasive) is the assertion of their working-class adolescent identity that is characterized by bluffing and talking nonsense.[102]

The group of students in Excerpt 9.18 transforms the teacher-designed identity into one that they desire in the absence of the teacher. The next section shows another intriguing situation in which the students at first resisted the teacher-designed and assigned student roles but then ended up conforming to the teacher's expectations and participated in the task actively.

From Resisting to Participating: Shifting Subject Positionings

With two illustrative cases, we intend to show changing pupil behaviors from resisting to actively participating in teacher-designed activities. The whole process reveals an intriguing form of student identity construction from assertion, negotiation, to transformation. It is important for readers to note the "local contingencies" (Pennycook, 2003, p. 529), or situated, contextual forces, that induced the changes. We begin with Ms. Berner's 3E.

The following excerpts were taken from the same lesson conducted in the English room. The context was introduced in Excerpts 7.14 and 8.15. The activity Ms. Berner conducted in the next three excerpts is the popular "Who, When, Where, and What" story-making activity in which students take turns to put down on a piece of paper an imaginary time, place, names of one male and one female, and what each of them says without looking at what comes before. The final product is a creative story very often with funny characters and an unexpected combination of events.

Excerpt 9.19 (a).   #Berner (3E, 02/03/99)

Ms. Berner is giving instructions on how to play the game.

1. NET: Okay, okay. (..) Don't discuss it, write it down, and, once you've written it down, fo:ld, the paper so that nobody can see, and pass it to the person on your left, okay? So a girl, write down a girl.
2. B1: [talking to his neighbor] **Lei se aa** <*You write it*>.
3. B2: **Gang-hai lei se laa** <*Of course you write it*>!
4. B1: **Zou-me jiu ngo se zek** <*Why should I write it*>?
5. NET: Quickly. (..) Quick.

Excerpt 9.19 (b).   This excerpt takes place a couple of seconds after Excerpt 9.19 (a). The transcribed data are placed in two columns to show two concurrent pieces of interaction. While the teacher is responding to some students' query, B1 is still trying to coerce B2 to do the writing for him.

1. NET: Right, fold it^ and pass it to the left, (..) Alright, the next person, I want you, to write down, place. School? Temple? Los Angeles? A place.

2.   [several pps joking in Cantonese]   B1: Bong-ngo se maai keoi aa <Write these for me>.

3. B3:   What is place?   B2: Se mut-je aa <Write
                                                           what>?

5. B4:   Se go dei-fong meng aa <Write a place B1: Kau-kei se go aa <Just
          name>.   write something>.

6. NET: A place like Ocean Park, City Hall,   B2: Jau dou ngo <Me
          Shatin New Town Plaza, in Hong Kong   again>?
          or outside Hong Kong, anywhere, a
          place, anywhere.

Some teachers might find B1 and B2's behavior difficult to understand because the activity was supposed to be a game (which implies the prospect of fun) and the English required was extremely simple. The students were free to put down any English words they knew. The activity can be said to be highly democratic in nature. However, B1 and B2 simply take writing down one English word or phrase as a big chore and are trying to avoid doing it and their strategy of avoiding is to cajole others to do it for them. Such reluctance reveals students' attitude toward learning English. However, as is shown in Excerpt 9.20, the students' attitude changes drastically after the game was played once. What caused such a change?

After the teacher read out the first round of stories, the whole group laughed at some of the nonsensical outcomes. When the activity was done the second time, the same B1 and B2 showed interesting changes in their behavior. Excerpt 9.20 shows their reactions.

Excerpt 9.20.   #Berner (3E, 02/03/99)

The teacher has just asked the students to put down the names of one male and one female.

1. NET: ...and then fold it, alright, pass it to the next person.
2. B2: **Gan zu dou me-aa** <*What comes next*>?
3. B1: **Si-gaan lo** <*The time*>.
4. [One boy is spelling Leonardo Di Caprio to his classmate.]
5. NET: And a place.
6. B: Toilet.
7. B: Kowloon Tong **lo** [Cantonese particle used in statement]
   [Many Ss are talking at the same time.]
8. B1: [asking his neighbor] Kowloon Tong **dim cyun aa** <*How do you spell Kowloon Tong*>?
9. B2: K-O-R-L-O-O-N [sic], (..) **aa, m-hai** <*Oh, no*>, K-O-W-L-N-O-O-N [sic]

10. NET: Right, the next, when.
11. [Ss laughing quietly among themselves; T occasionally laughs briefly; some Ss keep talking]
12. NET: Alright? Place (..) And then the next person what (.) SHE said
13. B: Can you go to the house? [Ss laugh]
14. NET: [laughs]
15. B2: Can I help yo::u? [makes funny sound by lengthening "you"]
16. [Other Ss laugh; one B says something in English, indistinct on the tape, probably about sexual issues]
17. NET: And then what HE said.
18. B2: Just to say hi.
19. NET: I hope that (???) be embarrassing.

Instead of avoiding and resisting as in Excerpts 9.19 (a) and (b), B1 and B2 in Excerpt 9.20 are actively participating in the task. Even though the students are expected to respond to the NET's initiations in writing, many have often self-selected to say their responses in their seats (turns 6, 7, 13, 15, 18). The students also pay attention to language. For example, B1 asks B2 the spelling of "Kowloon," and from turn 13 onward, the students are using mainly English to communicate. The marked change in verbal practice of the students is probably a result of their ultimate realization that they could actually express something they want to express by asserting a different form of their self or their identity that is not the same as the traditional one. The requirement for the imaginary characters to be of opposite sexes has created a space for this all-boys group to assert their male adolescent identity, which is so commonly characterized by interest in sex-related topics. The single-gender nature of the group has, to a certain extent, encouraged the students to talk about sex-related issues with no feeling of embarrassment. The teacher, although a female, projected sexually a rather neutral image because of her age and her way of behaving. For example, she often was the first person to laugh loudly at the students' sexually implicated utterances. The teacher's unconventionally receptive attitude toward students' overwhelming interest in sex may be due to the fact that English was used by the students, and what they expressed was not particularly obscene in nature. It seems that the teacher has become one of the students' peers who could share their in-culture. In this respect, the teacher's and the students' discourse practices were mutually reinforcing with interpenetrable effects. Both the teacher and the students made efforts to cross over to the other side of the border—the students using English to express own ideas, and the teacher joining in the fun talk about some taboo issues. This temporary opportunity for both sides to assert some subdued and noninstitutional identities (e.g., the teacher is institutionally expected to provide proper moral guidance to the students) may be a crucial force contributing to the active participation of the students in the task.

Similar changes in students' discourse behaviors have also been observed in a lesson by Mr. Williams. Similar to the case of Ms. Berner, we present two excerpts to show contrast. In the first excerpt, Mr. Williams was asking the students to write down on a piece of paper words and phrases showing opinions that they learned the day before. Most students seemed reluctant to do so, or they really could not remember what the words were. The teacher commented on the students' performance with satirical expressions. Then he asked students to fold the paper and keep it safe because the paper contains valuable knowledge.

Excerpt 9.21.   #Williams (4E, 22/04/99)

The excerpt begins with Mr. Williams asking the students how many expressions they have correctly put down.

1. NET: Jacky, how many did you get right? (..) Four **laa**!? [seems like a Cantonese particle, or an ending sound found commonly in Singapore English] Terrible! Rubbish! Calvin, (..) How many did you get right? (..) [A student seems to be responding but indistinct on the tape.]
   Only? (.) Dear ME! Emily, how many did you get right? (..)
2. Ss: Zero.
3. NET: Can't be zero cause she was cheating so it can't be zero.
   How many //do you get right?
4. B: //Oh I see. [Probably meaning "Let me see."] Only one.
5. NET: Only one. [T sighs to show he is disappointed] Simon, THREE, S-Simon, how many did you get right?
6. Si: Zero.
7. NET: ZERO! That's because you haven't written them in English, you've written them in Arabic, nobody can read that writing. Okay, now very carefully, very carefully, put the papers back in your desk. Remember, they OOH! (??) on the floor? These papers are like gold, don't lose them. F-fold, carefully fold it back together and put it in your desk.
8. B: (??)
9. NET: You must be joking. (0.4) Emily, is that a paper aeroplane? (..) Right (..)
   I don't think it's a good idea to have anything on the desk ...

The activity in this lesson was actually a prelude to the one that we present later. It is clear from the students' behavior that they are reluctant to follow the teacher's instruction. They show their reluctance and resistance not through verbal challenges but through nonlinguistic acts of defiance. Throwing a piece of paper that the teacher describes as gold onto the floor or making a paper airplane out of it are deliberate acts meant to defy the teacher's pedagogical arrangement and possibly his negative and ironic remarks about the students' ability to perform the task to his satisfaction (turn 1, "Terrible! Rubbish!"; turns 3 and 7). After this interaction, the teacher started the core activity, an opinion poll. The beginning of the activity is presented in Excerpt 8.8 when some students attempted to ridicule the teacher's teaching methods and appearance. Even though some of the comments were somewhat insulting in nature, students' interest and attention were beginning to be captured.

Polling students' opinions on whether the teacher is the best or not (see Excerpt 8.8) is only the appetizer, the attention getter. After all, some of the negative comments from the students may be impulsive and not well thought out. In the rest of Mr. Williams' lesson, the discussion moved from individuals, to the school, then to the society. Most topics that came later were serious in nature, often related to education issues such as "Hong Kong is a good place to live," "Violent Japanese comic books should not be sold to children," "Hong Kong students cannot enjoy their youth because they have too much homework." These topics were chosen, according to Mr. Williams after the lesson, because of their high degree of relevance to adolescents in Hong Kong. He was sure that students at this age group would have lots of opinions about these topics. Due to the length of the transcripts, we cannot present them all here. But it is important to point out that from commenting on their teacher, to their peers, then their school, and then the society, students were given ample opportunities to voice their opinions. Excerpt 9.22 shows how the teacher elicited opinions from the students on issues related to study and work by constantly challenging them with hypothetical assumptions (turns 3, 7, 10), and sweeping conclusions (turn 14). All these seem to be effective in prompting students to respond. Note that all the pupil response turns in Excerpt 9.22 are self-selected by the students whereas at the beginning of Excerpt 9.21, they are nominated by the teacher.

Excerpt 9.22.   #Williams (4E, 22/04/99)

1. NET: Why do you want to pass your exams?
2. B1: Find a good job.
3. NET: Good jobs, so all you people here do want a good job? Is that right? So aah if you go to uh United States, do the students do as much school work as you?
4. B1: [very softly] No.
5. NET: If you go to Australia, do the students do as much school work as you?
6. Ss: No, no.
7. NET: Right, so their standard is lower?
8. Ss: [very softly] Higher.

9. B2: No, (??)

10. NET: How does that work? (..) If you, you all work very hard, so your standard must be higher, than theirs. (...)

11. B2: Maybe not.

12. NET: Maybe not, why maybe?

13. B2: Maybe they are clever.

14. NET: SO this is the answer then. Hong Kong students have to work hard because they are stupid. [Some pps laugh.] Is that the answer?

15. B3: [sounding very sure] //NO

16. B4: //some of them

17. [The interaction is interrupted when the teacher has to discipline a student.]

Even though the class size was large (over 35 students) and students' English production was limited due to their weak English proficiency and lack of sufficient preparation, the sense of active participation in a discussion conducted in English is strong. The teacher was not lecturing, and the students were not just practicing target structures in a mechanical way. They were like more or less egalitarian friends engaging in a heated discussion.

In brief, what Excerpts 19 to 22 illustrate is how individuals (in this case, the students) may shift from one way to another way of thinking and behaving as the discourse shifts and as their positions within varying story lines are taken up (Davies & Harre, 1990, p. 58). The students' varying positionings were reflected in their discourse practices. However, it may not be totally appropriate to think of the students as having full agency role in creating those subject positions. To the authors, the teachers play an essential role in coconstructing the students' multiple identities or positions by creating a communicative space that allows the "possibility of choice" of discourse manifestations rather than simply reproducing authoritative academic discourse from textbooks. As suggested by Davies and Harre (1990, p. 59), "[t]he possibility of choice in a situation in which there are contradictory requirements provides people with the possibility of acting agentically."

SUMMARY

In this chapter, we presented classroom interaction data showing how teachers and students performed and sometimes contested their institutional roles as "teachers" and "students" constructed through repeated discursive practices. We show how the teachers solicited appropriate student involvement in the lesson tasks through a variety of strategies and functional acts. We show that in situations where there is an apparent need to exercise procedural control, to monitor students' progress, and to elicit task-related responses from students, the discourse strategies employed by individual teachers, or between the NETs and LETs in general, are often strategically different. The teachers' choice of linguistic forms for directive purposes reflect their perceptions of their own status in the setting, and their power relationship with the students and such relationship changes over time and across space (as shown in Mr. Williams' application of a wide range of directive discourse).

The data analyzed in this chapter also reveal that discourse strategies employed by the teachers that are effective in monitoring and motivating students are those that appeal to students' concern for face or affective feelings, desire for fun, desire for forging collective group spirit, and sense of institutional obligations. A willingness or an ability to negotiate with students in their L1 and to appeal to their familiar Hong Kong Canton pop cultures and genres when classroom management and/or motivation problems arise is also a clear asset, as in the case of Mr. Sze, who experienced the least amount of discipline and motivation problems among our cases. Actually, both NETs and LETs attempted to employ some or all of these strategies, but to varying degrees of success. In general, the LETs seemed to have a wider variety of these strategies at their disposal, probably due to their familiarity with the students' sociocultural contexts, pop and peer cultures, and their distinctive linguistic practices.

The teacher's image may also impact on students' behavior. Uncooperative students frequently challenged NETs such as Miss Logan, Mr. Williams, and Mr. Nelson by an overt display of oppositional discourse. This is probably due to the stereotypical perceptions of NETs by most students as being more lenient, open-minded, and democratic. Many students might think that they could take advantage of these characteristics of the NETs and have more free-willed activities in class. In some situations, the NETs' behavior has reinforced the students' perceptions (as shown in Mr. Williams' Excerpt 8.1). At critical moments, Mr. Williams, Miss Logan, and Mr. Nelson all attempted to assert their institutional identity and enforced the traditional teacher authority, but they were not always successful. Mr. Nelson was more fortunate to have a generally well-motivated high-ability class and the students restrained themselves from going too far. In Mr. Williams' and Miss Logan's cases, the working-class background, the lack of motivation to study hard, and the generally low English proficiency level of most of the students created more interaction problems. These issues very often arise from students' lack of middle class-oriented linguistic and cultural capital that the schooling system assumes and expects students to have (see Lin, 1999; Lin & Luk, 2002). The teachers' lack of competence in the students' L1 as the language for counseling and negotiation and lack of familiarity of students' everyday life cultures seem to have intensified the tensions. Our data analysis in this chapter also shows that when the students' familiar cultural genres and elements are built into the task design, students will be more likely to become interested in doing the task (e.g. Excerpts 8.20 & 8.22).

Students' role in task participation should not be overlooked. Active and meaningful participation in tasks cannot be induced by teachers' efforts only. How students respond to teachers' efforts to motivate them gives us significant insights about engaging unenthusiastic students in learning activities. From the excerpts presented in the second section, we show how students performed the teacher-designed roles in various ways that were closely linked with their identities. When students conformed to, transformed, or resisted such institutional roles, and when they switched between language codes, there was often the desire to assert a form of identity of their own choice, and this desire was often motivated by different forces such as those to express personal feelings, a concern of face, or a desire to challenge the teachers (who represent authority), or to make the alienating textbook discourse more lively and personally relevant. The complex mental functionings of the students point to the multilayered and often ambivalent and contested meanings of "studenting." "Teachering" with this awareness in mind should consider how a student-sensitive pedagogy can be best constructed and implemented.

QUESTIONS FOR REFLECTION AND DISCUSSION

1. As a NET/LET, reflect on your use of directives for procedural control. Identify any dominant patterns and discuss with others the impacts that different types of directives may have on different students.

2. How far do you agree that Ms. Hung's use of directives for advisory purposes reflect different cultural orientations between NETs and LETs?

3. Do you think that teacher–student relationships inside the classroom reflects an asymmetrical power structure? If yes, should it be changed? Why or why not? And if it should be changed, how?

4. Reflecting on your own teaching situation, have you adopted some of the communication strategies (e.g,. exercising authority, making concessions, appealing to students' face consciousness) mentioned in this chapter to motivate reticent and/or nonconforming students to participate in lesson activities? How effective were they? Share with other people some other strategies you have tried out but not mentioned in this book.

5. If you were Miss Logan in Excerpt 9.9, would you have made similar concessions? Why or why not? From your experience, would the strategies (e.g., negotiating with the students in their L1) used by Tracy work if she were in Miss Logan's situation?

6. As a NET/LET, do you see any difficulties in engaging in a dialogue for pedagogical purposes like what Ms. Berner and Mr. William did in Excerpts 9.20 and 9.22 respectively? Why? What are the major factors?

7. What is your general attitude toward the impact of local pop culture on students' school work? What can be some of the ways to capitalize on students' pop culture for pedagogical purposes?

10

Implications—Toward a Pedagogy
of Connecting for the Development
of Intercultural Communicative
Resources

I n this last chapter, we would like to draw implications from the data, findings,
and discussions in previous chapters for teachers', teacher educators', and
policymakers' references concerning teaching and learning a second language
in a cross-cultural setting. We center our discussion around two major issues
that give significance to the data and findings previously presented. The first
one concerns the role of "native" speaker communicative resources in intercultural
contexts. Part of such resources involves the ability to respond appropriately to others' utterances taking into consideration the sociohistorical backgrounds where the
utterances are situated. The other one concerns the impact of the plurality and multiplicity of students' linguistic and cultural experiences on their discourse practices.
We end this chapter by proposing a "pedagogy of connecting" with a view to developing students' intercultural resources.

REVISITING THE "NATIVE" SPEAKER COMMUNICATIVE RE-
SOURCES IN CROSS-CULTURAL SETTINGS

The fruition of the study reported in this book all began with an interest in "native"
speakers. As suggested in the Preface, the term "native speakers" in the book title
covers not just the native English-speaking teachers, but also the students as native
speakers of Cantonese, and the local teachers who are native speakers of Cantonese
and functionally native in English in classroom settings. However, in the fields of
TESOL and second language acquisition (SLA), a predominant attitude is to privilege the status and speech models of the native English speakers. People in most sit-

uations differentiate between a "native speaker" and a "nonnative speaker" typically by the speaker's "accent." It is said in the SLA literature that after the critical period (or puberty), it is very difficult for someone to acquire a native or native-like accent (generally referring to one of those accents used in the inner-circle English-speaking countries) of a second language. Thus, it is not surprising that most of the students interviewed in this study made reference to the "better" and "more accurate" English pronunciation of the NETs. Our point of interest in this section concerns whether and to what extent the target language native speakership of the NETs has facilitated their communicative performance in the cross-cultural classroom encounters with students not possessing that "nativeness."

Native Speakerism—A Myth or a Reality?

The controversies revolving around the native speaker notion are presented in chapters 2 and 3. A consensus that seems to be emerging over the last decade among sociolinguistic researchers (e.g., Jenkins, 2000; Rampton, 1990, 1995) is to deconstruct the native/nonnative speaker dichotomy with a view to playing down the ethnicity and biological aspects but stressing the proficiency and affiliation elements of what we used to conceive of as a native speaker. Despite attempts to redefine the native speaker notion and displace the debilitating connotation of "nonnative" with other more neutral constructs (see chap. 3), a widely accepted term has not yet been available. It makes one wonder whether throwing away the term would be the best way forward to counteract many laypeople's deep-rooted, but biased and one-sided views of the native/nonnative dichotomy.

It is mentioned in chapter 3 that Davies (2003) presented six characteristics in support of the reality of the native speakers. Findings from interviews with the teachers and students presented in chapter 6 also show that "NETs" existed as a real entity in the minds of the students and the LETs. To these students and teachers, who we believe could claim a considerable degree of representation of most students and teachers in Hong Kong, NETs were perceived to be different from most LETs in three major aspects: (1) NETs possess different types of linguistic resources, that is, in normal cases, they have a better (meaning, in more professional terms, more idiomatic and fluent) command of English, but lack knowledge in Hong Kong students' L1; (2) by having been brought up in overseas countries, NETs bring with them sociocultural ideologies more related to the inner-circle English world that are often different from those of the local teachers; (3) NETs inject a higher degree of "genuine Englishness" (or authenticity) in every communication with them because they are non-Cantonese speaking. As some students have reflected, talking with the LETs in English makes the English communication a bit artificial whereas successful communication with the NETs was taken to be the only reliable indicator for their satisfactory standards of English (for example, Mr. Williams' 4E).

Interestingly, the LETs also seemed to have no problem identifying themselves as belonging to a different category from the NETs because they also saw the differences between themselves and the NETs, not just in terms of their command of English and knowledge of students' L1, but the whole repertoire of sociocultural and sociohistorical identities and resources each type of teacher brings to the classroom contexts. Mr. Sze, for example, openly admitted possessing a lower level of English proficiency compared with that of Miss Logan. However, he took pride in his ability to employ students' L1 to establish rapport and relationship with students to facilitate their L2 learning and handle discipline problems. Being in command of both the target language and the students' L1 has given him much flexibility in fulfilling his duties as an all-around teacher. Ms. Hung shares similar views. On the one hand, she appreciated the efforts of Mr. Nelson in attempting a more student-centered teaching approach that many local teachers dare not attempt. On the other hand, she had good faith in herself as someone who could attend to students' personal growth problems, and most importantly, help students tackle the high-stake and competitive public examinations to enable them to pursue higher studies.

Privileging Situated Communicative Resources in Intercultural Communication

Even though the attitudes of the students and the LETs in this study seemed to have supported the realistic existence of some distinctive qualities of the NETs as "native" speakers of English, their hegemonic status as TESOL experts should be examined situtationally. The LETs' acknowledgement of the value of the local linguistic and sociocultural resources they themselves possessed points to the fact that there are communicative resources other than "native" speaker linguistic abilities that an effective L2 teacher must command. Data from chapters 7 to 9 already show that the LETs are in command of different types of "resources" (or acquired knowledge) as an English teacher in an EFL context such as Hong Kong. They have resources of the students' L1, they have resources of the students' experience in the local education system and sociocultural upbringing, and therefore, have resources about how to interpret students' learning styles, attitudes, and problems in the classrooms. As evident in Excerpts 7.1, 7.2, 9.11, 9.12, whenever the situations warrant it, they drew on such resources to address or respond to motivation and discipline problems. Such ability has to a certain extent been shown to have facilitated the teaching and learning.

On the other hand, the NETs have, at times, acknowledged their "nonnativeness" (or lack of resources) when issues concerning students' L1 linguistic and cultural features arose. For example, Ms. Berner shed her teacher status and assumed a learner role by following the Cantonese demonstration of her students (Excerpt 7.3). Mr. Williams and Miss Logan appealed for students' Cantonese translation service to prevent communication breakdown (Excerpts 7.5 &

7.6). During these events and over these moments, the NETs' target language "native" speaker attributes and resources did not do much to help.

People's relations to a "native speaker identity" therefore, should not be viewed as a static and fixed phenomenon, or a natural resource residing in any destined groups of people. "Nativeness" should be understood as something that is sociohistorically constructed, constantly evolving and transforming, and needs to be achieved and reachieved in moments of talk. In different situations, the same person can be more or less "native" (or possessing more or less situated resources) in one way or another. They may invoke or reject "nativeness" as part of their identity for the best possible interaction outcomes at a certain moment. A competent language user, according to Kramsch (1998b, p. 27), is someone who cannot only speak and write according to the sociocultural rules of one social group, but also possesses "the adaptability to select those forms of accuracy and those forms of appropriateness that are called for in a given social context of use." Such ability is considered the privilege of not the native speakers, but the intercultural speakers, which both NETs and LETs should appropriate through repeated engagements in relevant discourse. It is only through understanding the need for "situated communicative resources" rather than native speakerism in the target language that the dichotomy of NETs and LETs ceases to be an issue that hurts some people's professional pride. Policymakers on introducing any native English-speaking teachers' scheme should take care not to perpetuate the perception that only NETs' "nativeness" is fundamental to the teaching and learning of English.

The Plurality and Multiplicity of Students' Linguistic and Cultural Experiences

In explicating the interactive practices of the teachers and students in the last three chapters, a major theme that emerges from the dialogic processes seems to support the argument that students bring into the classroom multiple and varied linguistic and cultural experiences and these experiences are often translated into noninstitutionally sanctioned language practices and identities. How the students conform to, resist, contest, or transform their roles and responsibilities in a school setting speak to their attempts to assert and perform a set of identities that they desire, which may or may not be compatible with the institutionally assigned identities with their associated roles and responsibilities. As discussed in the introductory paragraph in chapter 9 (also see related discussion of performativity in chap. 5), identity and language practices are like a circular route: They are mutually constitutive, that is, one constructing and at the same time being constructed by the other. Who we are affects the way we use language, which in turn further (re)constitutes who or what we are. It is also discussed in chapter 5 that a person's identity should not be viewed as a coherent whole, but tends to be unstable, sometimes fragmented and conflicting. A person (or "subject" in Foucault's[103] sense) might deliberately perform identities that have or have not sprung from one's subjectivity (a conscious and unconscious sense of self). For example, some 4E students of Mr. Nelson deliberately displayed a naughty student identity (see Excerpts 9.5 & 9.13) and challenged the teacher (Excerpt 8.9) whereas during the interview, they explicitly asserted their high respect for the teacher. Or a person may resist performing identities that contradict their subjectivity. For example, in Excerpt 9.18, the two boys resisted enacting the good student identity like their female counterparts. In these cases, students' performance reveals how they would index their relation to the "others" in the external world, for example, a friendly and relaxed relationship between Mr. Nelson and his 4E prompted the students to tease the teacher (Excerpt 8.9). A rather boring teacher-designed task in Miss Logan's 2B derived illegitimate fun among peers (Excerpt 9.18).

From Bakhtin's sociocultural perspective, language learning is largely an act of appropriating others' words and turning and claiming them to be one's own by populating them with one's intentions, styles, and accents (or voices). Claiming others' words as one's internal voice involves taking up a position as one's own (or displays a form of self-representation or identity). The person "inevitably sees the world from the vantage point of that position and in terms of the particular images, metaphors, story lines and concepts which are made relevant within the particular discursive practice in which they are positioned" (Davies & Harre, 1990, p. 46). Therefore, identities and positionings affect how a person interprets the world and the meanings of other people's discourse practice.

It is shown in chapters 7, 8, and 9 that students displayed different forms of responses to the process of appropriation. Some just accepted others' discourses, accents, and voices (e.g., the traditionally authoritative discourses of teachers) conformingly. Some resisted wholesale internalization of the authoritative discourses of the teachers, but reaccentuated or reappropriated it so that it became populated with their own intentions, desires, and tones of voices (i.e., their own accents and social styles). In this way, they have made the originally authoritative discourses "internally persuasive" and appropriated them and claimed them as their own (Bakhtin, 1981; Lin & Luk, 2005). In the former case, however, the conforming students imitated a voice that may not have come from their own speaking "selves." They seemed to be made to speak in a way that is of somebody else's (here the teacher's) desire. This is what Michel de Certeau called the colonial master's desire to administer "pedagogical treatment" to cure slave boy Friday of his linguistic illness or problem (de Certeau, 1984). This is similar to the situation where someone is the "animator" but not the "author and/or principal" of an utterance in the configuration of speaking roles[104] (Goffman, 1981). The ways that different students take up speaking roles are believed to have a decisive impact on their development as language users and their orientation toward the language that they are learning: Will they conformingly imitate it and become the master's (the teacher's) voice, will they resist it, or will they penetrate and populate it with their own voices, accents, and intentions and in such a way appropriate it and claim it as their own language (Lin & Luk, 2005)? Language learning is therefore mainly a (re)construction, (re)negotiation, and (re)performance of identities. Miller (2000) argued that learning a new language is like constructing and performing a new identity as the learner tries to come to terms with new sets of ideologies and worldviews and establish social membership in a new community. Norton (2000) found that L2 learners' identity is often directly related to their investment (or in classroom jargon, *motivation* of the students) in the target language. Toohey (2000), researching on the topic of language socialization and young children, connected identity pursuits with outcomes of students' participation in learning activities:

> When children could find desirable identities in words, play in words, when those words allowed them to "answer back," and when the words of their community were open and accessible to them, then they transformed their participation, "developing a range of voices ... within and through [their] social identities in the many and varied interactive practices through which [they live] their lives." (p. 122, partly quoting Hall, 1995)

The importance of a sense of self and incentives for participation in second language learning has also been asserted by Pavlenko and Lantolf (2000). The metaphor of participation, as developed by Sfard (as cited in Pavlenko & Lantolf, 2000), stressed the importance of membership and membership immediately accentuates the importance of identity and self. To Pavlenko and Lantolf (2000), participation and (re)construction of selves have mutual influences. They argued that:

> A self is a coherent dynamic system that is in "continuous production," and which emerges as the individual participates in the (most especially, verbal) practices of a culture. Thus, for children, growing up culturally is about engaging in activities. (p. 163)

Whereas Pavlenko and Lantolf (2000) seem to be implying that there is one coherent self in every individual, we would like to highlight the multiple, mutually contesting but coexisting forms of identities (or different representations of the self) in any classroom interaction. In the next section, we show five prototypical kinds of identities[105] that students seemed to have accepted, constructed, and performed as analyzed in our classroom excerpts in the last three chapters. It should be noted that not all students reported in this book performed all the identities identified in the same manner and under the same circumstances. Some might only display certain identities in fleeting moments, some switched between identities, and some showed discrepancies in their cognizance of and actual enactment of certain identities. In any case, these prototypes must be taken as our theoretical shorthand, for lack of better words or models, to talk about what are often much more complex phenomena.

Multiple Identities of Students

A microanalysis of students' discourse practices in excerpts in the last three chapters has enabled us to arrive at five prototypical identities (IDs) of the students.

ID1. Learners of a Socially Important Language. From formal interviews and informal interactions with the students in this study, we noticed that most of them understood why, and accepted the fact that, they had to learn English even though some expressed difficulties in learning it well, or in developing an interest in it. A few high proficiency students explained to the first author that they had to learn English because it is an "international" language important to their future. Inside the classroom, students seemed to have displayed ID1 by responding to the teacher's initiation in English, and when they were engaged in the teacher-designed language learning activities (e.g., Excerpts 9.16 & the girls in 9.18). These students carried out the tasks as designed by the teachers, but not without some modifications to assert other senses of self, for example, by switching to L1 for personal communication with peers. During the interviews, most students perceived it to be their obligation to observe the teachers' instructions and do the lesson tasks accordingly; they believed that their English would improve if they paid more attention in class and practiced more. In this sense, they can be said to be asserting the good student identity. However, it should be noted that not all students displayed this identity conformingly. Some showed resistance to the institutional expectations of their fulfillment of this role. For example, B1 and B2 in Excerpt 9.18 avoided speaking English to their peers. Ms. Berner's 3E boys in Excerpts 9.19 (a & b) refused to take part in the story composition activity, and Mr. Williams' 4E disregarded the teacher's pedagogical instructions in the initial stage of the activity (Excerpt 9.21). It seems that varying degrees of student engagement with this identity reveals that the teacher might need to appeal to some other forms of identities that are more internally persuasive, if not desirable, to the students.

ID2. "Native" Speakers of a Language Closely Related to Their Everyday Sociocultural World. This identity is felt to be the most deep seated in the students. The local language (the students' L1) has planted the sociohistorical roots of the students' immediate life world and contributed to their self, or local perspectives. Evidence for this identity is found in the moment-to-moment switching between and mixing of codes during their interactions with peers and sometimes, the teachers. Even though the students could not always use their L1 to interact with their teachers, their thinking processes were inevitably first mediated (totally or partially) by their L1. Their reasoning and critical thinking usually began in the medium of their familiar L1. As observed during the data collection visits, the students always talked to their peers in Cantonese first before they responded to the teacher in (their often broken) English. It seems that the L1 peer talk acted like a rehearsal for the subsequent responses, or a request for assurances from their peers about the validity of their intended answers. Occasionally, a student would repeat the teacher's question in Cantonese to help prompt his or her classmates to understand it and respond to it. It is interesting to note that although most students to whom the first author spoke readily asserted ID2 among peers, they felt obliged to avoid displaying ID2 in front of their English teachers inside the English classrooms, with the perception or understanding that ID2 would usually be disfavored or discouraged by the teachers. The reason is that ID2 was considered counterproductive to their construction and development of ID1, which seems to be more important for their future. Such a perception of the debilitating effects of L1 in L2 classrooms may probably be a social construction through institutional and public discourses (see Lin, 1996a). The authors feel that it is not a desirable phenomenon for students to harbor such a mentality toward their L1. As argued by Cook (1999), both L1 and L2 knowledge are equally important resources for multicompetent language users. Over this point, we see the need for further empirical research to inform policymakers, teachers, and students of the potential strengths of appropriate L1-support for L2-learning (see Anton & DiCamilla, 1998; Canagarajah, 2005b; Lin, 2000).

ID3. Adolescents Closely Attached to Everyday Cantonese-Based Popular Youth Culture.   Closely aligned with ID2 is an identity of the students that reveals a subjective self that in every respect is heavily nourished by the local popular sociocultural ecology. It is shown in chapters 7 and 8 that much of the students' creativity and adeptness in manipulating the L2 linguistic signals to have fun came from their L1 linguistic and cultural resources. Even though some of the L1 associations that students made of the L2 reveal only what mainstream adults might call the "vulgar and degrading" interests of the students (for example, the allusions to sex and gang culture, see Excerpts 7.14, 8.10, 8.15), as teachers, the authors cannot deny the potential motivating effects of these topics in promoting meaningful language use (or "internally persuasive discourse"). It seems that what teachers can do is not to suppress or repress this desire of the students to assert these popular cultural youth identities, but to skillfully turn their desire into a motivation for them to express their L1-based culture in L2 as a first step to a gradual development of a diverse range of L2 speaking styles and registers. Critical media literacy can be built into the L2 curriculum to induce students to acquire the critical analytical skills to analyze the (implicit) sexist, racist, or homophobic ideologies (messages) of many popular cultural texts. On the other hand, if teachers do not engage students in critical dialogues about their pop youth cultural texts and instead just suppress or repress students' desires, students are likely to simply tune out to their teachers during the lessons. Acknowledging the importance of pop youth cultural identities in the lives of the students might be the first step toward building trust and dialogue between teacher and students.

ID4. Interlocutors in a Conversation That Involves Cross-Cultural and Interethnic Elements.   This identity, strictly speaking, is expected to appear most naturally during the NETs' lessons. The NETs, being non-Cantonese speakers and having newly arrived from western countries, inevitably bring with them sociocultural perceptions about how things should be done or seen in ways that were likely to be different from members of the local community such as the LETs and the students. Conversations between members of different (although at times overlapping) sociocultural life worlds, however, often involve the need to confront, and hopefully, resolve, potentially conflicting ideologies and ways of being and seeing (i.e., beliefs, attitudes, perceptions, habits, practices). This is evident in Excerpt 9.22 when the teacher challenges the students' longstanding concepts of the purpose and methods of studying in school by making reference to how adolescents handle school work in the west (also quite stereotypically). The students, on the other hand, express both their agreement and disagreement. Such ability and cultural confidence to participate in cross-cultural negotiations is becoming increasingly important in view of the ever-increasing opportunities for transnational and intercultural interactions in the globalized world (Harris, Leung, & Rampton, 2002; Lam, 2000; Warschauer, 2000). As evidenced in a survey conducted by Luk (2001), many junior secondary students welcomed the opportunities to be taught by a NET because they could learn more about **sai fong man fa** <*western cultures*>. During the interview with Mr. Williams' 4E class immediately after the lesson reported in Excerpt 9.22, two of the boys who were most vocal during the lessons said that they really liked the discussion they were engaged in with Mr. Williams. They felt that they were developing into competent English users.

Even though cultural differences may not always appear in dialogues with NETs, we have reason to believe that most students perceived their interactions with NETs to be different from those with LETs. The major difference, according to some students during the interviews, lies in the fact that they had to use an "other" language to interact. From their perception, anything that happened in the local setting was likely to be new to the NETs, and that had, to a certain extent, increased their desire to communicate with the NETs. Many students, of course, also seemed to enjoy communicating with the LETs, but the whole orientation and configuration of the exchange would be quite different. Although it may be more intimate to interact with the LETs, it seems more novel and exciting to interact with the NETs.

As explained in chapter 4, in a broad sense, cross-cultural encounters can refer to interactions between people coming from the same ethnic background, but from different age generations, gender, and social class backgrounds. It follows that cross-cultural elements also appeared in interactions between LETs and the students. For example, Ms. Hung's Year 3 students tended to behave very seriously in front of the teacher (probably responding to the teacher's elegant and cultured ways of speaking) but became more playful during group interactions and interviews with the first author, who seemed to be an insignificant other to them. As evident in Excerpt 8.14, students of 1B whose class teacher was Mr. Sze display rather different behavior in Miss Logan's lessons. In Mr. Sze's lessons, they seemed to be more aware of the need to conform to the expectations on student behavior of a Chinese teacher even though down at heart, they might actually enjoy uttering things that are taboo in schools. It shows that even young students are able to adapt their interactional styles, fashion different selves, and perform identities in different cross-cultural contexts.

ID5. Adolescents Developing Into Adults Who Are Capable of Independent Thinking. The construction of this identity involves a development of the cognitive and metacognitive skills and strategies to do critical thinking. For example, in

Excerpt 9.17, some of Mr. Nelson's students are challenging their peers with thought-provoking questions that might actually be intended for the teacher. By taking up the hypothetical positioning of a teacher, the students consciously or unconsciously conducted thinking independent of their student identity and began to assume a teacher's "voice" that represents that of an adult. In the lesson where Excerpts 8.8, 9.21 and 9.22 come from, although some students of Mr. Williams tended to follow their peers in choosing their stances, quite a few were bold enough to be the odd ones out. Even though such practice may only represent the students' ambivalent attitude toward the activity, or toward the whole context of learning, these students at least showed a desire to assert a sense of agency. The teacher, as expected, deliberately pursued the thinking of these "odd" ones. It is interesting to note that on a few occasions, these odd ones changed their standpoints after some enquiries by the teacher. This is crucial evidence showing how we constantly negotiate with the changing contexts in our process of making sense of our surroundings, and about how we should position ourselves, and be positioned in the surroundings.

Capitalizing on the Multiple Identities of Students

Given the intimate connection between identity and language learning, it is crucial for language teachers to understand "*how* the identities of learners are engaged in the formal language classroom" (Norton, 2000, p. 140). We would like to further advance the notion that in the process of constructing our sense of self and identities in interaction, our desire to assert ourselves may also enhance our urge to communicate and enhance the self-perceived value of the meaning of our utterances. As suggested by Pavlenko and Lantolf (2000), "[a] linguistic cross-over is from the perspective of sociohistorical theory an intentional renegotiation of one's multiple identities, which are reconstructed in communications with members of another discourse" (p. 172). Belay (1996) and Canagarajah (1996b) have also argued that our sense of self and the act to construct and negotiate different identities seem most robust and dynamic in contacts with people and ideologies from other discourse communities, or other cultures. It may be this urge to represent ourselves in front of "other" people that has facilitated our development of a diverse range of communicative resources. A similar point is made in chapter 1 when the authors talk about how their development as English users was influenced by personal interactions with English speakers from overseas.

As argued by Bakhtin, words become "one's own only when the speaker populates [them] with her/his own intention, her/his own accent, when s/he appropriates the word, adapting it to her/his own semantic and expressive intention" (1981, pp. 293–294; feminine pronouns added by the authors to make the language nonsexist). It therefore seems that tasks that require only an animator identity may not be the best means to develop students' communicative resources. Judging from the attitude of the students from resisting to participate in the last section of chapter 9, it seems that teachers should consider creating more communicative space in their teaching to allow students to speak their minds and be the authors of their words, and thus in the process, enable their students to gradually acquire and claim the foreign language as their own.

Lam (2000), in exploring how literacy in an L2 is related to the discursive construction of text identity via electronic means, shows that identity tends to be represented and repositioned when the text-creation environment is different. In her case study of a Chinese immigrant teenager's (with the pseudonym Almon) written correspondence with a transnational group of peers on the internet in America, she found that

> [w]hereas classroom English appeared to contribute to Almon's sense of exclusion or marginalization (his inability to speak like a native), which paradoxically contradicts the school's mandate to prepare students for the workplace and civic involvement, the English he controlled on the Internet enabled him to develop a sense of belonging and connectedness to a global English-speaking community (p.476)

We believe similar outcomes would appear with the identity in the speaking self (apart from the writing self). As evident in chapter 9, students in Mr. Williams' 4E and Ms. Berner's 3E classes demonstrated a change in their discursive practices and projected a diverse range of identities (institutional, social, and cultural) when they perceived the discursive orientation to be different from their conventional institutional experience that allows for more space for them to experiment with different identities.

Block (2002), in revisiting the role of "negotiation of meaning" in promoting communication, argued for the indispensable place of "identity" in the process of negotiation of meaning. He contended that interlocutors engaging in "negotiation of meaning are actually engaged in acts of identity affirmation, face saving, and outright survival" (Block, 2002, p. 124). Data from the present study further support an important mediating role of "self" and "identities" in learning a second/foreign language. In the present study, we have shown in Excerpt 9.12 how Mr. Sze's changing activity format may have resulted in a less face-threatening situation and a subsequent increased level of participation by some previously uncooperative students. The negotiation of meaning thus becomes a "negotiating of identity and face" (Block, 2002, p. 127). A willingness to engage in the L2 use comes with an affirmation of the value of the self. Of course, the intensity of this sense of identity and the need for face saving differ from people to people, but in a collective activity as that found in classroom learning, every individual member plays a significant role in affecting others.

As Pennycook (1994) has rightly pointed out, the major task for EFL teachers "is not, as some teachers believe, to find ever better ways of making students talk, but to understand in ever more sensitive ways why they talk the way they do, and why they remain silent" (p. 245). To understand the discourse development of L2 learners, it is important to understand the identity drive behind the discursive practice. An effective EFL teacher and curriculum would not be effective without responding to the plurality and multiplicity of learner identities.

However, in the majority of Hong Kong EFL classroom contexts, as observed by both authors, opportunities for students to capitalize on different aspects of their identities (particularly IDs3, 4 & 5) were extremely rare. Many classroom activities required students to participate with only their institutional identity as a student (operations-oriented activities as described in Lin, 1996b) and speaking in a way that is of the teachers' design and in the teachers' voices only. Students' participation was often very mechanical and passive. The way they reproduced the written words from the textbooks was usually monotonous and dull, often not following the natural rhythm and beat of everyday English speakers. Such situations were found to be present in both NETs' and LETs' lessons. Even though most students seemed to know that they needed to display their English learner identity in the teacher-designed activities, their local pop culture-oriented adolescent identities may drive them to display discursive practices that are incongruous to their English learner identity, resulting in what most teachers would consider to be oppositional behavior. It seems that teachers, instead of trying to ask for a unified coherent, conformist self from the students, should perhaps attempt to capitalize on the other kinds of identities of the students, and in this regard, we would like to propose a "pedagogy of connecting"

TOWARD A PEDAGOGY OF CONNECTING

In the past 20 years, researchers in second and foreign language education have increasingly turned to "critical pedagogy" (Freire, 1998; Giroux, 1983; Pennycook, 2001; Simon, 1987) for insights to understand student resistance in the second and foreign language classrooms. Critical educators proposed different pedagogies having as their main thrust the call for legitimizing the multiplicity and plurality of cultural experiences of students. For example, Norton (2000) captured Simon's (1992) pedagogy of possibility in this way:

> The challenge for the teacher is to develop a practice which, as Simon (1992) argues, acknowledges student experience as legitimate curricular content while simultaneously challenging both the engagement of student experience and student identity. (p. 145)

This critical pedagogical orientation has been taken up by Guilherme (2002) with a view to promoting critical citizenship with critical intercultural awareness. Several terms have been proposed to illuminate the essence of such a pedagogy. They included: the pedagogy of dissent, difference, dialogue, empowerment, and hope. These pedagogical ideas are particularly relevant to EFL/EIL teaching and learning contexts. An underlying assumption of these pedagogies calls for teachers to exercise their "emancipatory authority" (Giroux, 1988) by promoting, legitimizing, acknowledging, validating dissent and differences in voices as a means to counteract hegemonic ideologies often reproduced through institutions such as schools.

At this point, some TESOL practitioners may want to ask if ID1 (Learners of a socially important language) should still occupy a central role in the business of learning English as an international language. To what extent can teachers and students afford to marginalize ID1 for the sake of allowing other forms of identities to take the spotlight? For example, should Miss Logan just take B1 and B2's language play in Cantonese (Excerpt 9.18) as normal and let it happen every day?

We therefore would like to propose a pedagogy of connecting. Apart from emancipating and validating multiple identities so as to engage students in classroom tasks, teachers should also provide a space (both discursive and intercultural space) for students to see the connections between such emancipation of identities and effective learning in schools. Only allowing students to release their counter-ID1 identities by talking about **daa-gei** <*playing electronic games*>, **kau lui** <*courting girls*>, and finding **zau gung** <*visiting Duke Chau, i.e., sleeping*> (see Excerpt 9.18), for example, would not contribute very much to the ultimate goal of mastering the L2 for their future social mobility. In Lin's (2000) words, the students would forever be "encapsulated' in a dominantly L1-based local culture and linguistic environment and this may not be conducive to their development of intercultural competencies to communicate with non-L1 speakers, which has increasingly become a requirement of the better jobs and careers in an ever globalizing economy. A pedagogy of connecting requires teachers to proactively design, plan, and engineer learning activities so that students' multiple identities (whether institutionally endorsed or not) will be acknowledged and capitalized on in the classroom with an ultimate view to enabling students to see how their desire to release and assert noninstitutional identities (e.g., ID3) can actually contribute to an effective fulfillment of the institutionally endorsed ones (e.g., ID1 & ID4). Figure 10.1 portrays our configuration of the connecting model. It adopts the concept of a "reactor" in which atoms (L1 and L2 resources) are divided, joined, remixed, or transformed to produce power (the development of a repertoire of "intercultural communicative resources"). The following sections elucidate each component of the model beginning with the *pedagogical goal* (the bottom level of the figure).

To enable students to see the importance of achieving ID1 and ID4 in addition to displaying IDs 2, 3, and 5, a pedagogy of connecting should promote border crossing for the development of intercultural communicative resources. As Kramsch (1998b, p. 27) defined it, a competent intercultural speaker is privileged for her or his competence in "operating at the border between several languages or language varieties, maneuvering his/her way through the troubled waters of cross-cultural misunderstandings." Being able to operate at the "border" between several languages or language varieties means the intercultural speakers have at their disposal a repository of situated communicative resources in the language and cultural codes involved in the cross-cultural encounters to facilitate dialogic interactions with their interlocutors.

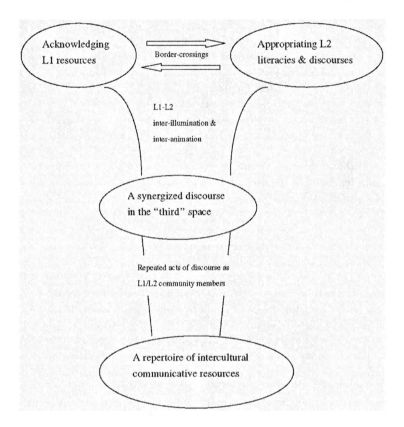

Figure 10.1.   Model of a pedagogy of connecting.

To develop this repertoire of intercultural communicative resources in EFL students requires resourceful intercultural TESOL practitioners who are aware of the need to coconstruct a "shared space of learning" (Tsui, 2004) with students through classroom discourse. Evidence of oppositional or resistant discourse practices of the students presented in chapters 7 to 9 reveals the phenomenon that teachers and students do not always share the same space of learning. The NETs (and sometimes the LETs) and their students seemed to be standing on different sides of the border. The results may be ineffective learning, or students' unwillingness to participate in class activities that were perceived by the students to be teacher-ethnocentric and decontextualized from the learners' feelings, beliefs, and experience (Kumeravadivelu, 1999). Without appropriate methodology, no matter how well the teachers would perform in grammaticality judgments, their ability to take students across the linguistic and cultural border from L1 to L2 is in doubt. Current critical classroom researchers in postcolonial situations such as Canagarajah (1999b) call for a "pedagogy of appropriation" that is viewed as a promising method to "enable students to appropriate the dominant codes and discourses according to their needs and interests" (p. 186). It is a pedagogy that would encourage students to "cross-cultural and discursive borders."

However, we would like to argue that such border crossing or "linguistic cross-over" (Pavlenco & Lantolf, 2000) should not be a road of no return. If a person crosses the border but never comes back, they will not make an effective intercultural speaker because they will then lose all the sociohistorical roots of their identities. It follows that effective intercultural speakers should be able to traverse the border between the L1 and L2 (or even L3, L4, etc.) as local contingency measures at moments of interaction, retaining L1-based sociohistorical linguistic and cultural heritage while appropriating the L2 sociohistorical linguistic and cultural resources as warranted. The tasks for TESOL practitioners, NETs and LETs alike, therefore, involve empowering students not just in terms of their ability to appropriate and reproduce normative grammatical utterances, but to claim agency and authorship in the language code(s) that they construct during dialogic processes by reaccentuating utterances of previous users and uses, and filling them with their own desires, intentions, and dialogic overtones (Bakhtin, 1981; Lin & Luk, 2005). Effective intercultural speakers must have a sense of ownership and agency over the language varieties they are employing in the interactions.

If intercultural resources (rather than target language native speakerism) are the ultimate goal for language learning for globalized communication, NETs, as well as LETs, should reflect on whether they are themselves resourceful intercultural speakers and how they could enable students to attain this goal. Alptekin (2002) proposed a model of intercultural EIL (English as an international language) pedagogy drawing on ideologies from Hyde (1998), Kramsch and Sullivan (1996), and Widdowson (1998) to replace the conventional model of communicative competence that strictly adheres to native speaker norms within the target language culture. In Alptekin's model, successful bilinguals with intercultural insights and knowledge should become the pedagogical models in EIL settings instead of monolingual native speakers. Developing students' intercultural communicative competence and enabling them to be both global and local speakers of English should be the pedagogical goals. Instructional materials should involve local and international contexts relevant to the learners' lives, and incorporate suitable discourse samples pertaining to native and nonnative speaker interactions. In many respects, Alptekin's model resonates with the thinking orientations in the present book, which emphasize a pedagogy of connecting local voices and global discourses.

At the top level of the connecting model (Fig. 10.1), we juxtapose L1 resources and L2 literacies and discourses for the crossing and connecting. Our contention is that a pedagogy of connecting should assist students to construct the identity of an L1 linguistic and cultural resource person in preparation for intercultural interaction. Some second language acquisition researchers tend to employ disparaging terminology to denote certain what we see as normal characteristics of the learning process. For example, they always talk of delearning the L1-based communication strategies that are usually perceived as linguistically deficient (although we must add that some SLA researchers did recognize the positive transfer of L1 in some contexts). It gives students the impression that their knowledge of the L1 is the source for all the major obstacles in learning the L2. With a pedagogy of connecting, this mentality should be changed. If teachers understand that it is natural that students like to draw on their L1-based cultural resources in response to the L2 learning tasks, teachers could invite students to draw up a list of self-chosen Cantonese (L1) idioms (e.g., **wan zau-gung** *<going to sleep>*, **caat-hai** *<to flatter>* (literally meaning 'shoe-shining'), and even **kau lui** (Cantonese slang meaning *<courting girls>*) and provide the English annotations to help non-Cantonese English users to understand the Cantonese popular culture with a view to facilitating cross-cultural communication. It is important to make students see the added value of knowing more than one language. The experience of learning a foreign language would, therefore, be additive, and not subtractive, nor a burden. This is also similar to the approach proposed by Lisa Delpit (1988) in helping African-American children in valuing their Black vernacular English (BVE) but at the same time explicitly getting them to discover the differences between BE and standard American English without denigrating their L1 (BVE). Being themselves L1-L2 bilinguals, LETs may seem to have a distinct advantage in promoting a positive self-image to the students as being resourceful in both L1 and L2. However, this attribute should not be confined to the LETs only. In the present study, NETs such as Ms. Berner had on several occasions acknowledged students' L1 resources and attempted to take them across the border based on that L1 (e.g., Excerpts 7.10 & 8.5)

The authors believe that students would be better able to notice the link between their L1 resources (which they seldom have any doubts about) and their successful appropriation of a foreign language if they could discern the potential for interillumination and interanimation between the two languages. The two languages can be viewed as having equitable linguistic and cultural status notwithstanding the hegemonic dominance of English. For example, teachers can openly engage students in a critical discussion of why English has become dominant, and how they can hold different views from the mainstream society without ignoring the need to learn English for social mobility, and not devaluing their own L1s. A pedagogy of connecting is one that actively engages students in seeing the connection between the languages and the meaning differences of the L1 and L2 cultural codes they encounter in the L2 learning process so that they could traverse back and forth between the L1 and L2 linguistic and cultural borders freely. EFL/EIL teachers always ask students to think in the target language. Although some students coming from a more L2-oriented sociocultural background (i.e., with family linguistic capital in Bourdieu's sense; see Lin, 1999) may be able to do so, most students would begin their thinking process in L1. When students are requested to express in L2, many of them would first formulate in L1 and attempt to translate them into L2. Some would feel very frustrated when they could not express themselves well in L2 because of insufficient L2 resources. To enable students to understand the challenges involved in mastering two languages, teachers should provide students with legitimate opportunities to respond to or reproduce in L1 those ideas written in L2. For example, students could be asked to act out an English play in Cantonese. They should be encouraged not just to act out the meaning, but to identify linguistic and cultural elements that are represented in the same way, or elements that are treated differently by the two languages as a reflection. This can enable students to understand the extent to which, and in what respects, the two languages can illuminate and animate one another. It is in this way that the students' metacognitive, metalinguistic, and cross-cultural awareness in their L1 (along the intra-mental plane) could contribute to their learning of an L2. This is particularly important as learning a foreign language involves appropriating or transforming the often alienating target language discourse (i.e., "authoritative discourse" in Bakhtin's sense; see previous discussion) and making it become an "internally persuasive," one's own discourse. Student resistance to learning may emerge without such internal relevance.

The result of an interilluminated and interanimated L1 and L2 may result in a "hybridized" discourse. From the authors' experience, a fundamental challenge to many TESOL educators practicing teaching in outer circle countries (Kachru, 1992) concerns frequent nonsensical, playful, and sometimes disruptive discourse practices of the students that often contain deviated L2 features blended with L1 overtones. Such discourse may represent students' resistant practices toward being forced to conform to the inner circle-based linguistic and cultural norms of interaction. Their strategies to counteract the undesirable business of learning English that is full of "authoritative discourses" are to go through it by turning it into parodic and self-invented, but more "internally persuasive," discourses characterized by hysterical laughter and nonsensical fun, or features of "carnival laughter" derived from verbal and language play as discussed in Lin and Luk (2005). It must be noted, however, that even though such discourse practices of the students may be resistant in nature, and not totally conducive to intercultural communication, they bear signs of linguistic crossover. Many students presented in chapters 7 to 9 were seen using a hybridized version of L1 and L2 in responding to their NETs' initiation. What potentials do these hybridized varieties have on students' development as competent intercultural speakers? We would like to enlist the notion of "third space" to interpret the emergence and significance of such practice.

"Third space" is a concept developed by postcolonial theorist Homi Bhabha that he uses to denote an indeterminate border area that "ensures that cultural signs are not fixed but can be appropriated, rehistoricized, translated, and reread" (Childs & Williams, 1997, p. 142). Bhabha sees the third space as the liminal (or unconventional) space that sits between fixed identifications, "a place of agency and intervention because it is here that all cultural meaning is constructed, and in that sense located" (p. 142).

We draw on this concept of "third space" to illuminate the discursive flexibility and creativity of some students in our data when they were engaged in self-initiated, and sometimes teacher-collaborated linguistic play, or when they were inserting subordinate L1 vernacular cultures into the dominant L2 discourses, or when they were asserting their transgressive identities by playfully challenging and contradicting the teachers with utterances that contravened the norms of behavior in the classroom in a Chinese society. When such acts were enacted, the linguistic and ideological references of either the L1 or the L2 the students uttered became unstable, flexible, and sometimes original, but at all times, imbued with students' strong quest for relevance to their personal interests, desires, and concerns, which results in a "third discourse" (a kind of discourse that defies the linguistic conventions of either L1 or L2). The concept of "third space" (or third place) has been currently used by some TESOL researchers to denote the kind of "linguistic exile" nonnative speakers create as a refusal to take roots, or an act to distance themselves from both one's native language and the foreign tongue (Kramsch & Lam, 1999, p. 63). To a great extent, students' third space discourse could be understood as their preferred medium through which they perform their acts of identity. In this regard, we propose that a pedagogy of connecting should acknowledge the communicative value of discourse practices situated in a "third space" because the potentials of further development from such hybridized discourse practices into intercultural communicative resources cannot be overlooked. The highly exultant experience of the students in using hybridized discourses synergizing both L1 and L2 to express their own meanings, as shown in the classroom excerpts in this book, may have long-lasting traces of memories in the students' minds and constructed an intriguing identity in the students as "native" speakers of hybrid intercultural linguistic varieties of which they could claim ownership. The initiatives of the students to practice code switching, code mixing, and "code crossing" (Rampton, 1995; see chap. 7), no matter how minimal, could become the first step for these students to develop into resourceful intercultural speakers.

Rampton (1995) discussed how code crossings tend to occur at moments of liminality (a concept developed by Victor Turner). Liminality is defined as the "interactive spaces where the dominant norms of everyday life are temporarily jeopardized or suspended" (Rampton, 1995, p. 167). At moments of liminality, there is a relaxation of the rules of interaction order, and constraints of ordinary behavior. Just imagine that in the middle of a conventional English lesson in Hong Kong with teacher-fronted whole-class IRF-type of interaction where students are required to respond to the teacher's initiation in English, the teacher suddenly leaves the classroom to bring something from the staff room. In most cases, the students would immediately break into informal chats with neighbors in Cantonese. The previously uptight facial expressions of some students experiencing language anxiety described in Tsui (1996) might become full of smiles and very relaxed. Liminal moments could of course appear the other way around, as when a group of people who are used to speaking among themselves in coarse language suddenly become very formal in their use of language due to the presence of a more conservative but important person.

A considerable amount of data in this study, in fact, helps to shed light on how liminal moments appeared in some otherwise traditional classrooms in Hong Kong. The discourse practices of the students (and sometimes the teachers as well such as Ms. Berner) in excerpts such as 7.14, 9.20, 9.22 and most of the excerpts in chapter 8 reflect characteristics of liminal talk during which language crossings occur. The interaction space that emerges during these liminal moments is largely least institutional and sociohistorically conventionalized, thus leaving a lot of indeterminate space in which students can manipulate, appropriate, and reappropriate the linguistic forms and ideological import from L1 to L2, or L2 to L1 to assert their creative, often playful meanings. It is interesting to note that the linguistic codes that were crossed sometimes involved languages other than the students' L1, or the target language. For example, there was evidence showing students' crossing to Putonghua, the national language of China. Given the popularity of Japanese in Hong Kong, it would not be strange at all if some Japanese phrases are used by students in their hybrid variety, even though no such instance has been captured in this study.

How can teachers create this "third space" and the liminal moments? Unlike communicative activities published for universal pedagogical applications, "third space" cannot be tailored according to a formula beforehand, but emerges through dialogic interaction of the teacher and the students when the opportunity comes. As pointed out by Kramsch (1993), many teachers tend to resign their teaching to the constraints of a lot of contextual factors, for example, overcrowded classes, a conservative educational culture, little academic or financial recognition.

> And yet, the classroom is not the totally socially controlled context it seems to be. As we have seen, it is constantly challenged by the learners themselves, in ways that are as varied as its potential meanings. What often constrains teachers is their fear of the imagination, of unexplainable and uncontrollable meanings, of paradox and ambiguity. If they listen to and explore further what their students are saying through their ill-formed utterances, their silences, their non-verbal language, they will discover where the forces of change are and where teachers can, as the saying goes, "make a difference." (Kramsch, 1993, p. 93)

To make the difference, teachers should develop a deeper understanding of the students' preferred worlds, cultures, identities, and voices. Lin and Luk (2005) argued that

> [t]eachers can engage themselves in what Bakhtin (1981, 1986, 1990) called the process of "transgredience," that is, the ability to step outside some existing practices and analyse from a vantage point the sociocultural sources and resources that constitute our own and others' actions. (p. 94)

It seems that both teachers and students would need to retreat to a "third space" sometimes to enable them to look at how they are positioned in the L1 and L2 interconnectedness from a vantage point.

Lastly, a pedagogy of connecting, like other forms of pedagogy, should not be viewed as the only pedagogical canon. It does not rule out tasks that focus on the formal properties of the language resources. These tasks, however, are not expected to be only mechanical pattern drillings, but to enable students to see the connection between mastering the building blocks of a language (e.g., its phonology, grammar, and lexis) and being able to express meanings effectively (as languages are sedimented products of repeated acts of discourse, see Pennycook, 2004). As pointed out by Cazden (1999), language socialization (as contrasted with language acquisition, see chap. 5, last section) involves the need to acquire knowledge about, and attitudes toward, language forms and functions (i.e., socialization about language) to substantiate their communicative performance.

CONCLUSION

It seems that "a pedagogy of connecting" poses challenges that have actually eclipsed the NETs/LETs dichotomy and constituted crucial issues for teachers under whatever labels to reflect on. It seems to be utterly important to provide opportunities for students to experiment with language crossings through constructing, using, and playing with linguistically and culturally synergetic ways of speaking, which are personally meaningful and socioculturally appropriate. We choose the word "synergetic" here as an alternative to "hybridized" to deanomalize the debilitating negative connotations of the latter in Chinese (**"zaap-zung,"** meaning "mixed breed"), and emphasize the added power of the constructed and constructing varieties that are imbued with students' desires, agency and identities.

Teachers could no longer restrict students' learning experience to the space within the four walls of the classroom, but should open up their minds to the meaning-making potentials of the ecological environments both inside and outside the walls of the classrooms and the environments' effects on the students' discursive practices.

To conclude, NETs should not be the enfranchised group to carry native speaker status and enjoy the accompanied power, authority, and privileges in foreign language learning environments. Achieving a response from their local students by engaging them in a dialogic learning process, and helping students to develop into effective intercultural speakers of English require resources in aspects other than the target language linguistic and cultural knowledge. Some of these other important resources are more likely to be possessed by LETs. It is therefore important for language policymakers and the public to understand that native speakerism is no convenient pregiven sure-win quality of NETs. For native speakerism to be effective in TESOL, it must be constantly learned, practiced, achieved, renewed, regained, relearned, and reachieved in different situated contexts.

QUESTIONS FOR REFLECTION AND DISCUSSION

1. From your experience as a second language teacher/student, have you identified some other types of identity constructed and asserted by the learners (or you yourself) in the classroom apart from the five mentioned in this chapter?

2. Have you ever tried using learners' L1 to motivate their L2 learning? If yes, did it work? To what extent? If not, what were the reasons for not using it?

Notes

[1]The official name of the NET Scheme in Hong Kong as shown in the job advertisements was "Native-speaking English" teachers, even though the term "native-speaker English teachers" is also commonly used almost as a homonym in academic papers. Adopting the term "native speaking" seems to be an attempt to tone down ethnicity and birthright and to emphasize proficiency and expertise. Besides, it was stated in the job advertisement in May 2004 that candidates "should be native-speakers of English or have native-speaker English competence." This requirement seems to have enabled speakers whose mother tongue is not English but who possess native-speaker competence to be eligible for the post. However, the Chinese translation of the scheme emphasizes English being the "mother tongue" (以英語為母語) of eligible applicants that seem to have highlighted the biological inheritance nature of NETs. Besides, in 2003, an ethnic Chinese who was brought up in Britain was rejected by a primary school head in his/her application to serve as a NET in primary school on the grounds that she or he did not look like a native English speaker. This incident shows that many people still harbor a narrow view of what constitutes a "native-speaking" English person.

[2]Education Department (1997, April 16). Administrative Circular No.27/97.

[3]Under the primary NET scheme introduced in 2000, two primary schools shared only one NET. Some prestigious primary schools, however, recruited more than one NET. Traditionally, what makes a school prestigious in Hong Kong is usually the English standards (often measured by public exam results) of its graduates.

[4]Cantonese is the first language of over 96% of the population in Hong Kong.

[5]The Secondary School Entrance Examination (SSEE) was a mechanism to screen primary school leavers for placement in secondary schools based on their performance in three tests on English, Chinese, and math. It was abolished in 1978 with the introduction of 9-year, universal, compulsory education from Primary One to Secondary Three.

[6]Public housing estates were built by the Hong Kong government for the lower income groups.

[7]Before 1998, up to 90% of secondary schools were the so-called Anglo-Chinese schools that claimed to teach most subjects in English. The one that the first author attended was also an Anglo-Chinese school. It became a Chinese medium school after 1998.

[8]The word "encounter" here is used to denote contacts that are unexpected and unprepared for; it may be a tension-filled but significant contact.

[9]Although English is important, only a pass (grade D or E) is required for entering into the University. That explains why some students invest comparatively less effort in English than in other content subjects.

[10] "A hen talking to a duck" （雞同鴨講）is a colloquial Cantonese idiom to analogize the mutual unintelligibility of speech between two human beings.

[11]Putonghua is the national language of Mainland China. It is similar to Mandarin in Taiwan. The two varieties are very similar but display differences in the sound and lexical systems.

[12]The mother tongue of up to 98% of people in Hong Kong was Cantonese, although the percentage has lowered in recent years (95% in 2002) due to massive new arrivals from Mainland China over the last few years.

[13]According to Bolton (2002), access to English increases through a mass education system. By 2001, the proportion of the population claiming to know English reached 43%, with 39% identifying themselves as speakers of English as another language.

[14]At that time, less than 20 schools had recruited EETs and most of these schools were government schools that were obliged to pilot new policy initiatives.

[15]The Education Commission was set up in February 1984 as a nonstatutory body to advise the government on the overall development of education in light of the community's needs. Consultation reports are released almost annually on current educational issues.

[16]There were 56 schools that had applied to join the NET scheme in 1997/1998, the year before the current NET scheme was launched.

[17]The major difference between the Enhanced NET scheme and its precedents lies in the fact that the NETs employed on the current scheme constituted extra manpower for the English panel in schools. This may be one reason why the Enhanced NET scheme generally met with less resistance from local teachers.

[18]The Education Department was incorporated under the Education and Manpower Bureau in 2003.

[19]The source of information is from Circular Memorandum No 173/98, issued March 25, 1998 by the Education Department.

[20]Some readers may find Lai's (1999) argument unconvincing after seeing that the official number of NETs of British nationality was 82 out of 334 in 1998. Although it was considered by Lai to be a significant increase from 58 in 1997, there were other factors resulting in the increase, the major one being the NET scheme in 1998 that was introduced on a territorywide basis whereas the previous ones were taken up by schools voluntarily. It is interesting, however, to note that the greatest provider of NETs in the 1998 recruitment was Australia, a former colony of Britain, with 123 out of 334.

[21]The concept of periphery and centre English users corresponds to Kachru's (1992) representation of the global spread of English with outer/expanding and inner circles respectively. The centre or inner circle refers to countries where English is the native and national language whereas periphery or outer circle refers to places where people use English as a foreign language.

[22]The terms "NS-NNS" were used in Long (1981) and Pica (1992) to refer to native and nonnative speakers.

[23]"Bound exchanges" are a type of subcategory of teaching exchanges in Sinclair and Coulthard (1975). They function to reiterate the head of the preceding free initiation so that the interaction could be extended. According to Tsang (1994, p. 45), three types of bound exchanges—reinitiate, repeat, and confirm "function to maintain the verbal interactions and prevent communication breakdown in the classes."

[24]See Widdowson (1993).

[25]In Gramsci's (1971, p. 28) sense, hegemony means "domination by consent." The ruling class' interest is presented as the common interest and therefore taken for granted. This is usually achieved through national apparatus such as media and education (see Ashcroft, Griffiths, & Tiffin, 2000, p. 116).

[26]The notion of "performativity" in language studies can be traced to Austin's (1962) book about doing things with words. According to Austin (1962), a performative utterance is one that performs an action at the same time that the utterance is issued provided that the persons issuing the utterance and the circumstances in which the utterance is issued are appropriate for the invocation of the particular actions and procedures (an important doctrine of felicities). Austin's theoretical underpinnings of the speech act theory were taken further by Bourdieu (1991) who identified institutional power and social relations as prerequisite felicity conditions to authorize a speaker to speak with the expected performative effects. It follows that a person must have the legitimate identity to effect a speech act. In this configuration, our identities (who we are) give meaning and power to words we utter. For example, it is generally held by the public in EFL countries that the English used by the White middle class from Britain, America, Canada, and Australia should be more accurate and standard. White middle class native Eng-

lish speakers from these places are therefore performing the act of establishing the "norms" and "standards" of English for the world's use. Other English speakers do not have this performative power because they lack the same identity (see related discussions of the linguistic and cultural privileges of the Whites in Kubota, 2005).

[27]The Language Proficiency Assessment for Teachers (LPAT for short) started to be enforced in 2001 to ensure that teachers of English and Putonghua all reach a publicly recognized benchmark level in terms of language proficiency. The test for the English teachers covers all four skills plus classroom language assessment. In the writing paper, one part requires candidates to identify grammatical errors from a student's composition and explain what grammatical features have been used incorrectly with appropriate metalanguage.

[28]It should be noted that there exist among prestigious and "standard" English varieties features of accent variations (see Bauer, 2003). Therefore, it is misleading to perceive all "native" speakers as speaking with only one correct accent.

[29]Apart from "discourse practice," the term "discursive practice" is also used in works on critical discourse analysis. The term is drawn from works of Foucault to emphasize the role of language as social practices. Although "discourse practice" and "discursive practice" are often used interchangeably, the latter generally signals an explicit interest in power relations within society (A Dictionary of Sociolinguistics, 2004).

[30]According to Li (2003), such practice of the Chinese shows a concern for food because "shortage of food has been a part of everyday life for a majority of the Chinese" (p. 80).

[31]The four aspects of culture in Scollon and Scollon (2001) are *ideology* (which includes beliefs, values, and religion), *socialization* (which includes education, primary and secondary socialization, theories of the person and of learning), *forms of discourse* (which include functions of language and nonverbal communication), and *face system* (which include kinship, the concept of the self, etc.).

[32]Interested readers may refer to Allwright (1988) and Kumaravadivelu (1999) for detailed critique of the interaction coding approach.

[33]"Intersubjectivity" is a sociocultural concept referring to how individual subjects relate to one another and gain understanding of one another. Wertsch (1998) defined it as "the degree to which interlocutors in a communicative situation share a perspective" (pp. 111–112).

[34]In Hong Kong, English carries the status of a "second language" in the sociolinguistic profile. However, the authors tend to avoid employing the terms "second language" experts and learners because there might be cases where English is not the second language of the teachers or the students. Therefore, we choose the term "target language."

[35]"Subjectivity" refers to the "conscious and unconscious thoughts and emotions of the individual, her/*his* sense of her/*him*self and her/*his* ways of understanding her/*his* relation to the world" (Weedon, 1987, p. 32, italics added).

[36]The aptitude test was abolished in 2001. Allocation of secondary school places is then mainly based on students' internal school results.

[37]In 2001, the five bands were reduced to three bands in order to minimize the labeling effects and the performance gaps between schools.

[38]Some schools also offer a commercial stream in which students study commercial subjects such as accounting.

[39]According to the general statistics on higher education in Hong Kong, the percentage of relevant age group being able to obtain first-year first-degree education increases from 15.0% in 1992/1993 to 17.0% in 2001/2002.

[40]"Subject constitution" is ideologically related to Foucault's (1997) "subjectivitiy" and "technologies of the self." It refers to a process that begins with knowledge of our "self" and the ability to work on it by regulating our bodies, our thought, and our conduct. Through these processes, individuals can transform their lives and achieve a degree of self-improvement (see Danaher, Schirato, & Webb, 2000).

[41]In Hong Kong, task-based teaching was introduced as part of a so-called target-oriented curriculum (TOC) reform (Carless, 1997, 1999; Mok, 2001). Also see note (46).

[42]The notion of "learner-centered" teaching is criticized by some classroom researchers. Holliday (1994), for example, quoted Hutchinson and Waters' (1984) view that a communicative approach should be "*learning*-centered" because the purpose of teaching should be to enable learning to take place.

[43]It should be noted that newly built schools after 1998 will have standard classroom size of $67m^2$ in a government initiative to create a more ideal school environment.

[44]The school was able to recruit two NETs by being a pilot Chinese medium school.

[45]A "seven-up" day means the teacher has to teach 7 (out of 8 or 9) consecutive periods on a teaching day.

[46]TOC refers to the target-oriented curriculum that is a form of outcomes-based education in which students progressed toward specified learning targets by carrying out tasks (Carless, 1997; Clark, Scarino, & Brownell, 1994; Morris, 2000). The theoretical framework is based on constructivist learning principles that assert that students needed to be involved in developing their own learning. Task-based teaching and learning were central to this philosophy. However, due to strong re-

sistance from teachers against its assessment mechanism, TOC was unofficially abolished but reincarnated as the task-based approach.

[47]Mrs. Bean is probably a female parallel of Mr. Bean, who is a popular British comedy figure.

[48]Every secondary school could apply for funding from the Education Department to set up an English corner/room for promoting English standard of the students. In some schools, only a corner was given. The allocation of a standard size classroom for the setting up of the English room in Ms. Berner's school reflected the principal's perceptions of the importance of English.

[49]During the data-collection visits, Mr. Nelson's class did not use the school textbook, but a magazine published in Spain for language teachers.

[50]Mr. Nelson studied Putonghua for 4 years in China.

[51]Five secondary schools and two primary schools were sampled for that study (which lasted from 1998 to 2000), and in each school, the NET and two to three local teachers were informants for the investigation. Their English lessons were observed and taped in three rounds of visits (about one week each time) at an interval of 4 to 6 months over a 2-year period.

[52]Miss Logan could not handle the discipline problem with 2E. The English panel head thus took up the teaching of half of the class (consisting of the naughtier ones), leaving the better ones with Miss Logan.

[53]Sampling students for the interview gave rise to many interesting phenomena. Most teachers identified the students and informed them of the details themselves. Ms. Hung, however, asked for volunteers during the lessons. As can be imagined, very few students volunteered themselves, but quite a few "volunteered" others. The latter's behavior was corrected by the teacher. Miss Logan identified the students but several turned her down. The first author needed to approach the students herself during the lesson and talked them into participating in the interview.

[54]The term "western culture" is used because in Hong Kong, people generally label festivals such as Christmas, Easter, and Halloween as 西方節日 <festivals coming from the west side>.

[55]Many Hong Kong citizens emigrated to English-speaking countries such as Canada and Australia in early 1990s after the Tienanmen Square Incident in Mainland China.

[56]"Missie" is a popular and informal way of calling their female teachers by students. Here the student mentioned "missie" instead of "ah sir" (male teachers) probably because there are more female English teachers than male.

[57]It should be noted that many teachers and students in Hong Kong perceive "activities" to be games or tasks that involve lots of movements and peer interaction. They seldom consider written exercises as activities.

[58]It is interesting to compare this proposed strategy with the least favorite activity in class—listening to the teacher talking about the textbook.

[59]During the visits, the first author observed an incident in which a student explained his problems to Ms. Hung in Cantonese while the teacher responded all along in English. The pupil looked puzzled at times (fieldnotes).

[60]The syllabus states that English should be used as much as possible not only for instructional purposes, but also for carrying out daily classroom routines, organizing teaching activities, and providing optimal opportunities for engaging learners in authentic situations where English is used for genuine purposes of communication.

[61]In normal classrooms in Hong Kong, students sit in rows. However, this lesson took place in a special room where students could sit in groups around large tables. Such kind of setting is felt to be more conducive to small group interactions. The group of girls initiating the conversation were sitting around one such table very close to the teacher's desk.

[62]ERS refers to the extensive reading scheme that is a government-resourced initiative to promote reading habits in primary and secondary schools. During ERS lessons, students are free to choose to read books classified under different grade levels.

[63]"G" is one of the grade levels in the reading scheme.

[64]Common repair strategies include repetition, reformulation, and linguistic simplification of utterances (see Crookes & Gass, 1993).

[65]G1 here is the same girl as G2 in Excerpt 7.7. It seems that this girl was quite enthusiastic in providing language broker service to her peers.

[66]Some students were able to provide "Wendy [sic]" and "Pizza Hut" in English. We will attribute the reason to the inherently different nature of these restaurant names as being born native English terms. Wendy's and Pizza Hut are more popularly known by their English names in Hong Kong. To the students, these may be terms that were born to be English, just like their native English teacher. These names are not so much L2 or L3 to the students, but just something they have acquired because they are in their everyday life.

[67]The student may actually mean "the other group" when he said "next group."

[68]"Zero" here is the real name of the student. According to Mr. Williams, Zero chose this name because he always scored zero marks in tests and exams, and most teachers thought that he was lazy. Due to the difficulty in finding a pseudonym that expresses the same connotation, we decided to keep the real name.

[69]The authors are not suggesting that the comprehension tasks for this book were poorly set because we have not seen them. We are only suggesting that there is such a possibility.

[70]"Sunday" was the name of a mobile phone company in Hong Kong.

[71]From the authors' vague memory of the TV commercial, which was no longer on show for several years, the background seemed to be somewhere in Hong Kong.

[72]The hiring of teaching assistants was funded by the Hong Kong government. These ELTAs are usually English-speaking preuniversity teenagers.

[73]The class was a remedial class, with Ms. Berner and a local teacher each taking care of 20 students. Ms. Berner had got all the boys. In this particular lesson, with the help of the ELTA, Ms. Berner was conducting the activity with only about 10 students.

[74]See Cook (2000, pp.114–115) for details of the classification.

[75]It is highly likely that these young students had been affected by local Cantonese movies that make funny, exaggerated, and nonsense phonological associations about people's names.

[76]Wong X Wai is an aged former female movie star who always dressed up in a colorful and exaggerated way. Her image was often the object of ridicule by the public and the mass media.

[77]Instances of social interaction for fun did occur between Miss Logan and her students during this study. Miss Logan told the first author that her 2B class gave her a toy as a birthday present after asking her about her favorite cartoon character. The first author had also observed three senior-form girls joking with Miss Logan outside the staff room by placing some cold and wet toy in her hands. However, the recorders inside the classroom have not captured these social interactions.

[78]"Illocutionary" and "perlocutionary" are two types of speech acts coined by J. L. Austin's (1962) *How to do Things with Words* to describe what we do in saying something, such as apologizing, describing, and so forth (illocutionary); and the purpose or effect of the utterance (perlocutionary).

[79]In his article, Guthrie contrasted the language use of a monolingual English teacher and a Chinese-English bilingual teacher teaching a class of Chinese students in America. There were instances when the monolingual teacher shushed the students when they spoke Cantonese to each other even though they were actually on task.

[80]It is a common practice for Hong Kong students to address their male teachers as **ah sir**, and female teachers as "missie."

[81]When the first author showed Mr. Williams Excerpt 8.7 and asked if he would mind if I present the Excerpt as it is and thus reveal his real first name, Mr. Williams agreed immediately. He told the first author that he really appreciated the creativity of the student.

[82]YKT is a pseudoacronym of the school.

[83]Perhaps being the only female (and young looking) in the classroom, the first author attracted some attention from the students. During recess, some students were eager to know what she was and the reason for her observations there. Some students volunteered to be interviewed and refused to leave even after the interview was over. This does not mean that they had any sexual interest in the first author, but being students in a boys-only school, their curiosity about females is understandable.

[84]From the first author's observation, "How come?" was a pet phrase of Mr. Nelson and many students imitated the way Mr. Nelson said it in class.

[85]Some young students (male and female) would compliment on female teachers' clothing styles, but they seldom would comment on male teachers' appearance.

[86]The first author observed that whenever the teacher approached the girl, she would start giggling, and always covered up her face with a book and talked to the teacher like a spoiled young girl would do with her boyfriend.

[87]For example, the students compared Elsa's waist measurement to that of a bucket, and a kind of essence oil well known in Hong Kong that has the middle part of its container being the biggest in measurement.

[88]In most secondary schools in Hong Kong, there are seven to eight English lessons in a 6-day cycle. Miss Logan's school practiced a 7-day cycle system and had nine English lessons every cycle.

[89]Miss Logan was surprised when the first author told her that Mr. Sze had already covered the topic, in more or less the same way as she did, the day before. This incident shows that the NET and LET working in the same school teaching the same class seldom had any collaboration and communication in terms of curriculum design and day-to-day teaching.

[90]The standard pronunciation of the second character should begin with a nasal /n/. However, many Cantonese speakers replace it with a lateral. Some linguists attribute the cause to a lazy tongue.

[91]"Discourse strategies" can be distinguished from "communication strategies" in that the latter focuses on mutual attempts of two interlocutors to agree on a meaning in situations where linguistic and sociolinguistic rule structures do not seem to be shared. It emphasizes more how communication can be maintained by strategies such as paraphrase, borrowing, topic avoidance, or L1-transliteration (see Tarone, 1983). Paralinguistic features such as gestures and facial expressions can also be used. Discourse strategies, on the other hand, concern the use of language to convey messages that may or may not aim at achieving mutual understanding.

[92]The students almost always responded in Cantonese, mixed with single-word English occasionally.

[93]This sounds like a Cantonese particle 哪 (/na:/) that serves a similar function as the framing word "now" in English. What Ms. Hung uttered was to me something in between the two phonologically.

[94]During formal reading conferences, students are summoned to the teacher's desk to do the conference. Mr. Williams was observed to have done conferencing more informally by walking around the classroom and talking to students in their seats.

[95]See the background information in the paragraph preceding Excerpt 7.14, chap. 7.

[96]The first author remembers that she learned these strategies from more experienced local teachers. Whether Miss Logan learned these from her past experience as a teacher or from local teachers in Hong Kong is beyond our knowledge.

[97]Most of these students interviewed said that they experienced communication problems at the beginning. However, the situation improved after several months because Miss Logan used lots of gestures and pictures to explain.

[98]It is interesting to draw readers' attention to Mr. Williams' recount of personal experience in "being taught" Cantonese by various minor staff in the school in the second interview (see chap. 6). That learning experience made him realize the students' difficulties in learning a foreign language and the importance of repeated drillings and demonstration. The second interview took place on the same day after the lesson presented in Excerpt 9.8. It might be the case that students' performance in the task had reminded him of his personal experience that enabled him to show such empathy during the interview.

[99]Houses in secondary schools are like student halls in the universities. In Ms. Hung's school, all students were assigned to a house labelled with color terms. The mentioning of "house" was a system devised by Ms. Hung to motivate students to answer questions. According to Ms. Hung, students responded more actively when they knew that they did so to gain merits for their house rather than for individual achievements.

[100]Quotation marks were put around "initiates" because the students concerned are actually animating some predetermined questions.

[101]"Finding Duke Chau" is a traditional Chinese idiom meaning "to go to sleep."

[102]"To talk nonsense" (講無厘頭話) has been a part of the youth culture in Hong Kong introduced by Canton pop film star Stephen Chow in the early 1990s.

[103]Foucault was a French philosopher in the 1950s who argued that forms of knowledge and humankind's sense of oneself (or subjectivity) are constructed by specific institutions, discourses and practices.

[104]In Goffman's (1981) configuration, an individual may take up or shift between three roles in uttering a given linguistic expression—(1) the "animator," or "the sounding box"; (2) the "author," or "someone who has selected the sentiments that are being expressed"; or (3) the "principal," or "someone whose position is established by the words that are spoken" (p. 144).

[105]An earlier version of four of the five identities was reported in Luk (2005a).

Appendix: Conventions of Transcription

Symbols	Meaning
NET	Native English speaking teachers employed on the NET Scheme in Hong Kong
LET	Local Cantonese-English teachers in Hong Kong
T	The teacher in that particular excerpt
B1, B2, ...	Different male students in consecutive turns distinguishable by their different voices
B	An unidentifiable male student
Bs:	Several male students
G1, G2,...	Different female students in consecutive turns distinguishable by their different voices
G	An unidentifiable female student
Gs:	Several female students
Ss	A number or the whole class of students
faat ming <To invent>	Transcription of Cantonese[1] utterances followed by English translation
[ ]	Researcher's comments
(XX)	Uncertain hearing
(???)	Indecipherable utterances
.	Falling intonation followed by noticeable pause (as at the end of declarative sentences)
(..)	Short pause
(...)	Medium pause of up to 5 sec
(o.6/7/8,...)	For wait time longer than 5 sec, the pause will be represented by figures showing the number of seconds involved. Wait time longer than one minute will become (1.0) and so on
,	Continuing intonation
?	Rising intonation, usually a question

---

[1]Spoken Cantonese from the data was transcribed using the system of Cantonese transcriptions developed by the Linguistic Society of Hong Kong (1997).

^	High pitch utterances, as used when the students anglicize the Cantonese words
!	High falling pitch showing exclamations
:	Lengthened syllable (usually attached to the vowels); extra colon indicates longer elongation
-	Self-halting, or abrupt cutoff
CAPS	Emphatic and strongly stressed utterances
XXX	Underlined utterances are words read out from texts, including textbook materials, worksheets, or students' written works
=	Contiguous utterances or latching
//	Overlapping utterances
<XXX>	Utterances made with a greater voice volume compared with that of the preceding and following ones
A-B-C-D	Sounding out the letter names of a word
{....}	Untranscribed section of the excerpt

References

Adamson, B., & Li, S. P. T. (1999). Primary and secondary schooling. In M. Bray & R. Koo (Eds.), *Education and society in Hong Kong and Macau* (pp. 35–57). Hong Kong: Comparative Education Research Centre, the University of Hong Kong.

Alfred, G., Byram, M., & Fleming, M. (Eds.). (2002). *Intercultural experience and education*. Clevedon, England: Multilingual Matters.

Allwright, D. (1988). *Observation in the language classroom*. London: Longman.

Alptekin, C. (2002). Towards intercultural communicative competence. *ELT Journal, 56*(1), 57–64.

Amin, N. (1999). Minority women teachers of ESL: Negotiating White English. In G. Braine (Ed.), *Nonnative educators in English language teaching* (pp. 93–104). Mahwah, NJ: Lawrence Erlbaum Associates.

Anton, M., & DiCamilla, F. (1998). Socio-cognitive functions of L1 collaborative interaction in the L2 classroom. *The Canadian Modern Language Review, 54*(3), 315–342.

Arthur, J. (1996). Code switching and collusion: Classroom interaction in Botswana primary schools. *Linguistics and Education, 8,* 17–33.

Ashcroft, B., Griffiths, G., & Tiffin, H. (2000). *Post-colonial studies: The key concepts*. London: Routledge.

Austin, J. L. (1962). *How to do things with words: The William James lectures delivered at Harvard University in 1955*. Oxford, England: Clarendon Press.

Austin, T. (1998). Cross-cultural pragmatics—Building in analysis of communication across cultures and languages: Examples from Japanese. *Foreign Language Annals, 31*(3), 326–341.

Bakhtin, M. M. (1981). *The Dialogic imagination: Four essays by M. M. Bakhtin* (C. Emerson & M. Holquist, Trans.). Austin, TX: University of Texas Press.

Bakhtin, M. M. (1986). *Speech genres and other late essays* (V. W. McGee, Trans.). Austin, TX: University of Texas Press.

Bakhtin, M. M. (1990). *Art and answerability*. Austin, TX: University of Texas Press.

Bakhtin, M. M. (1994). Folk humor and carnival laughter. In P. Morris (Ed.), *The Bakhtin reader* (pp. 194–205). London: Arnold.

Barton, D., Hamilton, M., & Ivanic, R. (Eds.). (2000). *Situated literacies: Reading and writing in context*. London: Routledge.

Barratt, L., & Kontra, E. H. (2000). Native-English-speaking teachers in cultures other than their own. *TESOL Journal, 9*(3), 19–23.

Bauer, L. (2003). *An introduction to international varieties of English*. Hong Kong: Hong Kong University Press.

Belay, G. (1996). The (re)construction and negotiation of cultural identities in the age of globalization. In H. B. Mokros (Ed.), *Interaction and identity* (Vol. 5, pp. 319–346). New Brunswick: Transaction Publishers.

Bernstein, B. B. (1971). *Class, codes and control* (Vols. 1–3). London, Routledge & Kegan Paul.

Biggs, A. P. & Edwards, V. (1994). "I treat them all the same"—Teacher–pupil talk in multiethnic classrooms. In D. Graddol, J. Maybin, & B. Stierer (Eds.), *Researching language and literacy in social context* (pp. 82–99). Clevedon; Philadelphia: Multilingual Matters.

Biggs, J., & Watkins, D. (1996). The Chinese learners in retrospect. In D. Watkins & J. B. Biggs (Eds.), *The Chinese learner: Cultural, psychological and contextual influences* (pp. 269–285). Hong Kong: CERC & ACER.

Block, D. (2002). 'McCommunication': A problem in the frame for SLA. In D. Block & D. Cameron (Eds.), *Globalization and language teaching* (pp. 117–133). London: Routledge.

Bloome, D., Carter, S. P., Christian, B. M., Otto, S., & Shuart-Faris, N. (2005). *Discourse analysis and the study of classroom language and literacy events*. Mahwah; NJ: Lawrence Erlbaum Associates.

Bloome, D., & Willett, J. (1991). Toward a micropolitics of classroom interaction. In J. Blase (Ed.), *The politics of life in schools: Power, conflict, and cooperation* (pp. 207–236). Newbury Park, CA: Sage.

Bolton, K. (ed.) (2002). *Hong Kong English : Autonomy and creativity*. Hong Kong: Hong Kong University Press.

Bolton, K., & Hutton, C. (2002). Media mythologies: Legends, "local facts" and triad discourse. In C. Barron, N. Bruce, & D. Nunan (Eds.), *Knowledge and discourse: Towards an ecology of language* (pp. 147–164). Harlow, England: Longman.

Bond, M. H. (Ed.). (1996). *The handbook of Chinese psychology*. Hong Kong: Oxford University Press.

Bond, M. H., & Hwang, K. K. (1986). The social psychology of Chinese people. In M. H. Bond (Ed.), *The psychology of the Chinese people* (pp. 213–264). Oxford, England: Oxford University Press.

Bourdieu, P. (1991). *Language and symbolic power*. Cambridge, MA: Harvard University Press.

Boyle, J. (1995). Hong Kong's education system: English or Chinese? *Language, Culture and Curriculum, 8*(3), 291–304.

Boyle, J. (1997a). Imperialsim and the English language in Hong Kong. *Journal of Multilingual and Multicultural Development, 18*(3), 169–181.

Boyle, J. (1997b). Native-speaker English teachers of English in Hong Kong. *Language and Education, 11*(3), 163–181.

Breen, M. P. (1986). The social context for language learning—a neglected situation? *Studies of Second Language Acquisition, 7*, 135–158.

Breen, M. P., & Candlin, C. N. (1980). The essentials of a communicative curriculum in language teaching. *Applied Linguistics, 2*, 89–112.

British Council. (1989). *Expatriate English language teachers pilot scheme—Hong Kong* (Final evaluation report). Hong Kong: Author.

Brown, J. S., Collins, A., & Duguid, P. (1989). Situated cognition and the culture of learning. *Educational Researcher, 18*(4), 32–42.

Brown, G., & Yule, G. (1983). *Discourse analysis*. Cambridge, England: Cambridge University Press.

Bruner, J. S. (1990). *Acts of meaning*. Cambridge, MA: Harvard University Press.

Brutt-Griffler, J., & Samimy, K. K. (1999). Revisiting the colonial in the postcolonial: Critical praxis for nonnative-English-speaking teachers in a TESOL program. *TESOL Quarterly, 33*(3), 413–431.

Brutt-Griffler, J., & Samimy, K. K. (2001). Transcending the nativeness paradigm. *World Englishes, 20*(1), 99–106.

Burnaby, B., & Sun, Y. (1989). Chinese teachers' views of western language teaching: Context informs paradigms. *TESOL Quarterly, 23*(2), 219–238.

Byram, M. (1989). *Cultural studies in foreign language education*. Clevedon, England: Multilingual Matters Ltd.

Byram, M., & Fleming, M. (Eds.). (1998). *Language learning in intercultural perspective: Approaches through drama and ethnography*. Cambridge, England: Cambridge University Press.

Caillois, R. (1969). The structure and classification of games. In J. W. Loy & S. Kenyon (Eds.), *Sport, culture and society: A reader on the sociology of sport* (pp. 000–000). London: Macmillan. (Original work published 1955)

Cameron, D. (1997). Performing gender identity: Young men's talk and the construction of heterosexual masculinity. In S. Johnson & U. H. Meinhof (Eds.), *Language and masculinity* (pp. 47–64). Oxford, England: Blackwell.

Canagarajah, A. S. (1993). Critical ethnography of a Sri Lankan classroom: Ambiguities in student opposition to reproduction through ESOL. *TESOL Quarterly, 27*(4), 601–626.

Canagarajah, A. S. (1999a). Interrogating the "native speaker fallacy": non-linguistic roots, non-pedagogical results. In G. Braine (Ed.), *Non-native educators in English language teaching* (pp. 77–92). Mahwah, NJ: Lawrence Erlbaum Associates.

Canagarajah, A. S. (1999b). *Resisting linguistic imperialism in English teaching.* Oxford, England: Oxford University Press.

Canagarajah, A. S. (2000). Negotiating ideologies through English: Strategies from periphery. In T. Ricento (Ed.), *Ideology, politics and language policies* (pp. 121–132). Amsterdam: John Benjamins.

Canagarajah, A. S. (Ed.). (2005a). *Reclaiming the local in language policy and practice.* Mahwah, NJ: Lawrence Erlbaum Associates.

Canagarajah, A. S. (2005b). Accommodating tensions in language-in-education policies: An afterword. In M. Y. A. Lin & P. W. Martin (Eds.), *Decolonisation, globalisation: Language-in-education policy and practice* (pp. 194–201). Clevedon, England: Multilingual Matters Ltd.

Candlin, C. N. (1997). General editor's preface. In B. L. Gunnarsson, P. Linell, & B. Nordberg (Eds.), *The construction of professional discourse* (pp. ix–xiv). London: Longman.

Candlin, C. N., Lin, A. M. Y., & Lo, T. W. (2000). *The discourse of adolescents in Hong Kong* (City University of Hong Kong Strategic Research Grant #7000707). Hong Kong: City University of Hong Kong.

Carless, D. (1997). Managing systemic curriculum change: A critical analysis of Hong Kong's target-oriented curriculum initiative. *International Review of Education, 43,* 349–366.

Carless, D. (1999). Perspectives on the cultural appropriacy of Hong Kong's target-oriented curriculum (TOC) initiative. *Language, Culture and Curriculum, 12*(3), 238–254.

Carless, D. (2003). Factors in the implementation of task-based teaching in primary schools. *System, 31,* 485–500.

Cazden, C. B. (1986). Classroom discourse. In M. C. Witrock (Ed.), *Handbook of research on teaching* (pp. 432–463). New York: Macmillan.

Cazden, C. B. (1988). *Classroom discourse: The language of teaching and learning.* Portsmouth, NH: Heinemann.

Cazden, C. B. (1999). Socialization. In B. Spolsky (Ed.), *Concise encyclopedia of educational linguistics* (pp. 63–65). Amsterdam: Elsevier.

Cazden, C. B. (2001). *Classroom discourse: The language of teaching and learning.* Portsmouth, NH: Heinemann.

Chacon, C., Alvarez, L. C., Brutt-Griffler, J. & Samimy, K. K. (2003). Dialogues around "revisiting the colonial in the postcolonial: Critical praxis for nonnative-English-speaking teachers in a TESOL program. In J. Sharkey & K. E. Johnson (Eds.), *The TESOL quarterly dialogues* (pp. 141–150). Alexandria, VA: Teachers of English to Speakers of Other Languages.

Chaudron, C. (1983). Foreigner talk in the classroom—an aid to learning? In H. W. Seliger & M. H. Long (Eds.), *Classroom oriented research in second langauge acquisition* (pp. 127–145). Rowley, MA: Newbury.

Chief Executive, the Honourable Tung Chee Hwa. (1997). Building Hong Kong for a new era. Address to the provisional legislative council meeting. Hong Kong: The Hong Kong Special Administrative Region of the People's Republic of China.

Childs, P., & Williams, R. J. P. (1997). *An introduction to post-colonial theory.* London: Prentice Hall.

Clark, H. H. (1996a). *Using language.* Cambridge, England: Cambridge University Press.

Clark, H. H. (1996b). Communities, commonalities and communication. In J. J. Gumperz, & S. C. Levinson (Eds.), *Rethinking linguistic relativity* (pp. 324–355). Cambridge, England: Cambridge University Press.

Clark, J., Scarino, A., & Brownell, J. (1994). *Improving the quality of learning: A framework for target-oriented curriculum renewal.* Hong Kong: Institute of Language in Education.

Cook, G. (2000). *Language play, language learning.* Oxford:: Oxford University Press.

Cook, V. (1999). Going beyond the native speaker in language teaching. *TESOL Quarterly, 33*(2), 185–209.

Coupland, J. (2000). Introduction: sociolinguistic perspectives on small talk. In J. Coupland (Ed.), *Small talk* (pp. 1–25). London: Longman.

Crookes, G., & Gass, S. (1993). *Tasks and language learning: Integrating theory and practice.* Clevedon/Philadelphia: Multilingual Matters.

Crystal, D. (1998). *Language play.* London: Penguin Books.

Curriculum Development Council. (1983). *Syllabus for English* (Forms I–V). Hong Kong: Government Printer.

Curriculum Development Council. (1999). *Syllabluses for secondary schools: English language Secondary 1–5.* Hong Kong: Government Printer.

Danaher, G., Schirato, T., & Webb, J. (2000). *Understanding Foucault.* London: Sage.

Davies, A. (1991). *The native speaker in applied linguistics.* Edinburgh, Scotland: Edinburgh University Press.

Davies, A. (2003). *The native speaker: Myth and reality.* Clevedon, England: Multilingual Matters Ltd.

Davies, B., & Harre, R. (1990). Positioning: The discursive production of selves. *Journal for the Theory of Social Behaviour, 20*(1), 43–63.

de Certeau, M. (1984). *The practice of everyday life.* Berkeley: University of California Press.

Delpit, L. D. (1988). The silenced dialogue: Power and pedagogy in educating other people's children. *Harvard Educational Review, 58,* 280–298.

Donato, R. (1994). Collective scaffolding in second language learning. In J. P. Lantolf & G. Appel (Eds.), *Vygostskian approaches to second language research* (pp. 33–56). Norwood, NJ: Ablex.

Donato, R., & McCormick, D. (1994). A sociocultural perspective on language learning strategies: The role of mediation. *The Modern Language Journal, 78,* 453–464.

Education Commission. (1995). *Education Commission Report No. 6.* Hong Kong: Author.

Education Department. (1990). *Report on the interim evaluation of the effectiveness of the management of the expatriate English language.* Hong Kong: Author.

Ellis, G. (1996). How culturally appropriate is the communicative approach? *ELT Journal, 50*(3), 213–218.

Ellis, R. (1994). *The Study of Second Language Acquisition.* Oxford, England: Oxford University Press.

Epstein, J. S. (1998). Introduction: Generation X, Youth culture, and identity. In J. S. Epstein (Ed.), *Youth culture: Identity in a postmodern world* (pp. 1–23). Malden, MA: Blackwell Publishers.

Erickson, F. (1984). What makes school ethnography ethnograpic? *Anthropology & Education Quarterly, 15,* 51–66.

Evans, S. (1996). The context of English language education: The case of Hong Kong. *RELC Journal, 27*(2), 30–55.

Evans, S. (1997). Teacher and learner roles in the Hong Kong English language classroom. *Education Journal, 25*(2), 43–61.

Fairclough, N. (1992). Introduction. In N. Fairclough (Ed.), *Critical language awareness* (pp. 1–29). London: Longman.

Fairclough, N. (1995). *Critical discourse analysis: The critical study of language.* London: Longman.

Fasold, R. (1990). Sociolinguistics of language. Oxford, England: Blackwell.

Ferguson, C. (1983). Language planning and language change. In J. Cobarrubias & J. Fishman (Eds.), *Progress in language planning* (pp. 29–41). Berlin: Mouton.

Flanders, N. A. (1970). *Analysing teaching behaviour*. Reading; MA: Addison-Wesley.

Foucault, M. (1997). *Ethics: Essential works of Foucault 1954–1984* (Vol. 1). London: Penguin.

Freire, P. (1998). *Teachers as cultural workers*. Boulder, CO: Westview Press.

Gabrenya, W. K. J., & Hwang, K. K. (1996). Chinese social interaction: Harmony and hierarchy on the good earth. In M. H. Bond (Ed.), *The handbook of Chinese psychology* (pp. 309–321). Hong Kong: Oxford University Press.

Gandhi, L. (1998). *Postcolonial theory: A critical introduction*. New Delhi, India: Oxford University Press.

Garfinkel, H. (1967). *Studies in ethnomethodology*. Toronto, Canada: Prentice-Hall.

Gee, J. P. (1996). *Social linguistics and literacies: Ideology in discourses*. London: Taylor & Francis.

Gee, J. P. (1999). *An introduction to discourse analysis: Theory and method*. London: Routledge.

Gibbons, J. (1984). Interpreting the English proficiency profile in Hong Kong. *RELC Journal, 15*(1), 64–73.

Giroux, H. A. (1983). *Theory and resistance in education: A pedagogy for the opposition*. South Hadley, MA: Bergin & Garvey.

Giroux, H. A. (1988). *Teachers as intellectuals*. New York: Bergin & Gavey.

Godfrey, P. (1992). Josiah's school drops English. *Window, 2*(19), 32–36.

Goffman, E. (1981). *Forms of talk*. Oxford, England: Blackwell.

Goffman, E. (1986). *Frame analysis*. Boston: Northeastern University Press.

Gramsci, A. (1971). In Q. Hoare & N. Smith (Eds.), *Selections from the prison notebooks of Antonio Gramsci* (Q. Hoare & N. Smith, Trans. & Eds.). London: Lawrence & Wishart.

Guilherme, M. (2002). *Critical citizens for an intercultural world: Foreign language education as cultural politics*. Clevedon, England: Multilingual Matters Ltd.

Gumperz, J. J. (1982). *Discourse strategies*. Cambridge: Cambridge University Press.

Guthrie, L. F. (1984). Contrasts in teachers' language use in a Chinese–English bilingual classroom. In J. Handscombe, R. A. Orem, & B. P. Taylor (Eds.), *On TESOL '83 "The Question of Control"* (pp. 39–52). Washington, DC: TESOL.

Haastrup, K., & Phillipson, R. (1983). Achievement strategies in learner/native speaker interaction. In C. Faerch & G. Kasper (Eds.), *Strategies in interlanguage communication* (pp. 140–158). London: Longman.

Habermas, J. (1987). *Theory of communicative action: Vol.2. Lifeworld and system: A critique of functionalist reason*. Boston: Beacon Press.

Hakkarainen, P. (1999). Play and motivation. In Y. Engestrom, R. Miettinen, & R.-L. Punamaki (Eds.), *Perspectives on activity theory* (pp. 231–249). Cambridge, England: Cambridge University Press.

Hall, J. K. (1993). The role of oral practices in the accomplishment of our everyday lives: The sociocultural dimensions of interaction with implications for the learning of another language. *Applied Linguistic, 14*(2), 145–166.

Hall, J. K. (1995). (Re)creating our worlds with words: A sociohistorical perspective of face-to-face interaction. *Applied Linguistic, 16*(2), 206–232.

Hall, J. K. (2000). Classroom interaction and additional language learning: Implications for teaching and research. In J. K. Hall & L. S. Verplaetse (Eds.), *Second and foreign language learning through classroom interaction* (pp. 287–298). Mahwah, NJ: Lawrence Erlbaum Associates.

Halliday, M. A. K. (1978). *Language as a social semiotic: The social interpretation of language and meaning*. London: Arnold.

Hancock, M. (1997). Behind classroom code switching: Layering and language choice in L2 learner interaction. *TESOL Quarterly, 31*(2), 217–235.

Harris, R. (1989). *The worst English in the world* [Inaugural lecture by the chair of English language]. The University of Hong Kong.

Harris, R., Leung, C., & Rampton, B. (2002). Globalization, diaspora and language education in England. In D. Block & D. Cameron (Eds.), *Globalization and language teaching* (pp. 29–46). London: Routledge.

Haworth, A. (1999). Bakhtin in the classroom: What constitutes a dialogic text? Some reasons for small group interaction. *Language and Education, 13*(2), 99–117.

Heap, J. L. (1976). What are sense making practices. *Sociological Inquiry, 46*(2), 107–115.

Heap, J. L. (1985). Discourse in the production of classroom knowledge: Reading lessons. *Curriculum Inquiry, 15*(3), 245–279.

Heap, J. L. (1992). Seeing snubs: An introduction to sequential analysis of classroom interaction. *Journal of Classroom Interaction, 27*(2), 23–28.

Heras, A. I. (1994). The construction of understanding in a sixth-grade bilingual classroom. *Linguistics and Education, 5,* 275–299.

Holliday, A. (1994). *Appropriate methodology and social context.* Cambridge: Cambridge University Press.

Holliday, A. (1999). Small cultures. *Applied Linguistics, 20*(2), 237–264.

Holliday, A., Hyde, M., & Kullman, J. (2004). *Intercultural communication: An advanced resource book.* London: Routledge.

Holquist, M., & Emerson, C. (1981). *Glossary for the dialogic imagination: Four essays.* Austin: University of Texas Press.

Hong Kong Yearbook. (2002). Retrieved April 12, 2006, from http://www.info.gov.hk/yearbook

Hopper, P. (1998). Emergent grammar. In M. Tomasello (Ed.), *The new psychology of language* (pp. 155–175). Mahwah, NJ: Lawrence Erlbaum Associates.

Howatt, A. (2004). *A history of English language teaching.* Oxford, England: Oxford University Press.

Hughes, M., & Westgate, D. (1998). Possible enabling strategies in teacher-led talk with young pupils. *Language and Education, 12*(3), 174–191.

Hundeide, K. (1985). The tacit background of children's judgements. In J. V. Wertsch (Ed.), *Culture, communication and cognition: Vygotskian perspectives* (pp. 306–322). Cambridge, England: Cambridge University Press.

Hutchison, T., & Waters, A. (1984). How communicative is ESP? *English Language Teaching Journal, 38*(2), 108–113.

Hyde, M. (1998). Intercultural competence in English language education. *Modern English Teacher, 7*(2), 7–11.

Hymes, D. (1974). The ethnography of speaking. In B. Blount (Ed.), *Language, culture, and society* (pp. 248–282). Cambridge, MA: Withrop.

Ivanic, R. (1998). *Writing and identity.* Philadelphia: John Benjamins Publishing Company.

Jenkins, J. (2000). *The phonology of English as an international language.* Oxford, England: Oxford University Press.

Jin, L., & Cortazzi, M. (1993). Cultural orientation and academic language use. In D. Graddol, L. Thompson, & M. Byram (Eds.), *Language and culture: Papers from the annual meeting of the British Association of Applied Linguistics.* Clevedon, England: British Association of Applied Linguistics (BAAL) and Multilingual Matters.

Johnson, K., & Tang, G. (1993). Engineering a shift to English in Hong Kong schools. In T. Boswood, R. Hoffman, & P. Tung (Eds.), *Perspectives on English for professional communication* (pp. 203–216). Hong Kong: City Polytechnic of Hong Kong.

Joseph, J. E. (1996). English in Hong Kong: Emergence and decline. *Current Issues in Language and Society, 3*(2), 166–179.

Kachru, B. B. (1986). *The alchemy of English: The spread, functions and models of non-native Englishes.* Oxford, England: Pergamon.

Kachru, B. B. (1992). Teaching world Englishes. In B. B. Kachru (Ed.), *The other tongue. English across cultures* (2nd ed., pp. 355–365). Urbana, IL: University of Illinois Press.

Kramsch, C. (1991). Culture in language learning: A view from the United States. In K. De Bot, R. B. Ginsberg, & C. Kramsch (Eds.), *Foreign language research in cross-cultural perspective* (pp. 217–240). Amsterdam: John Benjamins.

Kramsch, C. (1993). *Context and culture in language teaching.* Oxford, England: Oxford University Press.

Kramsch, C. (1995). The cultural component of language teaching. *Language, Culture and Curriculum, 8*(2), 83–92.

Kramsch, C. (1998a). *Language and culture.* Oxford, England: Oxford University Press.

Kramsch, C. (1998b). The privilege of the intercultural speaker. In M. Byram & M. Fleming (Eds.), *Language learning in intercultural perspective: Approaches through drama and ethnography* (pp. 16–31). Cambridge, England: Cambridge University Press.

Kramsch, C. (2000). Social discursive constructions of self in L2 learning. In J. P. Lantolf (Ed.), *Sociocultural theory and second language learning* (pp. 133–154). Oxford, England: Oxford University Press.

Kramsch, C. & Lam, W. S. E. (1999). Textual identities: The importance of being non-native. In G. Braine (Ed.), *Non-native educators in English language teaching* (pp. 57–72). Mahwah, NJ: Lawrence Erlbaum Associates.

Kramsch, C., & Sullivan, P. (1996). Appropriate pedagogy. *ELT Journal, 50*(3), 199–212.

Kubota, R. (2005). Critical multiculturalism and second language education. In B. Norton & K. Toohey (Eds.), *Critical pedagogies and language learning* (pp. 30–52). Cambridge: Cambridge University Press.

Kwan, M. H. Y. (2000). Reconsidering language learners' needs: A critical look at classroom verbal play of a reading lesson in Hong Kong. In D. C. S. Li, A. Lin, & W. K. Tsang (Eds.), *Language and education in postcolonial Hong Kong* (pp. 297–316). Hong Kong: Linguistic Society of Hong Kong.

Lai, C. (1994). Communication failure in the language classroom: An exploration of causes. *RELC Journal, 25*(1), 99–129.

Lai, M. L. (1999). Jet and Net: A comparison of native-speaking English teachers schemes in Japan and Hong Kong. *Language, Culture and Curriculum, 12*(3), 215–228.

Lam, W. S. E. (2000). L2 literacy and the design of the self: A case study of a teenager writing on the internet. *TESOL Quarterly, 34*(3), 457–482.

Lantolf, J. P. (2000). Introducing sociocultural theory. In J. P. Lantolf (Ed.), *Sociocultural theory and second language learning* (pp. 1–26). Oxford: Oxford University Press.

Lau, E. (1991). The future tense. *Far Eastern Economic Review, 151*(4), 18–19.

Lave, J., & Wenger, E. (1992). *Situated learning: Legitimate peripheral participation.* Cambridge, England: Cambridge University Press.

Law, W. W. (1997). The accommodation and resistance to the decolonisation, neocolonisation and recolonisation of higher education in Hong Kong. In M. Bary & W. O. Lee (Eds.), *Education and political transition: Implications of Hong Kong's change of sovereignty* (pp. 41–64). Hong Kong: The University of Hong Kong.

Leontiev, A. N. (1978). *Activity, consciousness and personality.* Englewood Cliffs, NJ: Prentice-Hall.

Leung, C., Harris, R., & Rampton, B. (1997). The idealised native speaker, reified ethnicities, and classroom realities. *TESOL Quarterly, 31*(3), 543–560.

Li, D. (2002). Hong Kong parents' preference for English-medium education: passive victims of imperialism or active agents of pragmatism? In A. Kirkpatrick (Ed.), *Englishes in Asia: Communication, identity, power & education* (pp. 29–62). Australia: Language Australia.

Li, K. (2003). Chinese. In J. L. Bianco & C. Crozet (Eds.), *Teaching invisible culture: Classroom practice and theory* (pp. 53–100). Melbourne: Language Australia Ltd.

Lin, A. M. Y. (1990). *Teaching in two tongues: Language alternation in foreign language classrooms* (Vol. 3, Research Rpt. No. 3). Hong Kong: City Polytechnic of Hong Kong.

Lin, A. M. Y. (1996a). Bilingualism or linguistic segregation? Symbolic domination, resistance and code-switching in Hong Kong schools. *Linguistics and Education, 8,* 49–94.

Lin, A. M. Y. (1996b). *Doing-English-Lessons in secondary schools in Hong Kong: A sociocultural and discourse analytic study.* Unpublished doctoral dissertation, University of Toronto, Canada.

Lin, A. M. Y. (1997). Hong Kong children's rights to a culturally compatible English education. *Hong Kong Journal of Applied Linguistics, 2*(2), 23–48.

Lin, A. M. Y. (1999). Doing-English-lessons in the reproduction or transformation of social worlds? *TESOL Quarterly, 33*(3), 393–412.

Lin, A. M. Y. (2000). Lively children trapped in an island of disadvantage: Verbal play of Cantonese working-class schoolboys in Hong Kong. *International Journal of Sociology and Language, 143*, 63–83.

Lin, A. M. Y. (2001). Symbolic domination and bilingual classroom practices in Hong Kong. In M. Heller & M. Martin-Jones (Eds.), *Voices of authority: Education and linguistic difference* (pp. 139–168). Westport, CT: Ablex.

Lin, A. M. Y. (2005). Doing verbal play: Creative work of Cantonese working class schoolboys in Hong Kong. In A. Abbas & J. Erni (Eds), *International cultural studies: An anthology* (pp. 317–329).Oxford, England: Blackwell.

Lin, A., & Luk, J. (2002). Beyond progressive liberalism and cultural relativism: Towards critical postmodernist, sociohistorically situated perspectives in classroom studies. *The Canadian Modern Language Review, 59*(1), 97–124.

Lin, A. M.Y., & Luk, J. C. M. (2005). Local creativity in the face of global domination: Insights of Bakhtin for teaching English for dialogic communication. In J. K. Hall, G. Vitanova, & L. Marchenkova (Eds.), *Contributions of Mikhail Bakhtin to understanding second and foreign language learning* (pp. 77–98). Mahwah, NJ: Lawrence Erlbaum Associates.

Lin, A. M. Y., & Man, E. Y. F. (in press). *Bilingual education: South East Asian perspectives.* Hong Kong: Hong Kong University Press.

Lin, L. (1994). Language of and in the classroom: Constructing the patterns of social life. *Linguistics and Education, 5,* 367–409.

Linguistic Society of Hong Kong. (1997). (A Cantonese Transcription Chart). Hong Kong: Linguistic Society of Hong Kong.

Littlewood, W. (2002). Cultural awareness and the negotiation of meaning. In C. Lee & W. Littlewood (Eds.), *Culture, communication and language pedagogy* (pp. 25–36). Hong Kong: Language Centre, Hong Kong Baptist University.

Long, M. H. (1975). Group work and communicative competence in the ESOL classroom. In M. K. Burt & H. C. Dulay (Eds.), *On TESOL '75: New directions in second language learning, teaching and bilingual education* (pp. 211–233). Washington, DC: TESOL.

Long, M. H. (1981). Input, interaction and second language acquisition. In H. Winitz (Ed.), *Native language and foreign language acquisition (Annals of the New York Academy of Sciences No. 379;* pp. 259–278). New York: New York Academy of Sciences.

Long, M. H. (1996). The role of the linguistic environment in second language acquisition. In W. C. Ritchie & T. K. Bhatia (Eds.), *Handbook of second language acquisition* (pp. 413–468). San Diego, CA: Academic Press.

Long, M. H., & Sato, C. (1983). Classroom foreigner talk discourse: Forms and functions of teachers' questions. In H. W. Seliger & M. H. Long (Eds.), *Classroom oriented research in second language acquisition.* Rowley, MA: Newbury House.

Luk, B. H. K. (1991). Chinese culture in the Hong Kong curriculum: Heritage and colonialism. *Comparative Education Review, 35*(4), 650–658.

Luk, J. C. M. (2001). Exploring the sociocultural implications of the Native English-speaker Teacher Scheme in Hong Kong through the eyes of the students. *Asia-Pacific Journal of Language in Education, 4*(2), 19–50.

Luk, J. C. M. (2003). The dynamics of classroom small talk. *Issues in Applied Linguistics, 14*(2).

Luk, J. C. M. (2005a). Voicing the "self" through an "other" language: Exploring communicative language teaching for global communication. In S. Canagarajah (Ed.), *Reclaiming the local in language policy and practice* (pp. 247–267). Mahwah, NJ: Lawrence Erlbaum Associates.

Luk, J. C. M. (2005b). Understanding and capitalizing on multiple identities of students in TESL/TEFL: Towards a pedagogy of connecting. In S. May, M. Franken, & R. Barnard (Eds.), *LED2003: Refereed Conference Proceedings of the 1st International Conference on Language, Education and Diversity.* Hamilton, New Zealand: Wilf Malcolm Institute of Educational Research, University of Waikato.

Luke, K. K., & Richards, J. C. (1982). English in Hong Kong: Functions and status. *English World-Wide, 3,* 47–64.

Mehan, H. (1979). *Learning lessons.* Cambridge, MA: Harvard University Press.

Miller, J. M. (2000). Language use, identity, and social interaction: Migrant students in Australia. *Research on Language and Social Interaction, 33*(1), 69–100.

Milroy, L. (1980). *Language and social networks.* New York: Blackwell.

Mok, A. (2001). The missing element of rational pedagogical reform: A critical analysis of the task-based learning English language syllabus. *Asia-Pacific Journal of Teacher Education and Development, 4*(2), 189–211.

Morris, P. (1992). Preparing pupils as citizens of the Special Administrative Region of Hong Kong: An analysis of curriculum change and control during the transition period. In G. A. Postiglione (Ed.), *Education and society in Hong Kong: Toward one country and two systems* (pp. 117–145). Hong Kong: Hong Kong University Press.

Morris, P. (1995). *The Hong Kong school curriculum: Development, issues and policies.* Hong Kong: Hong Kong University Press.

Morris, P. (2000). The commissioning and decommissioning of curriculum reforms: The career of the target-oriented curriculum. In B. Adamson, T. Kwan & K. K. Chan (Eds.), *Changing the curriculum: The impact of reform on Hong Kong's primary schools* (pp. 21–40). Hong Kong: Hong Kong University Press.

Morrison, K., & Lui, I. (2000). Ideology, linguistic capital and the medium of instruction in Hong Kong. *Journal of Multilingual and Multicultural Development, 21*(6), 471–486.

Norton, B. (1997a). Critical discourse research. In N. H. Hornberger & D. Corson (Eds.), *Encyclopedia of language and education* (Vol. 8, pp. 207–216). Dordrecht, The Netherlands: Kluwer.

Norton, B. (1997b). Language, identity and the ownership of English. *TESOL Quarterly, 31*(3), 409–429.

Norton, B. (2000). *Identity and language learning: Gender, ethnicity and educational change.* London: Longman.

Ochs, E. (1996). Linguistic resources for socializing humanity. In J. J. Gumperz & S. C. Levinson (Eds.), *Rethinking linguistic relativity* (pp. 407–437). Cambridge, England: Cambridge University Press.

O'Sullivan, T., Hartley, J., Saunders, D., Montgomery, M., & Fiske, J. (1994). *Key concepts in communication and cultural studies.* London: Routledge.

Pavlenko, A., & Lantolf, J. P. (2000). Second language learning as participation and the (re)construction of selves. In J. P. Lantolf (Ed.), *Sociocultural theory and second language learning* (pp. 155–178). Oxford, England: Oxford University Press.

Pennington, M. C. (1997). Projecting classroom language use in a group of bilingual graduates of a BATESL course. *Language, Culture and Curriculum, 10*(3), 222–235.

Pennington, M. C. (1999a). Bringing off-stage "noise" to centre stage: A lesson in developing bilingual classroom discourse data. *Language Teaching Research, 3*(2), 85–116.

Pennington, M. C. (1999b). Framing bilingual classroom discourse: Lessons from Hong Kong secondary school English classes. *International Journal of Bilingual Education and Bilingualism, 2*(1), 53–73.

Pennington, M. C., Lee, Y. P., & Lau, L. (1996). Communicating in the Hong Kong secondary classroom: The evolution of second language discourses. *Research Monograph, 7.*

Pennycook, A. (1994). *The cultural politics of English as an international language.* London: Longman.

Pennycook, A. (1998). *English and the discourse of colonialism.* London: Routledge.

Pennycook, A. (1999). Introduction: Critical approaches to TESOL. *TESOL Quarterly, 33*(3), 329–348.

Pennycook, A. (2001). *Critical applied linguistics: A critical introduction.* Mahwah, NJ: Lawrence Erlbaum Associates.

Pennycook, A. (2003). Global Englishes, rip slyme, and performativity. *Journal of Sociolinguistics, 7*(4), 513–533.

Pennycook, A. (2004). Performativity and language studies. *Critical Inquiry in Language Studies: An International Journal, 1*(1), 1–26.

Phillipson, R. (1992). *Linguistic imperialism.* Oxford, England: Oxford University Press.

Pica, T. (1992). The textual outcomes of native speaker-non-native speaker negotiation: What do they reveal about second language learning? In C. Kramsch & S. McConnell-Ginet (Eds.), *Text and context: Cross-disciplinary perspectives on language study* (pp. 198–237). Toronto: Heath.

Pierson, H. D. (1998). Societal accommodation to English and Putonghua in Cantonese-speaking Hong Kong. In M. C. Pennington (Ed.), *Language in Hong Kong at century's end* (pp. 91–111). Hong Kong: Hong Kong University Press.

Platt, E., & Brooks, F. B. (1994). The "acquisition-rich environment" revisited. *The Modern Language Journal, 78,* 497–511.

Poole, D., & Patthey-Chavez, G. G. (1994). Locating assisted performance: A study of instructional activity settings and their effects on the discourse of teaching. *Issues in Applied Linguistics, 5*(1), 3–35.

Purves, W. (1989, May 9). *Statement to shareholders.* Presented at the Annual General Meeting of the Hong Kong Bank, Hong Kong.

Quirk, R. (1990). Language varieties and standard language. *English Today, 21,* 3–10

Rampton, M. B. H. (1990). Displacing the "native speaker": Expertise, affiliation, and inheritance. *ELT Journal, 44*(2), 97–101.

Rampton, M. B. H. (1995). *Crossings: Language and ethnicity among adolescents.* London: Longman.

Rogoff, B. (1990). *Apprenticeship in thinking, cognitive development in social context.* New York: Oxford University Press.

Sacks, H., Schegloff, E. A., & Jefferson, G. (1974). A simplest systematics for the organization of turn-taking for conversation. *Language, 50*(4), 696–735.

Samovar, L. A. & Porter, R. E. (1995). *Communication between cultures.* Belmont, CA: Wadsworth.

Savignon, S. J. (1991). Communicative language teaching: State of the art. *TESOL Quarterly, 25*(2), 261–295.

Scollon, R., & Scollon, S. W. (2001). *Intercultural communication: A discourse approach* (2nd ed.). Cornwall, England: Blackwell.

Searle, J. (1965). What is a speech act? In M. Black (Ed.), *Philosophy in America* (pp. 221–239). Ithaca, NY: Allen & Unwin and Cornell University Press.

Sfard, A. (1998). On two metaphors for learning and the dangers of choosing just one. *Educational Researcher, 27,* 4–13.

Shore, B. (1996). *Culture in mind: Cognition, culture, and the problem of meaning.* New York: Oxford University Press.

Simon, R. I. (1987). Empowerment as a pedagogy of possibility. *Language Arts, 64,* 370–383.

Simon, R. I. (1992). *Teaching against the grain: Texts for a pedagogy of possibility.* New York: Bergin & Garvey.

Sinclair, J. M., & Coulthard, M. (1975). *Towards an analysis of discourse—The English used by teachers and pupils.* London: Oxford University Press.

Skehan, P. (1996). A framework for the implementation of task-based instruction. *Applied Linguistics, 17,* 38–62.

Even NETs fail the benchmark tests. (2003, June 14). *South China Morning Post.*

Stephens, K. (1997). Cultural stereotyping and intercultural communication: Working with students from the People's Republic of China in the UK. *Language and Education, 11*(2), 113–124.

Straehle, C. A. (1993). "Samuel?" "Yes, dear?" Teasing and conversational rapport. In D. Tannen (Ed.), *Framing in discourse* (pp. 210–229). Oxford: Oxford University Press.

Strauss, C., & Quinn, N. (1997). *A cognitive theory of cultural meaning.* Cambridge, England: Cambridge University Press.

Street, B. V. (1993). Culture is a verb: Anthropological aspects of language and cultural process. In D. Graddol, L. Thompson, & M. Byram (Eds.), *Language and culture* (pp. 23–43). Clevedon, England: BAAL & Multilingual Matters.

Sullivan, P. N. (2000). Playfulness as mediation in communicative language teaching in a Vietnamese classroom. In J. P. Lantolf (Ed.), *Sociocultural theory and second language learning* (pp. 115–132). Oxford, England: Oxford University Press.

Surry, M. (1994). English not spoken here. *Window, 3*(12), 32–37.

Swann, J., Deumert, A., Lillis, T. & Mesthrie, R. (2004). *A dictionary of sociolinguistics*. Edinburgh, Scotland: Edinburgh University Press.

Swann, J., Deumert, T. L., & Mesthrie, R. (2004). *A dictionary of sociolinguistics*. Edinburgh, Scotland: Edinburgh University Press.

Tang, C. (1997). The identity of the nonnative ESL teacher: On the power and status of nonnative ESL teacher. *TESOL Quarterly, 31*(3), 577–579.

Tang, G., & Johnson, R. K. (1993). Implementing language change in Hong Kong schools: An ecological approach to evaluation. *Journal of Asian Pacific Communication, 4*(1), 31–47.

Tannen, D. (1986). *That's not what I meant!: How conversational style makes or breaks relationships*. New York: Ballantine.

Tarone, E. (1983). Some thoughts on the notion of "communication strategy." In C. Faerch & G. Kasper (Eds.), *Strategies in interlanguage communication* (pp. 61–74). New York: Longman.

Tay, M. (1982). The uses, users and features of English in Singapore. In J. Pride (Ed.), *New Englishes*. Rowley, MA: Newbury House.

Tharp, R. G., & Gallimore, R. (1988). *Rousing minds to life: Teaching, learning, and schooling in social context*. New York: Cambridge University Press.

Tomalin, B., & Stempleski, S. (1993). *Cultural awareness*. Oxford, England: Oxford University Press.

Toohey, K. (2000). *Learning English at school: Identity, social relations and classroom practice*. Clevedon, England: Multilingual Matters.

Tsang, S. K. Y. (1994). *An analysis of teacher–pupil interaction in ESL classroom with reference to native speaking and nonnative speaking teachers*. Unpublished MA dissertation, Hong Kong Baptist University.

Tsui, A. B. M. (1985). Analysing input and interaction in second language classroom. *RELC Journal, 16*(1), 8–31.

Tsui, A. B. M. (1996). Reticence and anxiety in second language learning. In K. M. Bailey & D. Nunan (Eds.), *Voices from the language classroom* (pp. 145–167). Cambridge, England: Cambridge University Press.

Tsui, A. B. M. (2004). The shared space of learning. In F. Marton & A. B. M. Tsui (Eds.), *Classroom discourse and the space of learning* (pp. 165–188). Mahwah, NJ: Lawrence Erlbaum Associates.

van Lier, L. (1996). *Interaction in the language curriculum*. London: Longman.

van Lier, L. (1988). *The classroom and the language learner*. London: Longman.

van Lier, L. (2000). From input to affordance: Social-interactive learning from an ecological perspective. In J. P. Lantolf (Ed.), *Sociocultural theory and second language learning* (pp. 245–260). Oxford, England: Oxford University Press.

van Lier, L. (2001). Constraints and resources in classroom talk: Issues of equality and symmetry. In C. N. Candlin & N. Mercer (Eds.), *English language teaching in its social context* (pp. 90–107). London: The Open University, Routledge, Macquarie.

Vygotsky, L. S. (1986). *Thought and language*. Cambridge, MA: MIT Press.

Vygotsky, L. S. (1994). Extracts from thought and language and mind and society. In B. Stierer & J. Maybin (Eds.), *Language, literacy and learning in educational practice* (pp. 45–58). Clevedon, Avon: The Open University/Multilingual Matters.

Walker, E. (2001). Roles of native-speaker English Teachers (NETs) in Hong Kong Secondary Schools. *Asia Pacific Journal of Language in Education, 4*(2), 51–78.

Warschauer, M. (2000). The changing global economy and the future of English teaching. *TESOL Quarterly, 34*(3), 511–535.

Watson-Gegeo, K. A. (1988). Ethnography in ESL: Defining the essentials. *TESOL Quarterly, 22*(4), 575–592.

Watson-Gegeo, K. A. (1997). Classroom ethnography. In N. H. Hornberger & D. Corson (Eds.), *Encyclopedia of language and education* (Vol. 8, pp. 135–144). Dordrecht, The Netherlands: Kluwer.

Weedon, C. (1987). *Feminist practice and post-structuralist theory.* Oxford, England: Blackwell.

Wells, G. (1993). Reevaluating the IRF sequence: A proposal for the articulation of theories of activity and discourse for the analysis of teaching and learning in the classroom. *Linguistics and Education, 5,* 1–37.

Wertsch, J. V. (1991). *Voices of the Mind.* Cambridge, MA: Harvard University Press.

Wertsch, J. V. (1998). *Mind as action.* New York: Oxford University Press.

Westgate, D., & Hughes, M. (1997). Identifying 'quality' in classroom talk: An enduring research task. *Language and Education, 11*(2), 125–139.

Widdowson, H. G. (1993). The ownership of English. *TESOL Quarterly, 28*(2), 377–389.

Widdowson, H. G. (1998). Context, community, and authentic language. *TESOL Quarterly, 32*(4), 705–716.

Young, R., & Lee, S. (1987). EFL curriculum innovation and teachers' attitudes. In R. Lord & H. Cheng (Eds.), *Language education in Hong Kong* (pp. 83–97). Hong Kong: The Chinese University Press.

Yu, V. W. S. (1997). Encouraging students to read more in an extensive reading programme. In G. M. Jacobs, C. Davis, & W. A. Renandya (Eds.), *Successful strategies for extensive reading* (pp. 1–9): Singapore: Regional Language Centre, Southeast Asian Ministers of Education Organization.

Yu, V. W. S., & Atkinson, P. A. (1988). An investigation of the language difficulties experienced by Hong Kong secondary school students in English-medium schools: I. The problems. *Journal of Multilingual and Multicultural Development, 9*(3), 267–283.

Author Index

A

Adamson, B., 58
Alfred, G., xvi
Allwright, D., 38–39, 210
Alptekin, C., 199
Alvarez, L. C., 30
Amin, N., 23
Anton, M., 192
Arthur, J., 40
Ashcroft, B., 209
Atkinson, P. A., 59
Austin, J. L., 50, 140
Austin, T., 35, 209, 214

B

Bakhtin, M. M., 30, 37, 42–43, 45, 49–51,
    55, 140, 189, 194, 199, 201, 203
Barratt, L., 24–25
Barton, D., 53
Bauer, L., 210
Belay, G., 194
Bernstein, B. B., 38
Biggs, A. P., 119
Biggs, J. , 52, 126
Block, D., 195
Bloome, D., xv, 38, 40, 47, 50
Bolton, K., 13, 28, 107, 208
Bond, M. H., 52, 161, 164, 167
Bourdieu, P., 3, 37, 43, 161, 200, 209
Boyle, J., 13, 15, 19, 22, 27, 59
Breen, M. P., 55, 60
Brooks, F. B., 25
Brown, G., 36
Brown, J. S., 41
Brownell, J., 211

Bruner, J. S., 41
Brutt-Griffler, J., 22, 30
Burnaby, B., 24
Byram, M., xvi, 52

C

Caillois, R., 113
Cameron, D., 139
Canagarajah, A. S., xv, xviii, 12, 22, 28–29,
    44, 100, 114, 192, 194, 198
Candlin, C. N., 36, 55, 60, 114, 116, 126,
    129, 133, 137
Carless, D., 60, 62, 211
Carter, S. P., 50
Cazden, C. B., 38, 42, 53, 56, 114, 142,
    204
Chacon, C., 30
Chaudron, C., 26
Childs, P., xv, 201
Christian, B. M., 50
Clark, H. H., 37, 211
Collins, A., 41
Cook, G., 28, 123, 125, 128, 136–137
Cook, V., 26, 192, 214
Cortazzi, M., 52
Coulthard, M., 39, 141, 209
Coupland, J., 121
Crookes, G., 213
Crystal, D., 137

D

Danaher, G., 211
Davies, A., 22–23, 27, 186
Davies, B., 49, 182, 189
de Certeau, M., 189

Delpit, L. D., 3, 200
Deumert, A., 35
Deumert, T. L., 35
DiCamilla, F., 192
Donato, R., 24, 41–42, 47, 54
Duguid, P., 41

E

Edwards, V., 119
Ellis, G., 55, 86
Ellis, R., 42
Emerson, C., 49
Epstein, J. S., 108
Erickson, F., 6
Evans, S., 13, 61–63

F

Fairclough, N., 36, 142–143
Fasold, R., 36
Ferguson, C., 22
Fiske, J., 52
Flanders, N. A., 38
Fleming, M., xvi
Foucault, M., 43, 188, 211, 217
Freire, P., 196

G

Gabrenya, W. K. J., 52
Gallimore, R., 41
Gandhi, L., xv, 19
Garfinkel, H., 34, 38
Gass, S., 213
Gee, J. P., 24, 53, 86, 114
Gibbons, J., 47
Giroux, H. A., 196
Godfrey, P., 12
Goffman, E., 40, 161, 168, 170, 189, 217
Gramsci, A., 209
Griffiths, G., 209
Guilherme, M., xvi, 196
Gumperz, J. J., 37–38, 51, 142
Guthrie, L. F., 26, 121, 214

H

Haastrup, K., 100
Hakkarainen, P., 48
Hall, J. K., 24, 38, 41–42, 45, 49, 190

Halliday, M. A. K., 38
Hamilton, M., 53
Hancock, M., 25
Harre, R., 49, 182, 189
Harris, R., 12, 26, 193
Hartley, J., 52
Heap, J. L., 35, 38–39, 50, 83–84
Heras, A. I., 170–171
Holliday, A., 27–28, 35, 52, 60, 62, 211
Holquist, M., 49
Hopper, P., 30
Howatt, A., 62
Hughes, M., 40
Hundeide, K., 52
Hutchison, T., 211
Hutton, C., 107
Hwang, K. K., 52, 161, 167
Hyde, M., 52, 199
Hymes, D., 37–38, 45

I

Ivanic, R., 49, 53

J

Jefferson, G., 38
Jenkins, J., 22, 186
Jin, L., 52
Johnson, K., 13, 15–16, 18, 48
Johnson, R. K., 16
Joseph, J. E., 13

K

Kachru, B. B., 22, 28, 201, 209
Kontra, E. H., 24–25
Kramsch, C., 23, 35–36, 47, 55, 188, 197, 199, 202–203
Kubota, R., xix
Kullman, J., 52
Kumaravadivelu, 38, 43–45, 210
Kwan, M. H. Y., 62, 113–114, 164

L

Lai, C., 61–62
Lai, M. L., 14, 19–20
Lam, W. S. E., 193, 195, 202

Lantolf, J. P., 41, 47–48, 141, 190, 194, 199
Lau, E., 12
Lau, L., 41
Lave, J., 42
Law, W. W., 19
Lee, S., 28
Lee, Y. P., 41
Leontiev, A. N., 47
Leung, C., 26, 193
Li, D., 20
Li, K., 34, 210
Li, S. P. T., 58
Lillis, T., 35
Lin, A. M. Y., xv, 3, 12, 40, 43, 59, 61–62, 87, 91, 113–115, 137, 150, 155, 158, 161, 168, 183, 189, 192, 196, 199–201, 203
Littlewood, W., 37, 52, 91
Lo, T. W., 114
Long, M. H., xvi, 25, 39, 42, 54, 209
Lui, I., 59
Luk, B. H. K., 58
Luk, J. C. M., 2, 7, 18, 25, 29, 80, 90, 150, 155, 158, 160, 174, 183, 189, 193, 199, 201, 203, 217
Luke, K. K., 12

M

Man, E. Y. F., 59
McCormick, D., 24, 47, 54
Mehan, H., 39, 141
Mesthrie, R., 35
Miller, J. M., xv, 189
Milroy, L., 53
Mok, A., 60, 211
Montgomery, M., 52
Morris, P., 58, 211
Morrison, K., 59

N

Norton, B., xv, 43–45, 49, 190, 194, 196

O

Ochs, E., 37, 50–51
O'Sullivan, T., 52

Otto, S., 50

P

Patthey-Chavez, G. G., 39, 41–42, 48, 121
Pavlenko, A., 141, 190, 194
Pennington, M. C., xv, 41, 43, 62, 87, 113–114
Pennycook, A., xv, 20, 22, 27–28, 30–31, 43–44, 50, 59, 139, 177, 195–196, 204
Phillipson, R., xv, 19–20, 27–28, 100
Pica, T., xvi, 25, 209
Pierson, H. D., 12
Platt, E., 25
Poole, D., 39, 41–42, 48, 121
Porter, R. E., 35
Purves, W., 12

Q

Quinn, N., 37
Quirk, R., 28

R

Rampton, B., 26, 193
Rampton, M. B. H., xv, 19, 22, 28, 90, 186, 202
Richards, J. C., 12
Rogoff, B., 41

S

Sacks, H., 38
Samimy, K. K., 22–23, 30
Samovar, L. A., 35
Sato, C., xvi
Saunders, D., 52
Savignon, S. J., 25, 60, 141
Scarino, A., 211
Schegloff, E. A., 38
Schirato, T., 211
Scollon, R., xvi, 34, 37, 210
Scollon, S. W., xvi, 34, 37, 210
Searle, J., 38
Sfard, A., 190
Shore, B., 37
Shuart-Faris, N., 50
Simon, R. I., 196

Sinclair, J. M., 39, 141, 209
Skehan, P., 62
Stempleski, S., 33–34
Stephens, K., 52
Straehle, C. A., 123
Strauss, C., 37
Street, B. V., 34
Sullivan, P., 199
Sullivan, P. N., 42, 55
Sun, Y., 24
Surry, M., 12
Swann, J., 48

T

Tang, C., 27
Tang, G., 13, 15–16, 18, 48, 63
Tannen, D., 123
Tarone, E., 215
Tay, M., 22
Tharp, R. G., 41
Tiffin, H., 209
Tomalin, B., 33–34
Toohey, K., 190
Tsang, S. K. Y., 25, 54, 209
Tsui, A. B. M., 25, 54, 62, 113, 148, 198, 202

V

van Lier, L., 32, 39, 43
Vygotsky, L. S., 37, 41–42, 45, 56

W

Walker, E., 14, 16–17
Warschauer, M., 30, 193
Waters, A., 211
Watkins, D., 52, 126
Watson-Gegeo, K. A., 6
Webb, J., 211
Weedon, C., 211
Wells, G., 39
Wenger, E., 42
Wertsch, J. V., 49–50, 210
Westgate, D., 40
Widdowson, H. G., 28, 199, 209
Willett, J., xv, 38, 40, 47
Williams, R. J. P., xv, 201

Y

Young, R., 28
Yu, V. W. S., 59, 147
Yule, G., 36

Subject Index

Note: Page numbers ending in "f" refer to figures. Page numbers ending in "t" refer to tables.

A

Activity theory, 47–48
Activity types, 141
Agency roles, 168–173, 182
Assistant Language Teachers (ALTs), 14–15
Asymmetrical power relations, 53–54, 85–86, 137, 142
Authoritative discourse, 55, 141, 168, 189, 201
Authority, exercising, 148–153, 196–197

B

Bakhtin, Mikhail, 37
Banding system, 58–59
Bateson, Gregory, 37
Berner, Ms.
    academic history of, 63–64
    and lesson fun, 115–121, 130–131, 135–137
    professional beliefs of, 65–66
    and school context, 64–65
    and sense-making practices, 84–110
    strategies of, 143, 158–161, 170–172, 177–180
    students of, 77–80
Bhabha, Homi, 19–20, 201
"Big C" issues, 33–35
Bourdieu, Pierre, 37
Burke, Kenneth, 37

C

Cantonese language, 2–3, 13, 62, 185–186, 192
CCDA. See Critical classroom discourse analysis
Chinese medium of instruction (CMI), 14, 59, 64, 67, 73
Chomsky, Noam, 30
Class size, 48, 61, 65–66, 81, 173
Classroom interaction
    approaches to, 38–46
    and critical approach, 43–46
    and discourse analysis approach, 38–41
    and sociocultural analysis approach, 41–43
    understanding, 45–56
Classroom observations, 8–9
Classroom settings
    activities in, 47–48
    analysis of, 46–56
    identities in, 48–50
    interactive resources in, 50–53
    positionings in, 48–50
CLT. See Communicative approach to language teaching
CMI. See Chinese medium of instruction
Common ground, 37
Communication breakdowns, 95–97
Communication strategies, 54, 100–101, 199–200

Communicative approach to language
    teaching (CLT), 55–56, 60–62,
    65–66, 68
Communicative resources, 50–53,
    187–188
Concept formation, 83–84. *See also*
    Sense-making practices
Concessions, making, 153–161
Connecting, pedagogy of, 185, 196–204,
    198f
"Control talk, " 142
Critical classroom discourse analysis
    (CCDA), 43–46
Cross-cultural classroom interaction,
    38–56, 46f
Cross-cultural communication, 33–38. *See*
    also Communication strategies
Cross-cultural contacts, 5
Cross-cultural interactions
    in classroom settings, 50–53
    and English, 3
    and pedagogy of connecting, 197–199
    understanding, 33–44
Cross-cultural issues, 30–31
Cross-cultural resources, 185–205. *See*
    also Intercultural resources
Cross-cultural studies, 36–37
Cultural borders, 86–91
Cultural experiences, 188–190
Cultural issues, 33–35
Cultural models, 24, 37
Cultural perspectives, 34–35
Cultural stereotypes, 34, 52, 152
Culture, 33–37
Culture-based interaction breakdown,
    104–108
Curriculum culture, 60–64

D

Dialogic interactions, 49, 54–56, 197
Directive strategies, 141–148, 142t, 158,
    169–170, 183–184
Discourse
    authoritative discourse, 55, 141, 168,
        189, 201
    and culture, 36–44
    persuasive discourse, 55, 192, 201
    privileged discourse, 55

E

Education Commission Report, 14
Education logistics, 60–63
Education system, 57–63
EET. *See* Expatriate English Teacher
    (EET) scheme
EFL. *See* English as foreign language
EIL. *See* English as international language
Elicitation strategies, 141, 148–149,
    158–160, 163
ELT. *See* English Language Teaching
    (ELT) methodology
EMI. *See* English medium of instruction
English as foreign language (EFL), 2, 20,
    26–29, 195–198
English as global language, 12–13
English as international language (EIL),
    20, 38, 196–199
English Language Syllabus, 60, 81
English Language Teaching (ELT) meth-
    odology, 60–63, 67–68, 70, 74
English medium of instruction (EMI),
    59–60, 64, 67, 69, 72
English panel chairpersons (EPCs), 17
ESL/EFL students, 8
Essentialization of culture, 34
Ethnographic research, 5–9
Evaluation system, 58–59
Expatriate English Teacher (EET) scheme,
    13–15, 18–20. *See also* Na-
    tive-speaking English teachers

F

Face, sense of, 161–167

G

Global communication, 12–13, 21–32,
    199–200
Guidelines for NETs, 16. *See also* Na-
    tive-speaking English teachers
Gumperz, John, 37

H

HKSs. *See* Hong Kong students
Hong Kong, 11–20

Hong Kong education system, 57–63
Hong Kong primary schools, 1
Hong Kong students (HKSs), 9–11, 17–18
Hung, Ms.
  academic history of, 71
  and lesson fun, 132–133
  professional beliefs of, 71–73
  and sense-making practices, 84–110
  strategies of, 143, 146–147, 159–161,
    168–170
  students of, 78–80
Hymes, Dell, 37, 45

I

Identities, 48–50, 140
Ideological framework, 45–56
Implications of study, 185–205
Independent thinking, 193–194
Indexicality, 37, 51, 91, 105, 107
Informative strategies, 141–142, 163, 169
Institution-based interaction breakdown,
    108–110
Interaction breakdowns, 97–111
Interaction, studies of, 33–44
Interactive resources, 50–53
Intercultural communication, 36–37. *See also*
    Cross-cultural communication
Intercultural EIL, 197
Intercultural interactions, 35–36. *See also*
    Cross-cultural interactions
Intercultural resources
  in communication, 187–188
  development of, 185–205
  and global communication, 199–200
  and native speakerism, 186–188
  and pedagogy of connecting, 197–199
  and student linguist experiences,
    188–190
  see also Cross-cultural resources
Interethnic elements, 192–193
Interpretive procedures, 83–84. *See also*
    Sense-making practices
IRE/IRF discourse model, 39–40

J

Japan Exchange and Teaching (JET),
    14–15

L

L1 learners, 23–26, 186–187, 197–204
L2 learners, 24–26, 186–187, 190,
    195–204
Language policies, 12–13
Lessons
  fun with, 113–138
  making sense of, 83–111
  and phonological play, 114–118,
    136–137
  and social talk, 119–123, 137
  and taboos, 133–137
  and teasing, 123–133, 137
  and verbal challenges, 123–133, 137
LETs. *See* Local English teachers
Liminal moments, 203
Lin, Angel, 3–5
Linguistic borders, 86–91
Linguistic "brokers," 91–95
Linguistic experiences, 188–190
Linguistic imperialism, 18–20
Linguistic interaction breakdown, 97–104
Linguistic play, 114–118, 136–137
"Little C" issues, 33–35
Local English teachers (LETs)
  explanation of, 2–3
  and NETs, 186–188
  observing, 8
  views of, 16–17
Logan, Miss
  academic history of, 73
  and lesson fun, 133–134
  professional beliefs of, 74–75
  and school context, 73–74
  and sense-making practices, 84–110
  strategies of, 142, 148–158, 174–176
  students of, 79–80
Luk, Jasmine, 2–3

M

Makerere Report, 27
Making concessions, 153–161
Mediation, 36, 42–43, 47–48, 54–56,
    141, 191
Medium of instruction (MOI) policy, 59–60
Miscommunication, 37, 95–97, 101–104,
    110, 187

N

Native speakerism, 186–188, 199
Native speakers
  in cross-cultural settings, 185–186
  defining, 21–24
  and sociocultural world, 191–192
  views on, 30–32
Native speakership, 30–31
Native-speaking English teachers (NETs)
  arguments against, 26–27
  arguments for, 24–26
  cultural knowledge of, 26
  and EET scheme, 14
  effectiveness of, 24–30
  explanation of, 1–3
  goals of, 18–20, 26
  in Hong Kong, 11–20
  and LETs, 186–188
  perspectives on, 18–20
  recruiting, 12–14, 24
  roles of, 14–18
  sociopolitical privileges of, 27–29
  student views of, 11
  views of, 16–17
Nelson, Mr.
  academic history of, 68
  and lesson fun, 117–118, 126–128, 137
  professional beliefs of, 70–71
  and school context, 68–70
  and sense-making practices, 84–110
  strategies of, 143, 151–152, 164–165,
    172–173
  students of, 78–81
NETs. See Native-speaking English teach-
    ers
Nishida, Kitaroo, 37
Nonconforming students, engaging, 126,
    142–145, 148–167
"Nonnative speaker, " 186–188

P

Participants in study, 57–82
Passive students, engaging, 148–167
Pedagogical activities, 141
Pedagogical goal, 197
Pedagogical strategies, 196–205

"Pedagogy of connecting, " 185,
    196–204, 198f
"Performing students, " 168–184
"Performing teachers, " 141–167,
    182–184
Persuasive discourse, 55, 192, 201
Phonological play, 114–118, 136–137
Positionings, 49–50
Post-Colonial Hong Kong, 11–20
Postcolonial theories, 18–20
Power relations, 53–54, 85–86, 137, 142
Practical reasoning, 83–84. See also
    Sense-making practices
Preclassroom observations, 8
Privileged discourse, 55
Procedural control, 142–148, 182–184
Putonghua language, 12–13, 203

R

Resistant students, engaging, 150,
    177–182, 196–204
Reticent students, engaging, 148–167

S

Said, Edward, 19–20
Sapir, Edward, 37
Second language acquisition (SLA),
    185–186
Self-image, 161–167, 194–196
Sense-making practices
  and communication breakdowns,
    95–97
  and cultural borders, 86–91
  and interaction breakdowns, 97–110
  in lessons, 83–111
  and linguistic borders, 86–91
  and linguistic "brokers, " 91–95
  successful practices, 86–97, 110–111
  unsuccessful practices, 97–111
Sense-making resources, 84–86
Social talk, 119–123, 137
Sociocultural perspectives, 3, 30–37,
    41–43, 141, 189, 192–193
Sociocultural views, 36–37, 191–192
Sociohistoric issues, 30–31, 42, 46–56
Sociopolitical issues, 27–29
South China Morning Post, 17
SPEAKING model, 45

Spivak, Gayatri, 19–20
Stereotypes, 34, 52, 152
Strategies
  for communication, 54, 100–101,
      199–200
  for connecting, 196–205
  of teachers, 141–184
Streaming system, 58–59
Student identities, 140, 190–196. *See also*
      Student performance
Student interviews, 9
Student performance, 168–184
Student perspectives, 11
Students in study
  attitudes on English, 77–79
  cultural experiences of, 188–190
  English experience of, 77–79
  interviews with, 76–81
  learning strategies of, 79
  linguistic experiences of, 188–190
  views of teachers, 80–81
Studentship, 140, 168. *See also* Student
      performance
Study participants, 57–82
Subject positionings, shifting, 177–182
Sze, Mr.
  academic history of, 75
  and lesson fun, 122–123, 131–132
  professional beliefs of, 75–76
  and sense-making practices, 84–110
  strategies of, 143–146, 162–164
  students of, 81

T

Taboos, 133–137
Target language experts (TLE), 48–49
Target language learners (TLL), 48–49
Task-based learning (TBL), 60, 62

Teacher identities, 140. *See also* Teacher
      performance
Teacher interviews, 8–9
Teacher performance, 141–167, 182–184
Teacher rankings, 61–62
Teacher-designed activities, 148,
      168–173, 177, 196
Teacher-designed identity, 173–176
Teachers in study, 63–76. *See also* spe-
      cific teachers
Teachership, 140, 168. *See also* Teacher
      performance
Teasing, 123–133, 137
TESOL, 20–21, 26, 29, 185–186
"Third space, " 4, 201–203

V

Verbal challenges, 123–133, 137
Vygotsky, Lev, 37

W

Williams, Mr.
  academic history of, 66
  and lesson fun, 124–130, 137
  professional beliefs of, 67–68
  and school context, 66–67
  and sense-making practices, 84–110
  strategies of, 142–146, 152–155,
      165–169, 180–182
  students of, 77–80
Wittgenstein, Ludwig, 37

Z

Zone of proximal development (ZPD),
      41–42